A GRIM ALMANAC OF

GEORGIAN
LONDON

THOU
SHALT DO NO MURDER

POISON

INFANTICIDE

JUSTICE

A GRIM ALMANAC OF

GEORGIAN LONDON

GRAHAM JACKSON & CATE LUDLOW

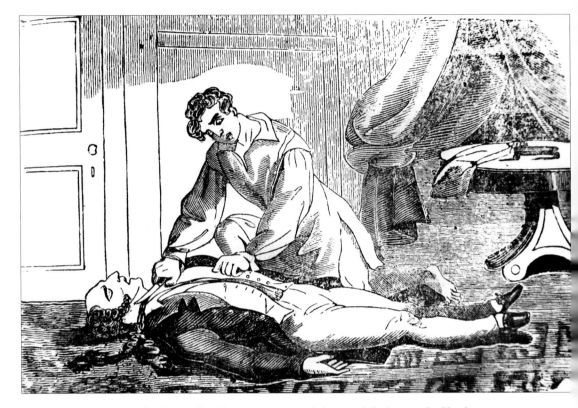

James Hall, who murdered his master in June, before carefully draining his blood into various pots and pans, and hiding his body. (*See* 18 June)

First published 2011

The History Press
The Mill, Brimscombe Port
Stroud, Gloucestershire, GL5 2QG
www.thehistorypress.co.uk

© Graham Jackson & Cate Ludlow 2011

The right of Graham Jackson & Cate Ludlow to be identified as the
Authors of this work has been asserted in accordance with the
Copyrights, Designs and Patents Act 1988.

British Library Cataloguing in Publication Data.
A catalogue record for this book is available from the British Library.

ISBN 978 0 7524 6170 0

Typesetting and origination by The History Press
Printed in Great Britain

CONTENTS

INTRODUCTION

The years between the accession of George I on 1 August 1714 – Queen Anne having succumbed to gout – and the death of George IV on 26 June 1830 was one of the most eventful centuries in British history. It was certainly one of the bloodiest: from the French Revolution to the Napoleonic Wars and the American Revolution, some of the key events which defined Britain occurred in this age. Many of the events need no introduction: the Battle of Waterloo, for example, or the Declaration of Independence.

This age was defined by four Georges: German-speaking George I (king from 1 August 1714 – 11 June 1727), whose reign started with a Jacobite rebellion and who was born on the day that the victim of another rebellion, Charles II, re-entered London in triumph; George II (king from 11 June 1727 – 25 October 1760), who promised his wife, on her deathbed, that he should not remarry – 'No, I shall have mistresses!'; George III (king from 25 October 1760 – 29 January 1820), the first George with English as his first language, whose reign saw the establishment of an independent United States and the battle against Napoleon – twice – and whose blindness, deafness and madness are legendary; and finally, George IV, the Prince Regent (who reigned as regent from 5 February 1811, and as king from 29 January 1820 – 26 June 1830). There are a few royal incidents in this book, including two of the most famous in the life of Queen Caroline, who unsuccessfully hammered on the door of what should have been her own Coronation (see 19 June).

The era began at the last dusk of the Golden Age of Piracy (and indeed, Mary Read of Bonny and Read fame was born in London) and was coloured a pleasing shade of crimson by the all-encompassing, notorious Bloody Code – a system which meant that, by 1815, a total of 220 offences carried the death penalty. Hundreds of Londoners stepped into the shadow of the Triple Tree at Tyburn – now the site of Marble Arch – or on to the gallows set up at Newgate's debtors' entrance (the site of London's hangings moved in 1783). Executions at Tyburn were marked by the roar of the crowd, the oaths of the men and women climbing into the cart to be hanged, and the swishing of missiles – dead cats, sticks, dead dogs, stones, offal, dung – flying thickly through the air as the cart creaked along the route from Newgate to Tyburn. A psalm was sung over the roar of the crowd, last speeches were made, cheers went up for a popular rogue – and oaths and boos for unpopular ones, such as Mrs Brownrigg, whom thousands of people wished into Hell – and then, as the feet of the prisoner left the wooden platform of the cart, the crowd would surge forward to fight for a souvenir, or for the body, which the surgeons needed and the family wanted to protect. After the Murder Act was passed in 1751, supplies became somewhat more plentiful, as the Act demanded that every murderer be dissected or hung in chains after death. This led to some colourful resurrections on the doctor's table.

Other methods of execution in this volume include: hanging, drawing and quartering, where the offender was choked, ripped open and his internal organs pulled out and burned in front of his eyes (after the genitals, of course); beheading with an axe, as in the case of Derwentwater and Kilmarnock; burning, as in the horrible case of Catherine Hayes; and decapitation after death, as in the case of the Cato Street Conspirators. In several instances, a bleeding skull was held aloft to the cry of, 'This is the head of a traitor!' Other corporal punishments included the pillory – a death sentence in itself in many cases – and the hot irons (burning on the hand for manslaughter), as well as whipping, which a London hangman once refused to perform until he got a pay rise.

It has not been possible to fit every grim event of the Georgian era into this book – the subject could fill many volumes: one volume on high life and royal scandals; one on politics and war; another on the brothels, gentlemen's clubs and sexual scandals of the day. We have chosen to concentrate, in this volume, mainly on crime in the capital – and what crimes they were! From the 'cupboard murderer', John Williamson, to the death of the Marrs (and another set of Williamsons) in London's East End – a Georgian serial killing that has never been conclusively solved – all manner of life and death is in this book. Almost all of the research has involved primary sources taken straight from the magazines and newspapers of the day, or from the trial records available at the magnificent Old Bailey Online.

We must thank the compilers of the phenomenal websites Capital Punishment UK (http://www.capitalpunishmentuk.org/) and georgianlondon.com, and also the people involved in the Old Bailey project: their exemplary research has made researching this book an absolute pleasure. We would also like to thank Neil R. Storey, who kindly provided some extremely rare images from his own collection for this volume. Graham and I both hope you enjoy reading it.

Graham Jackson & Cate Ludlow, 2011

JANUARY

Elizabeth Canning, who vanished on the evening of 1 January. Had a
London gypsy really stolen her underwear and locked her in a hay loft?

1771 On this day, John Joseph Defoe (grandson of Daniel Defoe, the author of *Robinson Crusoe*) was hanged at Tyburn, along with John Clark. They had been convicted of the highway robbery of Mr and Mrs Fordyce, who were travelling in their carriage to London. 'There were three pistols in the coach at one time,' said Mr Fordyce. 'They put a pistol to my head, and another to my wife; the third pistol was pointed to a gentleman sitting on the other side of the coach.' The thieves took their watches and their cash. The criminals were later identified, apprehended – Clark was cross-eyed, and hence very memorable – and tried at the Old Bailey, where they were found guilty and sentenced to death.

Fourteen years later, on this date, the first edition of the *Daily Universal Register* – later *The Times* – appeared in London.

1753 In 1754, the curate of the Savoy Chapel was arrested, tried, convicted, and sentenced to fourteen years' transportation for carrying out marriages without a valid license. 1,400 marriages were instantly dissolved.

The year before, on the evening of the 1st and through into the early hours of this day, Mary Squires and Susannah Wells may – or may not – have kidnapped Elizabeth Canning (18) and stolen her stays. According to Elizabeth's testimony at the Old Bailey, 'two lusty men' had grabbed her near the gate of Bethlem Hospital, stuffed a handkerchief in her mouth, tied her hands and dragged her along by 'her petticoats'. She then fell into a convulsive fit – which she had been prone to ever since an attic ceiling fell on her head. When she came to, she was entering a kitchen containing 'gypsey woman Squires'. She said the old lady had taken her by the hand and 'asked me if I chose to go their way [become a prostitute], saying, if I did, I should have fine cloaths.' Elizabeth said no. Her stays were cut off, and she was pushed into a hay loft. A broken jug of water and twenty-four pieces of bread lay on the floor. This, with a mince pie she had in her pocket, was all she had to live on for a month.

Notices were posted in the papers by her desperate parents, such as this, on 6 January 1753, in the *Daily Advertiser*:

> whoever can give any account where she is, shall have Two Guineas Reward... which shall be a great satisfaction to her mother. She is fresh coloured, pitted with the small-pox, has a high forehead, light eye-brows, about five feet high, eighteen years of age, well-set...

The truth of what happened has never been solved. Elizabeth claimed that she eventually pulled a board from a window and ran home. She gave enough information to suggest that she had been held at the house of Mother Wells in Enfield Wash, 'a house of very ill-fame', was carried there, and successfully identified her attackers and the room she was held in. The case came to trial at the Old Bailey, and both Mother Susannah Wells (who Elizabeth said she had seen through the window) and Mary Squires were found guilty and sentenced to death. However, many witnesses appeared to say that they had seen Squires in Dorset. Neither the judge nor the Lord Mayor of London,

Sir Crisp Gascoigne – whose coach windows were shattered by the mob for his support of the case – were happy with the verdict, and the death penalty was suspended for six weeks whilst they investigated – ending with a very surprising twist, when Elizabeth found herself on the other side of the dock on 24 April, on a charge of perjury.

Her story was full of inconsistencies. The room she named as her prison had a large and easily opened window, so low that one man shook his wife's hand through it: she 'thought it was fast', she retorted. Moreover, lots of visitors had been in and out of the room throughout that month, none of whom had spotted a half-naked kidnap victim hiding in the straw. Mr White, servant to the Lord Mayor, helpfully added that when he looked out the window, he saw 'a heap of human dung as high as a quart pot, which did not appear to have been trod upon; and upon the whole it did not appear to him that anybody had got out at that window'. Elizabeth also identified Mary Squires so quickly that she caused her own friends to doubt her – before she had even seen her face, in fact, causing the woman to reply, 'Lord Madam! I was 120 miles off at that time!'

Convincing arguments have been made for both the pro and the anti-Canning causes, both at the time and in more recent years. The truth of where Elizabeth spent a month of 1753 has never been discovered – but the Old Bailey decided that, wherever she was, it most certainly was not with Squires and Mother Wells, and she was found guilty. Elizabeth Canning was transported for seven years. She married in Connecticut, had five children, and died there in 1773.

3 JANUARY **1818**   A tragic accident befell Matthew Hirst (14) at the Three Hats, Islington Green, on this day, while he was playing with his brothers and sisters. He said, 'I will show you how they hang men at the gallows,' and looped a long rope attached to a ceiling hook around his neck. He climbed up onto a stool to make his demonstration particularly lifelike, but unfortunately he accidentally kicked the chair out from underneath him. The children, seeing his face black and distorted, ran to their mother, crying, 'Mat is hanging himself to frighten us.' The mother, thinking the children were playing, took no notice – until a porter went into the kitchen and found the boy suspended. When he was cut down he was quite dead.

4 JANUARY **1725**   'Captain' Charles Towers, a butcher covered with scars, and 'General' John Webb of the Wapping New Mint, were indicted this day for storming into the house of John Errington. According to an old statute, anyone who lived in the area of the Mint was immune from prosecution. All of the criminal families in the area had signed a book, and paid a small subscription fee, in order to join the 'New Minters', a group which swore to rescue any member who was arrested. Errington lived at the Red Lion on Wapping Wall, opposite King James's Stairs. At about 11 a.m., Towers, covered from his face to his waist in soot and grease, had burst into the house waving a giant quarterstaff. He cried out, 'Damn ye, you have got one of our prisoners, and we'll have him away!' Towers and Webb then ran into the room waving the list of 'New

Minters', and rescued the prisoner, John West, with many 'huzzas'. Towers tried to claim that he was simply a bit dirty, but the court found that he had deliberately disguised himself for the purposes of rioting in the streets, and he was sentenced to death. His colleague, who had not blackened his face, was released. According to the ordinary's report, Towers felt that 'Prisons were all so full that men died like rotten sheep, and he had rather go to the place whither he was going, than dwell under that Tyranny'. He said, 'I am going from a life of trouble and noise and confusion, to a world of quiet.'

1716   William Hammond of St Mary, 'Whitechappel', used a visit to his client Thomas Hollis, whom he was to shave, as an opportunity to abstract a silver spoon. The prisoner told the court that he had been drunk at the time – hardly an ideal qualification for a job involving throats and razors – and 'that it was his first Fact, and should be his last'. The jury reduced the value of the spoon for him, and he was whipped rather than transported.

5 JANUARY

1727   In early January of this year, the 'lunatic king' was first admitted to St Giles' Workhouse. This poor man became convinced that he was a king, and immediately appointed another lunatic as his prime minister, personal barber and servant. Sadly, however, one day the prime minister got so hungry that he ate his dinner before the lunatic king had come in – which made the king so angry that he attacked the prime minister on sight. The exiled prime minister shortly afterwards died of a fever, and the king, broken-hearted, refused to eat. He died of starvation a few weeks later.

6 JANUARY

1772   On 6 and 7 January, one of London's most famous hauntings took place in Stockwell. At about 10 a.m., as one Mrs Golding was sitting in her parlour, she heard the china and glasses in the back kitchen tumble down from the shelves and break. Her maid, Ann Robinson (20), rushed in and shouted that the stone plates were throwing themselves from the shelf. Mrs Golding went into the kitchen, and to her astonishment saw whole rows of plates and dishes flinging themselves onto the floor; an egg then flew across the room and hit the cat on the head. The next day, the ghost was back again: as the other servant, Mrs Mary Martin, went over to stir the fire, a pestle and mortar flew onto the floor next to her, followed by candlesticks, cups, brasses and many other small objects. The bewildered and terrified owners tried to save their goods by putting them onto the floor, but it was no good: the objects on the floor began to leap and jump like frogs, some flying 7 or 8ft in the air. Others smashed against the furniture, before the very furniture itself began to move! Bottles and hams hanging from the ceiling began to swing and leap to the floor, causing the whole family to flee in terror. When they returned to the house, a pot of water immediately began to boil of its own accord, before candles and other items flew at them. The only person who remained calm during these awful events was the servant, Ann, who told her mistress that 'these things could not be helped'. This made the family rather suspicious, suspicions which were borne out when Ann confessed, years later, to attaching 'long horse hairs' and wires

7 JANUARY

to the items as an elaborate and extremely clever practical joke. Every time she pulled on one of these invisible ropes, an item would fly into the air. The family had been too terrified to examine the possessed objects carefully, and so the trick had escaped detection. Ann later added that she had thrown the egg at the cat herself; her other tricks included adding chemicals to the pot of water to make it boil, and loosening the hams on their hooks so that they flew off at the slightest touch.

8 JANUARY **1806**   On 8 January, at about 10 a.m., the body of Lord Nelson began its last journey up the Thames from Greenwich Hospital. The procession of barges, all draped in black, was nearly a mile long, and guns were fired from the Tower as it passed; bells rang mournfully across London. The river had been cleared, but thousands of spectators lined the shore and crowded onto the boats moored at the side, or onto the bridges on the route, to watch the procession. At about 3 p.m., the body drew up at Whitehall, and more guns were fired. Trumpets were also sounded. An enormous hailstorm struck as the body was unloaded, but stopped as it reached the shore. Nelson was carried to Captain Hardy's room at the Admiralty, which had been draped all in black for the occasion.

The next day, muffled drum rolls called out London's mourners in their thousands. Troops, with black armbands, marched through the thronged streets in front of the six-horse carriage which was pulling Nelson's gilded coffin. The front of the carriage was a replica of the *Victory*. Roofs, chimneys, windows – all were crowded with hundreds of thousands of spectators. More than 200 mourning coaches and 400 carriages joined the body as it rolled to St Paul's. Twelve men from Nelson's crew carried the body into the cathedral, and a great storm of weeping broke out as he was carried to his grave inside. As darkness fell, 200 lamps were lit over the funeral bier and the coffin was slowly lowered out of sight. Earth rattled on the top as Handel's 'His body is buried in peace; but his name liveth forever more' was sung. Guns then rang out, and the staffs of

Lord Nelson's elaborate coffin.

The CAR on which the remains of LORD NELSON were conveyed to S.t Pauls Jan.y 9. 1806.

Nelson's funeral car. The motto roughly translates as: 'Let he who merits the palm possess it.' Nelson's coffin can be seen in the middle.

Nelson's household were snapped and placed on top of his coffin. His flag would have followed, but the crew carrying it ripped it into pieces to keep instead.

1760   On this day, pensioner Esther Monk confessed to the murder of her husband, coachman Richard, whom she had struck on the side of the head with a poker. She added that he was a very good husband, but that she had thought about it for several weeks after 'the Devil' suggested it to her. Neighbours said she was often 'very stupid', and 'in a strange way', and talked of drowning herself. She was acquitted by reason of insanity.

9 JANUARY

1765   On this day, thousands of destitute weavers asked the Houses of Parliament to ban foreign silks. Cheap foreign silks had decimated the demand for home-produced fabrics, and thousands of Englishmen and women went hungry as a consequence.

     Also on this day, but in 1727, a 12in-stab wound to the chest finally got the best of Edward Perry. At the end of December, as he was walking across St James's Park, drunken former Tower soldier Robert Hains (21) of 'Thieving Lane' in Westminster – the lane along which felons were transported to the Gatehouse Prison – came up and started 'meddling' with the party's women, seizing one by the throat and throttling her while attempting to kiss her. When the men protested, Hains drew his sword and stabbed Perry through the chest. The blade went all the way through the man's body and tore the thumb of Perry's wife, who was standing behind him. 'I am a dead man!' Perry shouted as he fell. Perry's lungs were ripped, and he died in great agony. Hains was hanged at Tyburn on 12 February.

10 JANUARY

1804   A strange case came to the Old Bailey today, when Francis Smith (29) was indicted for the murder of Thomas Millwood at Hammersmith. On 3 January, John Locke had bumped into Smith, who informed him that he

11 JANUARY

had just shot a ghost – the Hammersmith ghost, no less. The ghost was a man who had been running around the area, dressed up either in white or in calfskin, with horns on his head and glass eyes, frightening people. Servant Thomas Groom told the court that he himself had seen the ghost: as he was walking through the churchyard at about 8 p.m. or 9 p.m., 'some person came from behind a tombstone ... and caught me fast by the throat with both hands.' He had punched it, and it ran away. According to Old Bailey records, another woman had seen the ghost 'rise from the tombstones. The figure was very tall and very white. She attempted to run; but the ghost soon overtook her, and pressed her in his arms, when she fainted.' She was allegedly so frightened that she died.

Whole gangs of men had been out looking for the ghost. When the local watchmen crowded into the churchyard, they saw a man stretched out with a bullet hole in his jaw. Unfortunately, it turned out that the 'ghost' was the innocent bricklayer, Thomas Millwood. Thomas had already been warned to change his outfit after he had walked past a couple and frightened them so much that the man had threatened to punch him in the head. The intrepid ghost-hunter was sentenced to death, but saved from the gallows and sent to prison instead for one year.

Another ghost was said to haunt Hyde Park – a headless woman who leapt over the railings – though *London Lore* identifies this as the work of a couple of naughty boys with a projector.

12 JANUARY   1818   A fatal duel took place on this day, sparked by a quarrel in a London coffee house. The principals had forgotten where they were supposed to meet, and so the two seconds ended up fighting instead over which of the two would-be duellists was the coward. In a field by the Load of Hay, Chalk Farm, one second, Lieutenant Bailey of the 58th Foot, was shot through the intestines by the other. The injured man was carried to a nearby house, and shook hands with his opponent before he died. Bailey told his horrified killer, Mr Theodore O'Callaghan, that his first bullet had also grazed his leg: pulling up his trousers, he showed him where the bullet had passed through both legs of his trousers and one of his boots. O'Callaghan was arraigned on a capital charge, and was so grief-stricken that he could not read out his defence. He got three months' imprisonment.

Today in 1731, Mrs Goodchild, wife of a Charing Cross linen draper, had a fit. Unfortunately, she pitched forward into the fire and was burnt to death. She was two months pregnant.

13 JANUARY   1725   On this day, Mr James Wallis spied a pig sitting on top of a dung heap with part of a baby's body hanging out of its mouth. The head and the arms of the child had already been eaten. A local farmer suspected that his servant, Deborah Greening of South Mims, might know something of this horrible case, and she was eventually forced to admit that she had buried a stillborn baby in the aforementioned dung heap. The court therefore acquitted her of murder.

Six years later, Mary Martin was found lying in a field in Hoxton with a piece of knife sticking out of her head, and another under her left ear. Mr John Chapel of Bishopsgate Workhouse was committed to Newgate, and there confessed to the crime.

1716   *Dawks' Newsletter* of 14 January reported that 'the Thames seems now a solid rock of ice'. Booths, food stalls and a printing press were set up on the ice, and even royalty visited. A week later, it was frozen so solidly that four men roped themselves together and walked upstream for days across the surface. They then vanished somewhere on the river, and were never heard of again.

    On this day in 1762, William Tomlin (28) staggered into the Black Boy alehouse at Saltpetre Bank with his guts hanging out 'a great way'. The landlord pushed them back in, and took him to the hospital. Several foreigners were arrested in accordance with the description given by the dying man, and taken to see William in his sickbed. Eventually he claimed to recognise a young Portuguese man called Francisco Wilkins as the man who had stabbed him, after a fight over a woman. In broken English, Francisco explained that he was indeed with the attackers, but that he had no knife of his own. He was acquitted.

    14 JANUARY

1769   Mary Grindall (1) fell into the New River on this day. Her body was raked out of the water on the 16th, and carried along to the nearest public house on a board. The moment that her mother, Elizabeth Grindall, saw her child, she kissed it and cried, 'Let me wipe thy pretty face as I used to do. I wish you were alive again!' She wept 'very much'. It turned out that she had returned home the previous night without her child. When asked where it was, she 'fell a crying sadly and said it was in the water'. She was arrested, but after she had recovered from her shock, she told the following sad tale of her evening walk to Islington:

    15 JANUARY

> The moon shone very fine; and whether the child saw the light of the moon in the river I cannot say, but it gave a spring from my arm into the water, and I ran away directly, being sadly frightened.

Countless witnesses testified to her adoration of her daughter – 'She loved the child even to distraction: no woman in the world could love a child better,' said one. She was found not guilty of murder.

    Finally, today – a day for knowledge, for the British Museum opened on this day in 1759 – the *Gentleman's Magazine* claimed that a large turnip had been discovered in the exact shape of a man's head, a cast of which the Society of Phrenologists declared showed the tell-tale signs of 'acute mind and deep research'. However, when they asked to make further examination, the turnip's owner had to confess that 'he and his family had eaten it the day before with their mutton at dinner'.

16 JANUARY   **1735**   Moorfields servant Elizabeth Ambrook appeared in court on this day to answer a case of infanticide: she was accused of throwing her newborn out of a second-storey window. The neighbour had heard the window go up, and then saw 'something' fly out. He had poked it, and realised it was a dying baby. Ambrook said she had thought the house was on fire because of the pain she was in after giving birth, and had thrown the baby to save it from the flames. The 'grisle' of the child's soft skull was warped by the fall, and it died soon afterwards. His mother was sentenced to death.

On this same day, booksellers advertised a handy pocket-sized copy of a bestseller: *ONANIA; or, The Heinous Sin of Self Pollution, and all its Frightful Consequences, in Both Sexes*. This book included a...

> ...surprizing Letter from a young married Lady, who by this detestable Practice, became barren and diseased; and two astonishing Cases, in a Letter from a Clergyman, of a young Man and a young Woman, who to his own Knowledge, had so abused themselves thereby, that they died.

Other books advertised included a guide to home-curing venereal disease, and *The Life of Madam de Beamnount, a French Lady, who Lived in a Cave in Wales Fourteen Years Undiscover'd*.

17 JANUARY   **1777**   Rich widow Mary Eleanor Bowes, Countess of Strathmore – known to history as 'the Unhappy Countess' – tragically fell into the clutches of the notorious Andrew Robinson Stoney, a half-pay lieutenant aged 30. (The phrase 'stoney broke' is said to have been inspired by him.) They married on this day – and she regretted it shortly afterwards.

The husband's abuses included imprisoning the Countess in her own home, raping her maids and bringing prostitutes into the house. On one occasion, he held a knife to her throat, and threatened to cut it if she spoke another word. Mary Morgan, her maid, deposed that his treatment had been 'one continued scene of abuse, insult, and cruelty', and that he had burnt the Countess's face with a candle and beaten her with a stick. After the trial went against him, he contrived to kidnap the Countess to force her to return; he hounded her through the countryside, abusing her all the way, at one point threatening her with a red-hot poker. By this time the case was well known, and a nationwide search for the Countess was launched. Escape was thus impossible, notwithstanding that he avoided all roads and took his famished captive across moors and fields. A constable of the parish of Neasham deposed that when he saw Stoney, whose horse's bridle was being held by a country labourer, the prisoner attempted to shoot him. However, the constable promptly knocked the lieutenant off his horse with a stout cudgel. The court revoked all his rights over the Countess's property and sent him to prison in St George's Fields for the rest of his life. An acquaintance of his suggested the following epitaph: 'He was cowardly, insidious, hypocritical, tyrannical, mean, violent, selfish, deceitful, jealous, revengeful, inhuman, and savage, without a single countervailing quality.'

On this day in 1808, Horatio Viscount Trafalgar, Nelson's nephew, died of typhus. He was buried with his famous uncle in St Paul's.

1738   Covent Garden attorney Thomas Carr, who robbed William Quarrington of 93 guineas and a diamond ring in Shire Lane, near Fleet Street, went to the gallows with his partner, Elizabeth Adams, on this day. According to the Newgate Calendar:

> They were both remarkably composed for people in their dreadful situation, and just as the cart began to draw away they kissed each other, joined hands, and thus were launched into eternity.

(Shire Lane was a row of squalid houses at the time, with a reputation 'too black to be repeated'. It was so infamous that one murderer simply propped his victim against a door a little further up the street, and escaped capture for years.)

1743   On this day, sailor Thomas Rounce was hanged, drawn and quartered at Execution Dock after being captured aboard a Spanish ship – one which he had been forced to join to save his life. He was dragged to the site of execution by horses covered in ribbons, with the gleaming scimitar that was to cut off his head in front of him, and a silver oar paraded in front of that. As soon as he was hanged, he was cut down; his belly was ripped up, his heart pulled out and thrown on a fire, and his head was cut off. His quartered body was put in a coffin and given to his friends. It was the first such execution since 1708.
    On 19 January 1795, two ships freed from the ice on the Thames crashed into London Bridge. One lost all of its masts, knocked down two of the lamps and ripped through the central arch, shaking the whole bridge as it passed. It floated all the way to Somerset House, and beached there. The other boat lodged on the railings.

1802   In 1780, Joseph Wall accepted a post as governor of a Goree, an African colony. When he returned to London, rumours about his inhumane treatment of subordinates began to spread. He appeared in court at long last on this day, to defend himself against a charge of deliberately murdering one Benjamin Armstrong by tying him to a gun carriage and ordering him to have 800 lashes, of which he died five days afterwards. To his dismay, Wall was found guilty; he was executed on 29 January 1802. As the platform dropped, the rope slipped and the knot moved to the back of his head. He choked to death over an agonising twenty minutes. The rope was afterwards sold for 1s an inch.

1790   In 1790, 'a large stone was thrown with great violence into the King's carriage, during his majesty's journey to the House of Lords' by a half-pay lieutenant named James Frick, who was then sent to Bethlem Hospital. The stone did no injury to the King. On this circumstance, Peter Pindar wrote the following epigram:

Folks say, it was lucky the stone missed the head,
When lately at Caesar 'twas thrown;
I think, very different from thousands indeed,
'Twas a lucky escape for the stone.

It wasn't a good date for royals, as today, in 1809, St James's Palace caught fire, and £100,000 worth of damage was caused. However, this was a vast improvement to events on the other side of the Channel, where 'Citoyen Louis Capet', previously known as King Louis XVI, went to his death today in 1793. Sir Nathaniel William Wraxall read a note in St James's Palace which said, 'The unfortunate Louis is no more. He suffered death this morning, at 10 o'clock, with the most heroic courage.' He had attempted to resist, so the executioners had thrown him down onto the plank under the guillotine's blade, and tore his face.

22 JANUARY   1815   Mary Emmott (24) walked into Hackney church on this day and wandered into Mr Bridges' pew. The pew opener shooed her out, lest the ladies arrived and 'they be offended'. At the end of the service, Emmott was first out of the door – carrying the Bridgeses' Bible, which she had stolen. She told the court that she had abstracted it by accident, but was transported for seven years nonetheless.

23 JANUARY   1820   On this day, the Duke of Kent, Queen Victoria's father, was attacked by an inflammation of the lungs, and died.

Also on this day, but in 1815, Samuel Penney married Mary Davis in Surrey. Unfortunately, he already had a wife, Hannah Andrews, whom he had married six years earlier in St Giles' Church. Fortunately, however, the first wife was very young and the court did not have enough evidence to prove that the original marriage was legal, and Penney was acquitted.

24 JANUARY   1721   One of the most famous crashes in financial history occurred when the 'South Sea Bubble' finally burst. The directors were arrested on this day. The South Sea Co. had exclusive rights to trade in the Spanish colonies, and, as rumours of untold wealth began to spread, a bright scheme was laid: the company would lend the government money at an exceptionally good rate, and raise enough money to cover a massive proportion of the national debt by selling shares. More than £9 million was to be loaned. The idea of access to instant wealth suddenly gripped London. The stock madness was not helped by the main men behind the scheme, who whipped prices up. Single shares rose from £100 to £1,100. Then, when word got out that all the directors had sold up, and when people realised that the company couldn't possibly cover the cost of all those shares, the price suddenly dropped – and selling panic began. Small tradesmen suddenly found their stock was worth a tenth of what they had paid for it – if they could even find a buyer. In March 1721, the Chancellor of the Exchequer, John Aislabie, was sent to the Tower for his part in defrauding the public for his own profit, and the first Lord of the Treasury was also charged (but acquitted) of the same. The

Secretary of State was also implicated, and the entire property of his father, the Postmaster General, was seized.

In the brief wave of stock popularity, more than 200 weird and wonderful companies, called 'bubbles', started to sell shares in the most unlikely of schemes. These included the chance to buy shares in the profits of whale-fishing trips to Greenland; the importation of beaver fur; companies promising to 'inoffensively empty bog-houses'; trading in hair or the bleaching of hair; pox insurance; an 'air-pump' for the brain; and a company specialising in checking the virginity of prospective brides.

Things were even stranger on the other side of the Channel, as on this day in 1732, forty monks died after drinking from a barrel of wine in which a deadly viper had drowned, after it had wormed in through the bung-hole.

1789   In 1789, former teacher Mary Patmore of High Street, Mile End, St Dunstan's, died after her husband, stay-maker William, and his second wife, Rachel Walters, locked her in a soaking-wet garret (later attributed to the juices 'violently oozing' from the woman, and the spilling of her chamber pot) and starved her to death. On this day, churchwarden Henry Eyre went to the house to view the body, and found... **25 JANUARY**

> ...the appearance was the greatest scene of distress I ever saw. I saw a human body on the straw, and a few rags underneath, which were cut from her back all swarming with vermin: the appearance of the sight was extremely shocking ... her belly shrunk in, her ribs started.

Mortification had eaten down to her bones. The husband had told visitors that when she was dead he planned to sell her to the surgeons; he told others, if they happened to hear groaning coming from the attic, that it was nothing but a 'vagrant' he was sheltering. One lady visitor found the wife weeping on the floor, and crying, 'I'm very hungry, the child gnaws me!' Mary was pregnant, and in fact gave birth in her lonely attic. She then sank, and was discovered with 'each hand up to the side of her hair, fighting with death'. She died that night. The husband told his astonished lodger that he had found some men who, for a shilling each, would throw the body in the Thames for him. He had already sold her child, stillborn, to the surgeons for 4s. When the enormous poverty of the family was revealed – little money for food, and none for medical treatment – the pair were found not guilty.

1715   John Hurrel of St Botolph, Bishopsgate, was convicted of stealing 16 yards of cloth from a shop on 26 January, after he was seen to push up his coat sleeve, thrust his arm into a hole in the glass, and bring something out. He pawned the material, and the pawnbroker identified him. **26 JANUARY**

1715   Itinerant fruit-seller and gambler William Rose (19) of St Andrew's, Holborn, stole four pairs of stockings, after lifting the lock of a shop with a pocketknife. James Evans, who had turned King's Evidence to save himself, told how he had helped by throwing his coat over the shop boy when he **27 JANUARY**

came out of the cellar during the theft: he had hugged him fiercely to his chest, and cried out, 'Dear Jemmy!', kissing him to distract him. Both men were later captured, and Rose was hanged on 2 October 1717.

28 JANUARY **1785** Sir Ashton Lever advertised lottery tickets for the right to obtain his famous Leverian Museum collection from Leicester House, Leicester Square on this day; it cost 1 guinea per ticket. Natural curiosities by the thousand, many collected by Captain Cook on his travels, filled 1,300 glass cases. They included 200 'species of warlike instruments, ancient and modern', the tomahawk, 'the scalping-knife, and many more such desperate diabolical instruments of destruction, invented, no doubt, by the Devil himself'. The house had previously been known for its curiosities, including a moving painting which was alleged to be 4 miles long (but was actually 0.25 miles). It was a royal residence, most famous as the childhood home of George III. Prince Frederick died here – his father famously, on hearing the news, coldly finished his game of cards before informing his wife that their son was dead.

29 JANUARY

A coffin thief in action! This is one Jonas Parker, who took £5 worth of lead, in the form of a coffin, from Aldermanbury Church in 1778.

1820 King George III died at Windsor on this day, at the age of 81. He had been virtually blind for ten years, and spent his final years in seclusion at Windsor Castle, talking to invisible courtiers.

A plate engraved '29 Jan 1721' was stolen in 1732 by Aldgate gravedigger Thomas Middleton, and coffin-bearer Frances Warner, as part of a haul of 200lb of lead taken from the crypt of Bow Church, and eventually sold to John Newton. However, the provenance was hard to hide: 'One of my Men,' Newton told the court, said, 'this Lead smells so strong of dead Corps that it almost choaks me!' Newton went to the authorities, and both Middleton and Warner confessed that they hadn't been able to resist the sight of all that valuable metal. The vault had been so completely rifled that one corpse – recognised by its lame leg and the post-mortem stitches running up the chest – was found slumped on the floor: the entire coffin had been taken, and the sawdust from inside dumped next to him. Middleton was transported.

1789   On this day, the Regency was formally announced – and then the King recovered! The whole of London was illuminated in celebration, and, according to the *Gentleman's Magazine*, 'from one extremity to the other and far out into the surrounding suburbs there was one blaze of light'.

Also on this day, but in 1734, Judith Defour of Bethnal Green wrapped a piece of linen around her daughter's neck and left her, naked, to die in a ditch. The child was the bastard of a Spitalfields weaver. John Wolveridge heard an outcry in Bethnal's fields and ran towards the sound. There he found a child (about 2 years old) stretched out, with a 'black circle' about its neck, 'and a mark like the print of a thumb, under the right ear.' When the mother was found and asked how she could possibly be so barbarous, she confessed, 'in a violent agony of grief', that she had choked it so it would keep quiet whilst she stole the new clothing it wore. She had taken it out of the Bethnal Green Workhouse to do so. When she had noticed that the child was still alive, she had bashed its head with a stone. She had received 8*d* for her share in the stolen clothing. She claimed that a 'wicked creature' from the workhouse named Sukey had 'seduced' her into committing this heinous crime. Judith was sentenced to death. The ordinary at Newgate described her as 'Very hard-hearted ... I have not seen one more stupid, nor less thoughtful'. She confessed at the end that she...

> ...drank and swore much, and was averse to virtue and sobriety, delighting in the vilest companies, and ready to practice the worst of actions. She acknowledged the justice of her sentence, and died in peace with all Mankind.

1825   The *Examiner* on this day reported the suicide by poison of Italian flower-seller Christina Marie Briscolie (19). The inquest was held at the Three Cups, Oxford Road. Briscolie had been abandoned by her wealthy lover when their baby died. He afterwards rejected her pleas for money, writing, 'Who ever dreamt of meeting with such sublime feelings in the bosom of an Italian flower girl? ... The enclosed is the last assistance that you can expect of me.' After reading this, she 'wept all day and night' and spoke wildly. Briscolie informed a friend that she had 'settled everything this day, but it has cost me many tears'. She was shortly afterwards discovered lying slumped upon the floor of her room, her stomach filled with 'laudanum in a quantity greater than [the surgeon] had ever seen before'.

FEBRUARY

A trial in progress at the Old Bailey.
Two hanging men can be seen out of the window.

The famous Hogarth engraving of the Idle Apprentice at the Triple Tree, surrounded by orange-sellers and the rowdy, enormous crowds of a typical hanging.

1715   On this day, a very strange and very horrible attack occurred. Richard Griffith, of the parish of Hadley, had been sharing a stable with his fellow servant, Richard Davis. One day, Davis vanished. When their employer enquired after him, Griffith replied that he had not heard from the other servant. This news rather surprised her – but not as much as the discovery, a fortnight later, of the servant's body, missing its head, stuffed into a nearby dung heap. Another servant was horrified to discover the head perched precariously on the top of the pile, gleaming amid the ordure. The head had been picked clean by the hogs that lived in the field. All of the dead man's money was gone, as well as the silver buckles from his shoes. It all looked very black for Griffith, blacker still when he fled, and blackest of all when the investigators discovered that he had sold all of the deceased's clothes to a pawnshop. Griffith told the court that he had quarrelled with the prisoner and stabbed him in the head with a pitchfork that lay nearby. He was sent to the Triple Tree, lamenting his evil actions.

1 FEBRUARY

1785   Servant Sarah Panton, who worked at a pub in Poland Street, Soho, was examined today to determine whether she had just given birth to the naked baby found attacked and abandoned in a Hampstead hedge. Surgeon George Rodd was called to see the child, who had been taken to a chandler's shop at Kilburn. A rip ran down from the mouth to the chin, the neck had two wounds, and the top of its head and skull was covered with punched wounds. The cold had kept these wounds closed, but the moment that the child was brought into the house it started to bleed. Thomas Webb, surgeon of Coldbath Fields Prison, came to examine Panton – whereupon she burst into tears. Her employers noticed that she seemed much thinner, all of a sudden. The court could not prove that the child was hers, however, and so she was acquitted. The truth about the baby was never discovered.

2 FEBRUARY

1814   Three people were trapped on a piece of ice that floated free from the rest on this day, during another of the Thames' spectacular ice fairs. Above Westminster Bridge, two more young men stood on a piece that broke free:

3 FEBRUARY

they floated under the bridge at top speed, crying piteously for help all the way. One then sat – or fell – down and hurled them both to their deaths in the icy water.

Also on this day, but eleven years earlier, Peter Woulfe died at Barnard's Inn. This tall, thin man was the last true exponent of alchemy. His unusual method of curing any feeling of illness (by travelling all the way from London to Edinburgh – and back – by the mail coach) proved his undoing: he caught the cold that killed him on the way. According to the *Literary Gazette*, his room was 'so filled with furnaces and apparatus that it was difficult to reach his fireside'. A visitor once made the mistake of putting down his hat – and never found it again amongst the chaos.

4 FEBRUARY   **1796**   The *Gentleman's Magazine* reported on the execution of three murderous sailors – Colley, Cole and Blanche – who had murdered Captain Little. They were brought out of Newgate a little after 10 a.m, and taken to Execution Dock on a cart with a platform in the middle, where the three men sat. Two executioners sat behind them. They were hanged in the pouring rain, in front of an enormous crowd. They were dissected shortly afterwards.

5 FEBRUARY   **1732**   One of the most infamous murderers of the eighteenth century came to Newgate on this day, after cutting the throat of spinster Ann Price (17) in the Inner Temple, strangling Elizabeth Harrison (60) with a cord, and garrotting widow Lydia Duncombe (80) on 4 February. Ann, known as 'Nanny', was found sprawled in a pool of blood, her throat slashed three times from ear to ear; she seemed to have 'struggled hard for life'. Elizabeth – who had spent her whole life working for Lydia – was lying strangled on the bed, with scratches and the dark bruises of knuckles around her neck. Blood rushed from her nose, and a thin piece of bloody apron string had been wrapped so tightly around her throat that it bit into the skin. Lydia was on the floor, a thin string twisted around her spindly neck also. That same night, an employer grew suspicious of the demeanour of Temple laundress Sarah Malcolm (22), who knew the dead women, and searched her property. Hidden in a chamber pot, they found bloody clothing and a silver tankard, also covered in blood. 'You bloody murdering bitch you!' said the finder. 'Was it not enough to rob the people, and be damn'd to you, but you must murder them too? I'll see you hang'd, you bitch! You bloody bitch you!'

Sarah Malcolm, sketched in her cell by Hogarth.

When she was searched in the prison, Malcolm turned out to have bags of money hidden in her hair. She told the court that Mary Tracey, Thomas Alexander and James Alexander (two brothers) had murdered the women whilst she waited outside. James had hidden under the bed, and sneaked out in the night to let in the others. Sarah Malcolm was executed in Fleet Street, near to the scene of her crime, on 5 March 1733. She at first appeared quite calm, almost serene, and was reading a book – but then she burst into tears, and suddenly fainted. 'Just before the Cart drew away,' said the ordinary of Newgate, 'she look'd towards the Temple, and cryed out, "Lord have Mercy upon me, Christ have Mercy upon me, Lord Receive my Spirit," and then the Cart withdrew.'

1790   The *Gazette* reported: 6 FEBRUARY

Lady Wallace has in her possession a beautiful child about two years of age, who constantly accompanies her in her morning visits. Of this child she gives the following extraordinary account: that it was left at her door with a sum of £200 for its maintenance, but in all her enquiries she has never been able to discover its parents.

The article finished with a rather snide coda:

Her attention to the infant is increased by its bearing so very strong a resemblance to an illustrious family.

Also on this day, in 1800, the bladder of Evan Jones was fatally split at Holborn Bridge after an argument with a soldier over a game of dominoes. His killer was fined 1s.

1785   At about 8 p.m., a man knocked at the door of Mrs Abercrombie, in   7 FEBRUARY
Charlotte Street, Rathbone Place, calling out 'Post!' with a very loud voice. The maid immediately opened the door – and the man, accompanied by six others, all armed with swords and pistols, rushed into the house and robbed it. They then forced their way out the front and escaped.

Also on this day, but in 1729, Elizabeth Burgess of Whitechapel noticed her servant Jane Bostock coming out of the outhouse carrying a mop. Her suspicions were aroused; they were confirmed when the darkness within was searched with a stick and a dead baby boy was hooked out. Jane said that the child 'came from her in the House of Office [privy], and she could not help its falling down'. She was found not guilty.

1804   Forger Ann Hurle (22) was sentenced to death on this day. She   8 FEBRUARY
tried to speak as the halter was placed around her neck, but her voice failed her. The crowd grew louder and louder as the cap was pulled over her face. As the cart lurched forward, she gave a faint scream, and for two or three minutes after she was suspended she appeared to be in great agony, moving her hands up and down frequently.

Today, in 1722, clever and unscrupulous printer W. Chetwood of Russell Street, Covent Garden, made the most of recent sensation Moll Flanders by offering customers her true-life story, 'written from her own Memorandums', for just 5s.

9 FEBRUARY   **1774**   On this day, Ann Holding or Hawling attacked Elizabeth Tanner with a poker in the 'foul ward' of a London workhouse. The nurse heard a ruckus and came running, to find Ann – who had already been thrown out of the ward once for fighting over who got to sit nearest the fire – trying to break down the window, whilst shouting out that they were a 'parcel of pocky whores' and she planned to kill them all. The nurse sent Ann packing, but an hour later she was back – she had run to the fireplace and seized a poker, with which she struck Elizabeth on the face, declaring that she was a 'street-walking bitch'. Ann was tied up and locked in the morgue. Elizabeth, meanwhile, began to bleed at the mouth; she died a few weeks later. She had been about to be discharged. Her attacker was usually known as 'Mad Nan', and her defence was that her faculties were impaired: 'she is an inoffensive woman if not insulted,' said one witness, 'but when insulted she does not mind what she does; she is so weak in her understanding that a flower or piece of paper would divert her.' Ann was found guilty of manslaughter.

The next year, on this day, Massachusetts was declared in rebellion, and the American War of Independence began.

10 FEBRUARY   **1726**   On this day, Richard Witchell was drinking in the Hoop & Griffin Tavern, Thames Street, when Samuel Millington came in. Witchell immediately leapt up and informed the man that he was 'a scrub'. Words flew, and the two men took off their hats and wigs, and fell to scuffling on the floor. By a horrible accident, someone opened the door to see what was happening and caught Witchell's foot between the doorframe and the door. As he leapt up, the bone of his leg was ripped quite out of his shin – the surgeon found it hanging down whitely over his shoe. His ankle was shattered, the wound mortified, and, although the attending surgeon Charles Whadcock chopped off the limb, Witchell died two weeks later.

11 FEBRUARY   **1786**   At around 2 a.m., Mary Horseman of Kentish Town was woken by the sound of her 10-year-old son calling out that his father, London milkman Walter Horseman, needed her. Walter had been sleeping in the room above whilst his daughter was teething. Mary found her husband sitting on his bed. By the light of the moon, which was flooding through the large bay windows, she could see that he was quite black with blood, which covered him from his face to his waist. 'Lord bless me,' he said. 'Something has run over my face!'

'Run over your face?' she responded. 'Why, you are nothing but blood!' She ran for a candle, and, when she returned, the light revealed a truly hideous sight: her husband was cut to pieces, his forehead, eyes and nose smashed. His skull, which was broken, was described in court as 'cut and mangled in a desperate fashion'. The two sections of the skull had broken apart, and his eye sockets had been smashed into shards. The doctors who saw him knew instantly that there was nothing they could do.

As Mary wrapped a pillowcase around her husband's head, in an attempt to stem the bleeding, she discovered an ominous-looking stake of wood lying by the side of the drawers; a hole had been drilled in one end and filled with molten lead. It belonged to her apprentice, Joseph Rickards, an 18-year-old who had recently been dismissed from service for being too slow about his work. Next to the stick was an iron bar, taken from another room in the house, and this was quite covered with blood, 'jellied' on the bar with shreds and scraps of human flesh. A few farthings were all that was missing from the house. Walter Horseman lived until the 19th, but could give no account of what had happened to cause such dreadful injuries.

Rickards' landlady told the court that he had been out on the night of the murder; a watchman described meeting him near the Horsemans' house at 3 a.m. The two young lodgers in the third room of Horseman's house said that one of the tall cupboards at the end of their room was open when they woke, though it had been shut when they went to sleep. It was large enough for a man to crouch in or lie down inside. Rickards finally confessed on the 20th, claiming that he had secreted himself in the cupboard, and then crept out to batter his former employer to death, because Walter's wife, whose 'breasts he had laid hold of', had frequently kissed him and said she wished her husband dead. When the court found Rickards guilty, he stopped in the dock to say that his claims about Mrs Horseman were false, and that he did not know why he committed the crime. He was executed in Kentish Town on 27 February.

1790 On this day, William Higson's wife confessed that her husband was known locally as 'a second Brownrigg' because of the cruel way he treated his children. Blows were often heard echoing up the stairs of their lodging house – two or three times a day, every day. The ever-repeated word was 'Daddy! Oh daddy!' The next day, Mrs Higson's worries were proved true, when her husband cracked his 8-year-old son Joseph's head open with a poker. The next day, a neighbour heard him crying out sadly, 'Dear daddy, dear daddy!' When she visited, she found him moaning, with his head shockingly swollen. 'Has your daddy been beating you?' he had previously been asked. 'Yes,' he had replied, 'my daddy has a new way of beating me, because the neighbours should not cry out shame.' His father told the doctor who visited that the boy merely had 'a cold', even though the whole side of his face was bloody. 'His two eyes,' said the beadle who was called, 'were as big as a great turkey's egg cut in half.' This was because of all the blood pushing up against them, leaking from where his skull was cracked. The father was sentenced to hanging and dissection.

1726 A grand masked ball, given at the opera house, commenced at midnight. One particularly unlucky gambler lost £50, then £150. He was forced to hand over the money, bundled in four rouleaux (coins wrapped in paper), but the other gamblers grew suspicious and tore them open – to reveal nothing but halfpence inside. However, he proved so smooth-tongued in court that he was quickly released without charge.

At Puddle Dock (now the Mermaid Theatre), in 1732, the body of a man was found floating with a deep wound on his neck, and several other cuts and bruises. He was naked apart from the collar of his shirt, his shoes and his stockings.

12 FEBRUARY

13 FEBRUARY

14 FEBRUARY   **1732**   A horrible case came to an end at Tyburn gallows on this day. On 9 December, Charles Bird had woken up to hear his mistress, Jane, crying out in the room below: 'For God's sake, don't murder me! Pity me, for Christ's sake! For my poor family's sake!' Then she started to cry out Charles' name, louder and louder. 'God damn ye,' cried a deeper voice, 'what do ye want with Charles?' It was his master, waterman Robert Hallam (34), and, as Charles listened in horror, he heard the heavy sound of the metal fire tongs striking the pleading woman. A neighbour, Ann Anderson, was separated from this horrible scene by only a thin wall. She was woken by the row, and said wearily to her husband, 'Hallam's a beating of his wife again according to his custom.' Both Jane and Robert had recently begun to be unfaithful – Jane had slept four times with the lodger, and another time with a neighbour – and their relationship had fallen into violence and jealousy as a result. In fact, Jane was about to give birth, and Robert suspected that the baby was not his own. Ann heard a 'struggling and a rustling' towards the window, followed by a 'lamentable shriek' – and something flew out of the window. It was Jane. The husband ran, half dressed, into the street, carrying a candle: he told passers-by that his wife was drunk and a bitch, and manhandled her mangled form back into the house. As he was dragging her, Ann leant out of the window and roared, 'You villain! You have thrown your wife out of the window, and kill'd her!'

Ann found her friend cold and dead the next morning. Blood covered the wood by the window where she had tried to hold on to the frame. Ann told the magistrate at the trial that followed that she had once seen the poor wife's arms 'as black as your Lordship's gown' with bruises. Another neighbour told the court that Hallam had previously threatened to kill his wife, declaring, 'I'll send you and your infant to the Devil together!' Nine months earlier, he had appeared in court for threatening to rip his wife up with a kitchen knife. The wife's body was quite black, and the infant's head in her womb greenish with bruising. Hallam protested his innocence to the end, claiming that his wife had thrown herself out of the window to escape him.

15 FEBRUARY   **1724**   Alice Brumpton looked out of her window in Essex Court at 6.30 a.m. on this day and saw Constantine MacDennis, of St Clement Danes, dragging Frances Williams, his laundress, along the passageway outside; he stabbed her nineteen times with his sword, threw her onto the stones, and informed her that she was a witch and that he planned to burn her. He told the men who grabbed him that a murder had been committed in the Tower but he could not discover it because she had bewitched him. He also accused her of drinking all the milk in his house so that he could not make tea, throwing straw on his fire for magical purposes and magically causing him to have a rash. He was found not guilty of murder by reason of insanity.

16 FEBRUARY   **1821**   At 9 a.m., in a field between Chalk Farm Tavern and Primrose Hill (where the first Druidic revival meeting was held in 1717), two men fought to the death over slighting articles in a magazine. Mr John Scott, of York Street, Covent Garden, the editor of the *London Magazine*, fought Mr Christie, a friend of the editor of rival publication *Blackwood's Magazine*. The second shot fired hit Mr Scott in the groin, flew through his intestines and lodged on the other side. The surgeon, Mr Guthrie, extracted the ball, but the editor died on 4 March. His rival was tried and acquitted of murder.

1819   On this day, William Jennings (33) appeared at the Old Bailey to answer for his part in the death of Mary Ann Cormack (2). Mary's guardian was a Covent Garden soup-seller, and Jennings was a hustler offering a special kind of 'composition coal', which he claimed 'only the best gentlemen used'; it promised a wonderful fire for her soup. He gave her a black hatful of a strange soft rock. When she placed a hen's egg-sized lump on her fire that evening, it flew out like a rocket and set the rest of the rock on fire – and then the children's clothes, too. In a moment, all their clothes were on fire, and the heat grew so fierce that even the paint peeled from the walls. The soup-seller's eyebrows were burnt off, and another's eyeballs were scorched; poor little Mary was the worst afflicted, and died two days later. Jennings confessed that he had found the coal in the Strand, and was sentenced to three months in prison. · 17 FEBRUARY

1752   On this day, breeches-maker William Hill of Long Lane went to an apothecary to confess that he felt sadly ill. Old Bailey records show that he had been afflicted with a 'sad griping in his bowels', and 'turned yellow, grew very thin, and fell away from a very lusty man almost to nothing'. He became like a 'shadow', and could not even sit down for the pain in his insides. One day in March, he found a 'knob' of pure poison in his gruel; his niece, who lived with him, tasted it, 'and said it was very nasty stuff'. It turned out that his apprentice, Mary Carpenter (15), previously of Lambeth Workhouse, had been systematically poisoning his gruel with a dark green powder of vitriol – 'otherwise white copperas'. She was sent straight to the nearest compter, and confessed that she had poisoned him eight times, after her father had told her that the substance was very deadly. An ounce and a half could be had for a penny. Hill died on 1 May, and his guts were found to be 'very much distorted with wind'. His apprentice was found not guilty of murder, but the court directed that she be charged with poisoning. · 18 FEBRUARY

1728   Peter Bluck of Holborn appeared at the Old Bailey to answer a charge of murdering his daughter Anne (5) on this day. As he pleaded 'not guilty', the court noticed, to their astonishment, that he appeared to be quite mad. The motive was that he was afraid his two other children would treat the little girl badly, and so he had hung a noose of wire from his bed and hooked her tiny head through it. He had taken her down forty-five minutes later, and then told everyone she had died from an 'apoplectick' fit. Two and a half years later he confessed, and went to court. It turned out that he had given £400 to the minister to pray for him, and had nothing left to live on. As the only evidence against him was his own confession, and as he was quite clearly not in his right mind, the jury found him not guilty. · 19 FEBRUARY

20 FEBRUARY   1745   Weaver Edmund Gilbert (67) of Bethnal Green attacked his apprentice, Thomas Salter (14), with a hearth brush on this day, striking him on his side and his forehead and creating 'a great black place on his side'. Salter died on the 24th, but he could not tell anyone how ill he was because 'his tongue was so swelled that he could not speak'. 'About his lower rib on the right side ... was as black as my hat,' said his uncle. The woman who lived above the shop saw Thomas in his coffin; he was bruised in 'a barbarous manner from head to foot'. The neighbours testified that: 'There were such outcries, shrieks, and lamentations that made our hearts bleed to hear them.' Gilbert came to Tyburn on 7 June 1745, where he was judged 'a very morose spirit [who] used all those very ill over whom he had power', but 'died in peace with all men'.

Also today, but in 1795, Kyd Wake was tried at the King's Bench for following the King's coach, hissing, and throwing stones as part of a rabble of 200,000 people assembled at St James's Park to petition the King – somewhat ironically – for peace. The windows were smashed in St Margaret's Street, and the coach itself was almost destroyed on its return trip through Pall Mall. When the King left, with just two footmen, in his private coach, he was again attacked: men tried to pull open the doors, but a nearby party of Horse Guards saw the turmoil and galloped to the rescue. Wake got five years of hard labour and was pilloried in Gloucester.

21 FEBRUARY   1814   On this day, 'Colonel du Bourg' appeared in Dover claiming that Napoleon had been killed, and the war with France was at an end at last. French officers began to appear in the streets of London handing out peace flyers. These events had a significant impact on the London Stock Exchange: £1.1 million worth of shares were traded before the lie was exposed. Deliberate stock manipulation was suspected, and three people connected with that purchase were charged with the fraud: Lord Cochrane, a well-known naval hero and MP; his uncle, the Hon. Andrew Cochrane-Johnstone; and Richard Butt, Lord Cochrane's financial advisor. Captain Random de Berenger, who had posed both as du Bourg and as one of the French officers, was soon arrested, and a guilty verdict was returned against all of them. The chief conspirators were sentenced to twelve months of prison time, a fine of £1,000 each, and an hour in the public pillory. Lord Cochrane was also stripped of his naval rank and expelled from the Order of the Bath. He was saved from the pillory by Sir Francis Burdett, who told the government that if Cochrane was put in pillory, he would stand beside him. On his release from jail, Cochrane was accepted into the British Navy, and progressed to the rank of Admiral. He also had his titles restored.

22 FEBRUARY   1773   This afternoon, a long-running quarrel between Lord Townshend and Lord Bellamont, 'the Hibernian Seducer' (who had at least thirteen children by various different women), was finally decided in Marylebone Fields when Bellamont received a pistol ball near the groin. His Lordship ultimately recovered, after great suffering, but the extra ball remained lodged next to his spine. It can be assumed that no lasting harm came to his

Lordship's greatest asset, however, since he managed to father several more children after the duel.

Meanwhile, one of the strangest events in London history occurred on this day, when 5ft 10in Arthur Thistlewood (48) suggested to a small group of friends that a forthcoming dinner at Lord Harrowby's house in No. 39 Grosvenor Square would be an ideal opportunity to kill the Cabinet. Thistlewood managed to assemble twenty-seven men to further the conspiracy, which was to occur on the following night. A three-stall stable in Cato Street (afterwards Homer Street) was hired as a meeting place. The conspirators planned to knock at Lord Harrowby's door with an 'urgent letter', and then run in with hand grenades. When the grenades went off, causing total chaos, all the men were to charge into the dining room and slaughter the diners. Their victims' heads were then to be paraded along the Strand. The spontaneous mob that they thought would form was to seize the Bank, the Tower, the Mint and all other places of importance.

However, a man named Hidon was not the revolutionary he appeared to be, and accosted Harrowby and told him all. When the conspirators met, twelve

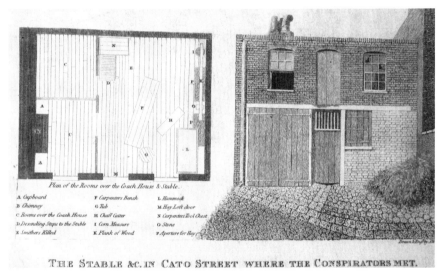

THE STABLE &C. IN CATO STREET WHERE THE CONSPIRATORS MET.

The stable where the Cato Street Conspirators met.

The attack on the Cato Street stable. The last words are captured: 'Oh God, I am...', as are the host of weapons lying on tables inside. The other speech bubbles say: 'Extinguish the lights!' and 'We are Peace Officers, lay down your arms!'

police officers of the Bow Street Runners were waiting in a public house on the opposite side of the street. At 7.30 p.m., the police burst in and arrested the conspirators. It was a desperate fight: the only way into the stable was up a narrow ladder, and the whole room was a mass of cutlasses, bayonets, pistols, sword belts and pistol balls. The room soon filled up with smoke from all the guns firing. In the confusion, Thistlewood killed a policeman called Smithers – whose last words were, 'Oh God! I am —'. Thistlewood managed to escape, along with a couple of the conspirators. One of the policemen was shot in the head, but the bullet ground across the side of his head, ripping the scalp as it went. Another was shot in the arm, but the bullet glanced along his arm, tearing the sleeve of his jacket from wrist to elbow. The next day, a London entrepreneur charged 1s to visit the stable. The escapees were all captured a few days later. Thistlewood was caught in White Street, Finsbury, and went to the Bloody Tower. He met his fate on 1 May.

23 FEBRUARY   **1716**   On this day, one of the most audacious escapes in history took place when William Maxwell, 5th Earl of Nithsdale, broke out of the Tower of London on the day before he was due to be executed. He was disguised as a woman, despite having an impressive beard. His eyebrows were powdered white, and rouge was dabbed over the beard to hide it. The escape was planned by his wife, and involved a clever deception carried out by Mrs Mills, whom the Countess lodged with (and who, being tall and pregnant, was almost the same size as the would-be escapee), and Mrs Morgan, who was very slim and so could carry a spare set of clothes stuffed up her top. Only one guest was allowed into the cell at a time, so the Countess sent in Mrs Morgan, who quickly handed over the spare outfit, followed by Mrs Mills (weeping dramatically and clutching a handkerchief over her face). Once inside, Mills changed into the clothes left by the first visitor and left. Nithsdale then changed into Mrs Mills' dress, clamped a handkerchief over his face and fled for the door, escorted all the way by his wife – who kept behind him so that the guards would not notice the way he walked. The sympathetic guards opened the doors for 'Mrs Mills', and the Earl quickly made his way to Dover, and thence to Rome.

24 FEBRUARY   **1716**   James, Earl of Derwentwater and Viscount Kenmure were executed on Tower Hill today for their part in the failed Jacobite rebellion of 1715. During the Lords' time in prison, so much money had flowed in from sympathisers that the rooms were allegedly swimming in wine, and extremely merry. Thus, security became rather lax, allowing Jacobite Thomas Forster to make false keys and escape Newgate on 10 April 1715; one month later exactly, fifteen men escaped by the age-old trick of hiding near the door and punching the first person who opened it. One escaped by the luckiest chance: he saw a piece of silver plate he recognised in a window by the prison, and realised that his family were inside – they helped him get away. Others were not so lucky, and were caught milling around in the streets, unsure where to go. Lord Winton broke out of the Tower, and escaped as well – as did Derwentwater's younger brother, Charles Radcliffe,

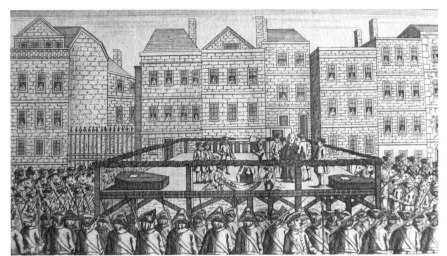

Execution of
the Rebel Lords,
Derwentwater
and Kenmure, on
Tower Hill. The
coffins, draped in
black, each had
nameplates already
attached, which the
Lords read before
they perished.

who was finally captured, in 1745, upon a pirate vessel and executed. No such chance for escape came to this unlucky pair.

They travelled from the Tower in a hackney-cab, and arrived to a black-draped room on Tower Hill. At the platform – also draped in black – both prayed. Then, after getting the executioner to remove a rough bit of wood from the block so it didn't hurt his neck, Derwentwater's head was removed with a single blow. All of the Earl's extensive estates went to the Greenwich Hospital, a revenue 'generally estimated at between thirty and forty thousand pounds per annum'. Viscount Kenmure prayed for the Pretender before his head came off with two blows.

1762 A proclamation was issued today in 1744, ordering all papists to **25 FEBRUARY** depart Westminster and the city, and 10 miles hence. Suspected papists who remained were to be put under house arrest.

Later on, in 1762, William Kent went into the vault at St John's in order to prove that the body in a coffin there really did belong to Fanny, his last wife's sister and his new wife in all but name. This was the final blow to the credibility of the Cock Lane Ghost ('the most bungling performance of the silliest imposture,' according to writer and social reformer Mrs Montague).

The ghost saga had begun when a lodger in Cock Lane, West Smithfield, had offered the landlord's 10-year-old daughter a bed – only to be disturbed by the echoing of loud rapping sounds in the night, like a cobbler at work. The story had begun to spread, and the ghost's tricks diversified to include scratching under any bed that the girl was placed upon, following her about, throwing her into fits, accusing locals of murder and answering callers' questions with well-timed knocks. Eventually, the girl in question was hog-tied to the bed (which was raised up like a hammock, with her arms spread out as wide as they would go), whereupon silence was renewed. She was threatened with Newgate, after which she was caught with a wooden board stuffed up her dress (which she had used to make the scratching noises). Her whole family was sent to prison.

'English Credulity, or the Invisible Ghost.' This cartoon satirises the Cock Lane debacle: blind magistrate Sir John Fielding can be seen entering (with the black cloth wrapped around his eyes) on the left, saying, 'I should be glad to see this sprite!' Other ministers look under the bed, containing the children, over which the 'spirit' hovers. (Courtesy of the Library of Congress, LC-USZ62-137506)

26 FEBRUARY **1724** A small boy called upon Mrs Ann Rondeau this day and said that a man wanted to speak to her at the sign of the Black Dog, Bishopsgate. Ann waited at the sign for quite some time, but, as no one appeared, she returned home. There she found her daughter sitting quietly in her chair, head leaning against the chimney piece. 'What,' she said, 'are you fast asleep?' She reached out and touched her daughter's hand, but it dropped heavily towards the floor. Mrs Rondeau realised, with a start, that her daughter's front was covered with blood: her throat had been slashed, and she was dead. The motive turned out to be love: the dead girl's husband, Lewis Houssart (40), had married again, but his new wife had learnt that he was already married and had thrown him out. 'I will make you sensible that I have no other wife,' he told her, and had marched off to manage his wicked deed. After a long appeal, which rested on facts such as the illegality of the case, given that his name was really Loui, not Lewis (which the court revoked, using examples of his own handwriting, where he had carefully written out 'Lewis'), he was hanged at the end of Swan Yard, Shoreditch, on 7 December 1724. 'When he arriv'd at the place appointed for his death,' said the ordinary, 'he turn'd pale, and was very sick...'

In another case, Mary Morgan, who worked at the Red Lion in Holloway, confessed (when friends noticed she looked a bit peaky) that she had just buried a baby in the garden. It was dug up and found to have two stab wounds – the bowels protruded from one of these. She was quickly found guilty of murder on this day.

27 FEBRUARY **1751** Robert Hore, an apprentice carpenter, left his master's horse outside a shop in Knightsbridge; when he came back, it was gone. A man saw someone riding past, hell for leather, but could not see what colour the horse was in the dark. The beast was eventually found at the George Inn in Hammersmith, left behind by a customer. When the customer explained that he had found the horse, worn out, wandering in the streets past Kensington, he was acquitted.

Hogarth's 1751 print of 'Gin Lane', set in St Giles' parish. Details include syphilitic sores on the prostitute's legs (centre front), a man who has hanged himself (in the window on the left) and the motto mentioned in the text (below) on the lintel of the archway on the bottom right.

1736   A duty was proposed on gin and spirits on this day, to try to halt their ruinous influence. The 'Historical Chronicle' of the *Gentleman's Magazine* had the following to say:

> We have observed some signs, where such liquors are retailed, with the following inscriptions, 'Drunk for a penny, dead drunk for two pence, clean straw for nothing'.

28 FEBRUARY

1735   On this day, melancholic Quaker shoemaker John Wright was baptised in an attempt to reconcile himself with God, as he was 'sure he would be damn'd'. However, it did no good: after becoming convinced that he would not go to Heaven, he made two unsuccessful suicide attempts (one an attempt to drown himself in St James's Park), and then decided that it was better to die at the hands of the law than at his own hand. He turned to a desperate string of crimes. In June 1738, an attempt to extort money from ironmonger William Dolley of Holborn went wrong: he decided to hand-deliver a letter demanding £30, and the shopkeeper simply grabbed him and sent for the watch. The letter said:

> We positively declare we will murder you, and yours, as sure as ever you were born ... if you refuse, we will wash our Hands in your Heart's Blood, and burn your House to Ashes.

His aunt testified to the Old Bailey that his father was 'a little disorder'd in his Brain', and that his sister was 'quite raving'. Wright was sentenced to death, but was afterwards respited.

29 FEBRUARY

MARCH

Drury Lane captured in all its glory in *Real Life in London*: falling bricks (guides to the city warned you to look up as often as possible), pawn shops, fallen women and soup-sellers galore.

1726 At dawn today an awful sight was discovered at Horseferry wharf, near Lambeth Bridge: a decapitated human head. A bloody pail was found nearby. This disgusting find was swiftly carried to St Margaret's churchyard in Westminster, where the mud was washed from its ashen cheeks, and its hair neatly combed. It was displayed on a pole, and thousands came to stare at this astonishing sight. All passing carts and coaches were stopped

The head in St Margaret's graveyard. (The first person I'd suspect would be the woman with the bucket! A hamper on the head was later used to transport dead bodies by London bodysnatchers Bishop and May; the smell caused quite a lot of comment.)

for several days afterwards in the hopes of discovering the rest of the body, but to no avail. Three weeks later, a jumble of arms, legs and thighs was found dumped by a pond in Marylebone. When the water was dragged, a white torso, wrapped in a blanket, was pulled from the depths. At last this dreadful churchyard spectacle was recognised – was it the head of chandler John Hays (or Hayes) of Tyburn Road?

Eventually, John's wife, Catherine (36), came to see the head for herself; by now it was bobbing in a jar of spirits. As soon as the glass vessel with its terrible contents was raised, she screamed, 'It is my husband's head! It is my dead husband's head!' She kissed the glass, and asked for a lock of the oily hair.

'You've had enough of his blood already,' said the surgeon – upon which Catherine fainted quite away. For it was indeed her dead husband's head, and Catherine had last seen it by flickering candlelight as her own son, tailor

The horrible moment when John Hayes' head departed ways from his body. Catherine is pictured carefully positioning the bucket. The bed in the background is depicted as distinctly rumpled, in accordance with the commonly held view that Catherine made love to one – or both – men whilst her husband lay a corpse. In reality, Billings burst into tears after the murder.

Thomas Billings (19), sawed it off. She had even helpfully held the pail to catch the falling blood.

John, an abusive husband, had been gulled into a drinking contest with Billings. When John had slipped into a drunken stupor, Billings had struck him twice on the head with an axe. Then Mr Thomas Wood, who was Catherine and John's lodger (and was also Catherine's lover), aided the pair by carefully slitting John's throat. The three fiends then proceeded to cut Mr Hayes into pieces so they could cram him into a long chest which Catherine had provided: first the head and the legs, then the thighs and the arms. Eventually, however, such a towering pile of jumbled chunks was formed that they over-spilled the wooden case. The two men had therefore begun a grim relay race: first the pail full of head and blood was carried to the wharf and slung into the darkness; then the limbs were carried, piecemeal, to the pond. All the way, a running patter about fetching this and that was held, to convince the neighbours that all was well – though the nearest neighbour heard the scrape of something heavy being dragged across the floor.

In court, where tickets were changing hands for up to 1 guinea, Catherine blamed cruel treatment, drink and the Devil for her crime, and announced solemnly, 'I'll hold up my hand and say I am guilty, for nothing can save me, nobody can forgive me.' Billings told the ordinary at Newgate that he had been 'sottishly intoxicated'.

Billings had decided to commit the crime after witnessing the husband beat Catherine: 'I'd be his butcher for a penny,' he had said. John had previously told Billings and Wood that humans had no souls; from this, they began to feel that it was no worse to kill him than to kill a dog or a cat.

Wood spent his days in the hold at Newgate, and – perhaps in a lucky escape – perished of a fever on 4 May before he came to Tyburn. Billings declared himself 'heartily sorry' for his sin, and came to the Triple Tree to be hanged on 9 May. Catherine was forced to watch him die. His body was then hanged in chains nearby.

Mrs Hayes had a more horrible fate in store. She was sentenced to be drawn on a hurdle, and there set alight and burnt to ashes. The thought terrified her: she fainted when the death penalty was announced, and cried and fretted constantly at the thought in prison. On 9 May 1726, she was taken to her death. The stake to which she was tied with links of iron had an iron collar, with a rope twisting around her neck onto which the executioner held. She begged the executioner to strangle her as the flames began to lick at the wood, but as he pulled upon the rope the flames roared up and scorched his hands. He let go, and Catherine vanished into the inferno. Three great shrieks were heard before she was swept from sight. Her sufferings were finally ended when the hangman threw a piece of wood at her head, shattering her skull and driving 'her brains plentifully out'.

Two further events marked this dreadful day: the stands for spectators, who numbered into the tens of thousands, broke under the massed weight, pitching two Londoners to their deaths. One prisoner, Mr Mapp, also managed to wriggle out of the halter around his neck in the cart, and made a brave dash for freedom across the heads of the crowd before he was captured.

Catherine Hayes set alight: this pictures the exact moment before the executioner was forced to let go of the rope, making Catherine one of the few women in British history to actually be burnt alive.

2 MARCH **1721** On this day, Peregrine Ball was playing football in Thames Street with another boy, John Wine (13), when a cart came rattling along. A wild kick sent the football firing up into the cart, and Wine ran into the street to get it. Horribly, he fell, and the cart sliced over the top of his belly: the child's backbone cracked under the weight. Peregrine and John (before he died the next day) insisted that the cart could have stopped, but many adult witnesses claimed it could not. The driver was therefore charged with manslaughter, burnt on the hand and released.

3 MARCH **1714** On this day in 1714, Nathaniel Parkhurst (or Perkhurst), a drunken prisoner at the Fleet Prison, stormed into the room of another prisoner, Lewis Pleura, crying, 'Damn ye, Sir Lewis, pay me the 4 guineas you owe me!' The watchman shortly afterwards heard a shriek of 'Murder!', and ran upstairs to find Pleura lying stark naked on the floor with Parkhurst sitting on him.

He was waving a sword, and a trail of blood led to the bed, the sheets of which were crimson with gore. The naked man had been stabbed eighteen or twenty times. Parkhurst was led from the room, but managed to struggle back into it so he could shout 'Damn ye, Pleura, are ye not dead yet?' He was hanged at Tyburn shortly afterwards.

1818 At about 8 p.m. the wind began to blow in London, and soon a perfect **4 MARCH** storm of rain, wind and lightning raged across the capital. The house of Mr Thatcher in Union Street, Chelsea, fell in upon him as he was sitting by his fireside reading and he was buried in the ruins. Neighbours managed to rescue him from the wreckage but he was very seriously injured. Trees were blown down in St James's Park and elsewhere across London. Mr Kinnaird, a Thames Police magistrate, was sitting in his back parlour with his family, at his house in Holborn, when a stack of chimneys fell in on them. They had just a moment's time for escape. The chair in which Mr Kinnaird was sitting was broken into slivers, as well as the table on which he was leaning. A kitchen at the back of Lady Hayes' house in Somerset Street was rendered one mass of ruins by a large wall falling into it. After some time, the body of Mary Mauntie, the cook, was recovered from the rubble, her head dashed to atoms and her body greatly disfigured. The bodies of the housemaid and the laundry maid were also dug out, but some signs of life were apparent in both of them – although they were most dangerously bruised. One had her thigh broken and was burnt about the shoulder, and the other was more seriously burnt.

1819 In the Court of King's Bench, Guildhall, a German quack doctor **5 MARCH** named Hube tried to sue a client named Phelps, of Crown Court, Cheapside, for failing to pay for his totally spurious cure for cancer. Hube had his case thrown out of court on this day.

1746 Law enforcer Mr North received an unsigned letter which advised **6 MARCH** him to look under the floorboards at 'Johannah' Wood's lodging in Hudson House. There he found a loose board. 'Here's the nest!' cried North – and lifted out a pair of flasks filled with earth, two pieces of good metal and thirty-six forged coins wrapped in paper. The evidence was not enough to convict Wood of high treason, but she was bound over for a new trial for uttering 'false and counterfeit coin'.

1804 Thomas Pitt, 2nd Baron Camelford (29) – the cousin of Pitt the **7 MARCH** Younger – was an adventurous sort: he was once flogged on board ship after attempting to trade a piece of broken barrel-hoop for sexual favours in Tahiti. He also loved duels, and often treated his horses cruelly in London's streets in the hope that someone would call him out. He said that his friend Captain Best was 'a scoundrel, a liar and a ruffian' at the Prince of Wales' coffee house, after Camelford's mistress, Symons – formerly Best's mistress – told him that Best had said some deeply unflattering things about him. (It was a lie – Best had turned down one of her advances.) They met in the fields behind Holland House. Camelford fired first, but missed; Best then fired, and his Lordship fell at full length. He seized his rival by the hand, and exclaimed, 'Best, I am a dead man; you have killed me, but I freely forgive you.' Camelford was found by gardeners, lying in the waterlogged field with a bullet lodged in his spine (after it had passed through his lungs).

8 MARCH   **1769**   Today, Elizabeth Chudleigh, maid of honour to the Princess of Wales, married naval lieutenant Evelyn Pierrepont, Duke of Kingston (though some reports give the date as the 3rd) in St George's, Hanover Square. Unfortunately, she already had a husband – Captain Augustus John Hervey, Lord Bristol. When Evelyn died, she found herself facing a charge of bigamy at Westminster Hall on 5 April 1776. This case was the sensation of the age. She argued that she had applied for, and received, a special dispensation license from the Ecclesiastical Court to remarry. Dr Collier, who in particular had told her it would be fine, sadly could not appear for her: he was trapped in his room with a debilitating attack of gout. Elizabeth lost

The trial of the Duchess at Westminster Hall.

the case – and if she had not been allowed to plead 'benefit of the Peerage', she would have been burnt on the hand with a hot iron. However, to her prosecutors' despair, the court decided to leave her with all the money from the marriage, even though it was not a valid one. She travelled the world in the most magnificent style, and died, at 68, on 20 August 1788. She left more than £200,000.

Also today, but in 1756, James Egan and James Salmon were pilloried in Smithfield for giving false testimony. Stones, brickbats, potatoes, dead dogs and cats, and 'other things' flew so fiercely that both men's heads swelled to an 'enormous size'. Londoners then leapt up and pulled their clothes so they were almost strangled, before a stone smashed into Egan's head and killed him. All three of his compatriots (two more men were pilloried elsewhere) died soon afterwards in Newgate.

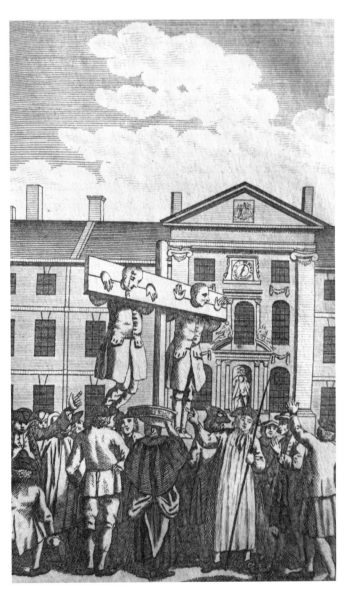

Egan in the pillory; the wound that was to lead to his death is visible on his face.

9 MARCH **1792**   Samuel Taylor, and his wife Jane, killed Thomas Partridge today, as he was walking with friends through Catherine Wheel Alley. Taylor and his wife came up and 'damned and blasted several times, and [used] many bad expressions'. Partridge was then thrown onto the floor – while Samuel's wife called out 'Stab him, stab him!' The watch came and took the attackers away, leaving Thomas leaning on a post, with his hands folded over his side. 'Oh Lord, I am a dead man ... I can feel all the blood trickling from my side!' he said. When his friend unbuttoned his jacket, 'the blood flew out all over [him] entirely'. The friend filled his wound in with cobwebs, but he languished – recovering, then sinking again – and died on 18 December. Both attackers were found guilty of manslaughter and imprisoned for a year.

10 MARCH **1792**   Botany-mad John, 3rd Earl of Bute – George III's tutor and later prime minister – died on this day, aged 78. He was, thanks to a 4s tax on cider, among other things, extremely unpopular; in fact, Chambers' biography has it that, 'Few ministers have been more hated than Lord Bute was by the English nation.' He spent £80,000 on his Hampshire home, which was so near to the cliffs that it eventually fell from them – as did he, in November 1790, when he slipped whilst collecting plants. The injuries he received were thought to have contributed to his death two years later.

11 MARCH **1811**   Edward Beazley (13) threw acid at Mary Ann Sutton in Fleet Street today, ruining her pelisse and her gloves. As she was walking along at about 8.30 a.m., she suddenly realised that the back of her clothing and her gloves were burnt. Then Edward ran up and slapped her face – leaving a burning sensation. His hands were covered with the liquid too. She had never seen him before. Edward confessed that he had attacked six couples that day, but promised not to do it any more if they would only let him go. He was whipped in Newgate.

12 MARCH **1745**   Nurse Lucy Acor, of Blackfriars, battered and starved tiny infant Mary Page (1) to death, leaving her 'in filth and excrements' in a drawer. Her landlady, who took over the care of the child, told the Old Bailey, 'The child was so neglected, that the bones were through the skin; and there were holes through the skin.' Acor frequently went out and left the child behind. The magnificently named Sarah Death told the court that the infant was originally kept on top of an old pillowcase, with a reeking pair of old breeches draped over it. The last time she saw it:

> ...it was in a most dreadful situation; I helped to clean the child's head, and the cap was eat into the head; I was forced to cut it with the scissars; it was very disagreeable, and quite devoured with vermin.

Doctor Vaux told the court that, in his opinion, the child was of 'diseased' parentage and sickly constitution, and the court therefore found Lucy Acor not guilty of murder.

Also on this day, but in 1716, a highwayman named James Goodman was executed – but not before he had done his utmost to escape from justice. When the sentence was passed, he leapt over the barrier in the Old Bailey and ran, successfully eluding the people chasing him, despite being heavily loaded with irons. However, he was caught in the strangest of ways: about a month later, he tried to have a man who had cheated him charged with theft. While he was sitting in a Holborn alehouse, waiting for the lawyers to arrive, he was recognised; the Newgate guards were called, and the man was dragged back to receive his punishment.

1790 On this morning, the effects of a vicious assault in Plow Street, Whitechapel, by Thomas Hewett Masters on his stepdaughter Mary Lovedon (6) took hold. The girl's mother, Esbeck Lovedon, went to buy a bullock's heart from Whitechapel Market. When she returned, her landlady remarked that it was odd she had seen neither husband nor child that morning. Five minutes later, Esbeck came running down the stairs, saying, 'Oh! Mrs Tate. My child is dead! My child is dead!' The girl was lying in bed, sadly bruised in every part 'to the finger ends'. The bowels were ripped, a large quantity of blood had fallen into her belly, and 'the whole scalp was one continued act of violence'. The court found Masters guilty of murder, and sent him to his death. **13 MARCH**

1757 In 1757, Robert Brazil knelt on a shop counter to reach a shelf, where he took five gowns. When the shopkeeper quizzed him later, he confessed, and shamefacedly escorted the man to the pawnshop, where he had sold the goods. 'I have nothing to say, but leave myself to the mercy of the jury,' he said at his trial. They sentenced him to death. **14 MARCH**

1723 On this day, Christopher Layer, die-hard Jacobite, went to his death. He had planned to murder the King, and seize the Prince of Wales and his children in order to place 'King James' upon the throne. At his trial, he complained of being so heavily weighted with chains that he could neither sleep nor write his defence; the court retorted that the chains, which had been specially sent up from Newgate, were to prevent his escape – which he had previously managed by scrambling through a high window – and they would not take them off: they would only have to put them all back on again. Layer was drawn to Tyburn on a sledge, dressed all in black, and used his last moments before he was hanged, drawn and eviscerated to warn the crowd that only damnation awaited the supporters of the usurper King George, and that they had best take up arms against him at once. His head remained on Temple Bar for many years afterwards. According to legend, Layer's head was bought by a London antiquary and buried with him, tucked neatly under his right hand. Other legends claim that it ended up under the floor of a London pub. **15 MARCH**

1733 Sir Robert Walpole beat up an actor at Haymarket Theatre during this month, after the man inserted an improvised joke about one of Walpole's policies into a performance of *Love Runs all Dangers*. **16 MARCH**

17 MARCH   **1800**   Today, the axle tree of Mrs Hunt's carriage broke while she was travelling along Bond Street. The coachman was thrown off the box and the wheels, passing over his head, killed him on the spot. The coach overturned, and the women inside were slightly bruised.

In 1803, £500 was subscribed to the Royal Jennerian Society for the purposes of 'exterminating the small-pox by the introduction of the vaccine innoculation [*sic*]'.

18 MARCH   **1740**   Jenny Diver, the greatest of all London's pickpockets, stepped onto the scaffold this day. She was finally captured when a woman she'd robbed caught hold of her dress and held on like grim death at Walbrook. 'Jenny Diver', named for her ability to dive stealthily into any pocket she chose, was born Mary Young. When she first arrived in London as a young orphan, she came by chance to the lodging house of Irish expert thief Anne Murphy. Anne introduced her to a company of St Giles' pickpockets, and she quickly became the finest of them all at the wicked art. She allegedly practiced for two hours a day. One of her most famous tricks involved putting on a pair of false arms, so she could rob two people at once. She was caught and transported more than once, but always returned to her old hunting grounds in the end. She cleverly spent her days before transportation using her illicit wealth and connections to buy up all the stolen property she could get her hands on. This was transported to the New World, making her, on her arrival, an extremely wealthy woman. On one occasion when she was transported – under the alias Jane Webb – she had robbed more than twenty people in one day upon London Bridge. Her spirits failed in Newgate's press yard, but she rallied in the cart and, after fervent prayers, was launched into eternity. She is buried in St Pancras' churchyard.

19 MARCH   **1784**   Between 6 p.m. and 7 p.m., two foreigners were attacked by a mob opposite the door of Drury Lane Playhouse. The mob surrounded them, crying out, 'Pickpocket! Pickpocket!' Under this pretence, they pulled them backwards and robbed them of everything they had in their pockets. One of the gentlemen, besides his money, lost his hat and one of his shoes; having found means to secure his watch, the villains cut and bruised him in a shocking manner, in the hope that he would drop it. Two of the soldiers on guard at last came to their assistance and rescued them.

20 MARCH   **1727**   Sir Isaac Newton, who amongst his many achievements sent master coiner William Chaloner to the gallows, died on this day. In a memoir, Newton wrote:

> I do not know what I may appear to the world, but to myself I seem to have been only like a boy playing on the sea-shore, and diverting myself in now and then finding a smoother pebble or a prettier shell than ordinary, whilst the great ocean of truth lay all undiscovered before me.

Two years later, in 1739, George Broderick and two friends assaulted William Reynolds on the King's Highway near Shoreditch. Reynolds was rattling along in a coach when three horsemen stopped it, and ordered him out. They put a gun to his head, and swore they would 'shoot his brains out' if he refused. He tried to claim that he had no rings – whilst surreptitiously wiggling his ring off with his glove – but one man saw. They ripped off his glove and took the ring. In court, the thieves claimed that they had given the proceeds to 'the Prisoners in Bedlam'. Broderick was hanged.

1829 The famous Duke of Wellington met the Earl of Winchilsea at   21 MARCH
Battersea Fields after the Earl wrote a letter, published in several newspapers, accusing Wellington of having 'insidious designs for the infringement of our liberties, and the introduction of Popery into every department of the state'. Wellington shot at the Earl but missed, whereupon the Earl raised his pistol and fired his shot into the air. Honour was then declared satisfied, and the Earl wrote a public letter of apology in the next edition of the *Standard*.

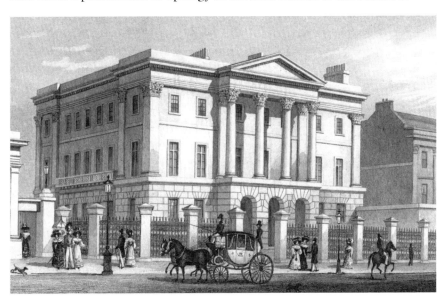

Apsley House, home of the Duke of Wellington.

1718 Today, as servant Thomas Parks was strolling through Cheapside,   22 MARCH
Robert Milksop stole his periwig, which had a value of 30s. Parks whipped around the second that Milksop touched the box containing the wig: Milksop dropped it and ran, but to no avail. He was chased, caught, and ultimately hanged.

1815 On this day in 1815, a London cook was arrested; as writer Judith   23 MARCH
Flanders has pointed out, the woman, cook Eliza Fenning (22) of No. 68 Chancery Lane, was later hanged, despite no proof that a crime had taken place. Fenning worked for the Turner family, and one day asked to make some of her speciality for the family – yeast dumplings. Mrs Turner agreed, though she observed that the dough was of rather a strange consistency. The dumplings, when they appeared, were observed to be 'black and heavy'

in appearance. After eating just a small piece of dumpling, Mrs Turner found herself feeling very faint – an excruciating pain began, followed by her head, as she put it, swelling 'extremely'. In court, Mr Orlibar Turner described how his wife (and shortly after, his son) fled the table on the night in question. He soon afterwards found his son crouched in the passage: he had brought up his dinner, and his eyes were 'exceedingly swollen; very much indeed'. Three minutes later, the illness struck the elder Mr Turner.

'The effect was so violent,' said Turner later, 'I hardly had time to go into my backyard before my dinner came up.' When asked if the vomiting was of a common kind, he replied, 'I never experienced anything before like it: it was terrible indeed.' The next morning, the Wednesday, an object of menace was discovered – the brown pan with which the dumplings had been made, still coated with dough. Mr Turner noted a white powder at the bottom of it, which he showed to several people in the house. This, he suggested, was arsenic. From his pocket, on the stand, the elder Mr Turner withdrew the knife and fork with which he had eaten that day. They were covered with a 'blackness', and had since rusted – another sign, he claimed, of the presence of the poison. The jury returned with a verdict of guilty, and the miserable girl was carried from the bar convulsed with agony, and uttering frightful screams. Eliza came to the gallows dressed all in white, with laced boots and a white cap. Her body was then carried through the streets of London, with the pall carried by six young women dressed likewise all in white: 'Many thousands accompanied the procession, and the windows, and even the tops of the houses, as it passed, were thronged with spectators.' She was widely believed to be innocent, and arguments still rage about the case to this day.

24 MARCH **1784** 'The town was this morning,' said the *Gentleman's Magazine*, 'thrown into a great ferment by one of the most extraordinary burglaries on record.' Robbers took the Great Seal of England from the Lord Chancellor's house in Great Ormond Street:

> The great seal consists of two parts about the size of a small plate, one folding over the other and the impression made by it is on both sides of the wax. The seal is composed mostly of silver, in value about 30l, but the workmanship amounts to a great deal more.

The theft was reported to Bow Street, and a man by the name of Levi was afterwards arrested on suspicion of melting down the seal – but, as the constables had not waited for a warrant before they carried him off, they had to pay him compensation for false imprisonment!

25 MARCH **1746** On this day, as Scottish servant Matthew Henderson was tying up his hair to go to bed, a sudden mad impulse to murder his mistress, Lady Dalrymple, swept over him. They were alone in the house. He crept up the stairs and entered her bedroom – where he chopped the cleaver into her sleeping form. His mistress sat up, electrified, and screamed out, 'Lord! What is this!' He struck down again, and she began to mutter words he could not understand and scrambled across the bed. She finally rolled onto the floor, and he followed, chopping remorselessly, until at last her body lay slumped by the curtains; they were found drenched with red, and slashed to ribbons. A horrible rattling sound from Lady Dalrymple's throat followed Henderson as he fled. He threw the meat cleaver into the privy, and then returned to sit, blood-drenched and terrified, on his bed. Eventually, he decided that he should rob the house, and, by the time he reached the street, laden with rings and watches, he was so frightened that he could hardly walk. He fled for his wife's house at Holborn. When he returned the following morning, his feigned surprise at the horrible charnel-house within was not to protect him for long.

Henderson quickly afterwards confessed at the Gatehouse Prison, and was hanged on a special gibbet at the end of Oxford Street. His corpse was left in chains by Edgware Road. He struggled a great deal as he hung. When the death warrant came down, he looked surprised, and said, sadly, 'I did not expect to die so soon.' If anyone spoke to him in the prison chapel, he would call out, 'Were there 10,000 hells, I deserve them all for the murder of my mistress!'

The motive for this murder is one of the oddest in London's criminal history: about eight days before, as he was dressing his master, Henderson had happened to step backwards and crush her Ladyship's toe. She had given him a filthy look, and, when he was alone, she had cornered him and said, 'Sirrah, how did you dare to tread upon me! Matthew, I'll turn you out of doors, for you have behaved very rudely to me!' She had boxed him upon the ear and left – and that was the last that she ever said about it. However, Matthew had brooded on the affair, until at last, caught up by a sudden frenzy, he reached his deadly resolution.

1807 On this day, William Wilberforce, Member of Parliament, woke for the first time with the knowledge that he had achieved his life's ambition, and had brought about the end of the slave trade. His speech to the house, twenty years before, had signalled his intention to declare war upon this odious trade: 'Never was a more complete system of injustice and cruelty exhibited to the world. To whatever portion of this odious traffic you turn your eyes you find neither consolation nor relief.' **26 MARCH**

1795 Today, naval lieutenant and 'nephew of God' Richard Brothers was committed to a private madhouse at Islington. He had been charged with 'unlawfully, maliciously, and wickedly writing, printing, and publishing various fantastical prophecies, with intent to create dissentions and other disturbances within this realm'. The publication in question was 'A revealed knowledge of the Prophecies and Times ... Wrote [*sic*] under the direction of the LORD GOD, And Published by his Sacred Command'. In it he revealed that the true age of the world was 5,913 years, and that the true Messiah was himself. He also confided that the... **27 MARCH**

...very loud and unusual kind of Thunder that was heard in the beginning of January 1791 was the voice of the Angel mentioned in the Eighteenth chapter of Revelation ... [which] roared through the streets, and made a noise over London like the falling of a mountain of stones.

Indeed, the whole city would have been burnt by the fire of God, but for his intervention. He informed readers that Wilberforce, Charles Fox and Sheridan had received his particular prayers, as worthy men; the Countess of Buckinghamshire needed none, for she (like him) was descended from David, King of Israel. He also informed readers that he had personally seen Satan, 'walking leisurely through London, his face had a smile, but under it his looks were sly, crafty and deceitful.' He predicted the destruction of all kings, the downfall of the navy, and the restoration of the Jews under their new 'prince and prophet', himself.

28 MARCH **1822** An animal called a 'Bonassus' (a bison) was exhibited in the Strand. A neighbour wrote a letter of complaint to the 'annoyance jury' this day:

> I am so annoyed by next door neighbour the Bonassus and with beasts, that I cannot live in my house for the stench of the beast is so great, and there is only a slight partition betwixt the houses, and the beasts are continually breaking through into my different rooms and I am always loosing [*sic*] my lodgers in consequence of the beast. First a monkey made its way in my bedroom; next the jackal came into the yard, and this last week the people in my second floor have been alarmed in the dead of the night by a monkey breaking through into the closet and are going to leave in consequence – this being the third lodgers I have lost on account of the beast ... I am quite pestered with rats and I am confident they came from the exhibition and in short the injury and nuisance is so great as almost impossible to describe ... Gentlemen, your early inquiry will oblige your servant, T. W.

> N.B. and if I mention anything to Mr James [the owner of the beast] he only abuses me with the most uncouth language.

29 MARCH **1715** William Bonner stole a silk handkerchief from James Coe on 29 March. As Coe was coming along Cornhill, he felt a hand in his pocket. Casting his eye down, he saw the prisoner lift his handkerchief, and deliver it to another man – whereupon Coe grabbed him. Bonner was found guilty of theft and whipped.

30 MARCH **1813** On this day, the day before the burial of the Duchess of Brunswick (George III's sister), the new vault in St George's Chapel, Windsor, was being prepared for her coffin's reception. Here, a fabulous discovery was made: three ancient coffins, one in lead and two in stone. The Prince Regent was told, and immediately went straight down to see them. Inside the first they found Charles I, 'as perfect as when he lived'. The nose was gone, but one eye stared back at the astonished regent before it melted in the air. The pointed beard was intact. Many of the teeth remained, and the wax poured on to

protect the body from the air had completely covered the ear, so that it remained exactly as it had been in life. They lifted up the body, and the head slowly toppled from it – revealing the irregular marks where the headsman's axe had split the skin. It appeared to have been glued back together after death. They lifted the head up, and found it was quite damp. It gave paper a greenish-red tint when pressed to it. The tendons of the neck were quite firm, and pores could be clearly seen in the skin. Beautiful dark brown hair covered the back of the scalp; the beard had a redder hue. The hair at the back was chopped short 'for the executioner's convenience'. The head was replaced and the coffin soldered closed again. The second coffin proved to contain Henry VIII, and contained nothing but the skull, and the bones of the arms and legs, in a perfect state. The coffin had been smashed in the middle, letting in the air. The last was Jane Seymour, and was not touched, out of respect. Until this moment, the exact spot where Charles' body had been interred was a historical mystery. Halford kept the fourth vertebrae of Charles I, severed cleanly by the headsman's axe, as a memento. One of Henry's fingers became a knife-handle.

The head of Charles I sketched after its discovery by the Regent. The perfect beard and abundance of hair was much remarked upon.

The Prince Regent, later George IV.

1715 Ex-soldier Matthew **31 MARCH**
Cornwall (23) stole 112lb of tobacco and seventy-seven plates and dishes, many on this day. On these, he could have had a very splendid last supper before he was hanged on 11 May. According to the ordinary's account, he told the court that 'he was sorry for what he had done, but could not now undo it, otherwise than by begging Pardon of GOD and Man, as he did'.

APRIL

The discovery of Oliver Cromwell's head was one of the wonders recorded at the British Museum in April. Here is James Poro, one of the first marvels to join the museum's collection: his portrait, complete with parasitic twin, was drawn especially for Hans Sloane during James's 1714 tour of the capital.

1763   On April Fools' Day, the following was reported in London   1 APRIL
newspapers:

> On Saturday last a number of people assembled at White Conduit House
> in order to see a man fly to Highgate in a new machine and back again in
> an hour; but the mob, after waiting in vain, recollected that it was the first
> of April, and all returned FOOLS to their respective houses.

* * *

On 18 February 1761, one John Muzard called on Mrs Ann King at her
house in Leicester Square to invite her to an opera. When he arrived to pick
her up on the 19th, he discovered Mrs King gone and her lodger, French
enamel painter Theodore Gardelle, waiting with the news that she had
travelled to Bristol or Bath that very day.

Earlier that morning, Ann Windsor, Mrs King's servant, had opened the
shutters of her windows at about 7 o'clock, and had then gone to fetch
some snuff for Mr Gardelle. When she returned, fifteen minutes later, the
house was silent, and she could see no one – not even when she looked into
Mr Gardelle's room (which she usually cleaned). Her mistress's room was
now locked. She made some tea and toast in the kitchen, and then she heard
footsteps walking overhead. Mr Gardelle walked down out of the garret, and
blushed the instant he saw the servant. He had a bruise on his face as large as
a shilling, and a great bump over his left eye (caused, he claimed, by a lump
of wood slipping out of the firewood pile as he was attempting to light a fire).
He had changed his clothes since last she saw him – and he quickly sent her
on another errand. When she returned, he informed her that Mrs King had
gone, and that her services were no longer required. She told him that she
did not believe him, as her errand had not taken long. However, she told the
Old Bailey that her mistress had been a 'very merry gentlewoman', and she
thought that Mr Gardelle had been 'bold' with her; she wondered if Mrs King
might have dismissed her in a fit of shame. Therefore she accepted the 5 or 6s
Gardelle offered her, packed up her goods and left.

Servant Thomas Pelsey, who also lived in the house, noticed a knife in
Gardelle's room, and asked him what it was for. Gardelle ignored him. Then
Pelsey noticed a strange smell, which Gardelle was trying to dispel by opening
all the windows. 'Somebody has put a bone in the fire,' Gardelle claimed.
A new charwoman (laundress) by the name of Mrs Pritchard, hired that
week, found she needed water to clean with, and went to the washhouse
to get it. In the stinking water tub inside, she felt something soft – a great
many things that were soft. Puzzled, she asked Pelsey to help fetch them
out. They waited until Gardelle had left and then, by candlelight, pulled out
two soaking, stained blankets, a pair of sheets and a curtain. None of them
were from Gardelle's room – but where could they have come from, and why
was he washing them? The mystery was about to deepen, for the following
day the servant got up at 10.30 a.m. and found the curtain hanging over
the banister, and the dirty sheets in the washhouse freshly rung. They were

Frenchman Theodore Gardelle putting Mrs King on the fire. His crime was discovered after her body parts were found in the roof on her attic – but her skull and hands were burnt.

later hung up in the room of the missing woman. Convinced that something was amiss, a carpenter was called in, and a grim search began. The search terminated in the 'necessary' (the privy) – where human bowels were found. Between the attic and the ceiling, they discovered dismembered lumps of flesh: genitals, a breast, part of a body and some bones, all neatly tucked away. Ashes were in the fireplace – filled with shards of human bone.

The prisoner, in his defence, described the moments after the maid had left on her first errand. Mrs King had heard him walking in the house, and called out 'who is there?' When she saw him, she said some harsh words. 'For want of other words' (his English being bad), he called her an 'impertinent woman'. She struck him, and in return he pushed her – and her foot caught on a ruck in the oil-cloth on the floor and tripped her, causing her head to be smashed against the corner of the bed. He tried to help her but she became frightened, misunderstanding his intentions – and then she began to retch blood. In a panic, he pulled the bedclothes over her to stop the bleeding (and hide her from his sight), but as he did so he began to get dizzy – and he fainted away, next to his victim. When he came to she was dead, and he staggered to the door, hitting his face on several things as he went and causing the bruises that so alarmed the servant. He told the court, at his trial on 1 April, that:

> I was in such a condition, I did not know what to do ... I have no reason to offer [for clemency], but that the accident was not voluntary. I had no intention to murder this woman, it came by accident. What I did afterwards with the body I look upon to be more wicked than what I did by giving her the blow.

He tried to kill himself in New Prison, first by an overdose of opium and then by swallowing coins, but to no avail: he was executed in the Haymarket, near Panton Street, 'and his body hang'd in chains on Hounslow-heath'.

1759 Mary Edmondson, a farmer's daughter from Yorkshire, went to live with her widowed aunt, Mrs Walker, in London. Today she was heard to cry, 'Help, murder! They have killed my aunt!' The people who came running found Mrs Walker, with her throat cut, lying with her head by the table. Mary claimed that four men had committed the crime, but the court found her guilty of the murder. She was sentenced to death. **2 APRIL**

1721 Martin Grat returned from the plantations before his time of transportation was up, and was sent to the gallows on this day. He could neither read nor write, and was a fisherman on the Thames before he turned to picking pockets. Records state that he was 'greatly frighted, lest his Body should be cut, and torn, and mangled after Death, and had sent his Wife to his Uncle to obtain some Money to prevent it'. Before he died, he said he 'hoped God would take Pity on him, a poor ignorant and foolish Fellow, and not throw him into Hell'. **3 APRIL**

1813 A large building in Skinner Street – and one with rather a notorious reputation for the riotous balls held there – which was due to be the £25,000 prize in the lottery, caught fire on this night. Six storeys came down, the back walls crumbling down on top of the building and the front ones crashing into the street, bruising two firemen. **4 APRIL**

1811 In the beginning of the year 1811, the swans of the Serpentine River went missing; their bodies were found on its banks, stripped of skin and feathers. Eventually, a man called Moses was discovered to have sent the swans' skins to a man called Ryder to be made into Christmas decorations. On this day, Ryder was brought up to the bar of the sessions-house at Hicks's Hall, charged with having received into his possession six swans' skins, knowing them to have been stolen. When asked why he wanted the swan skins, Ryder replied that they were for the decoration of fine young Christian ladies. The skins fitted the corpses exactly. He was found guilty, fined and imprisoned. **5 APRIL**

1803 On this day, as the handsome Lieutenant-Colonel Montgomery and Captain MacNamara (36) were riding in Hyde Park, each followed by a Newfoundland dog, the dogs fought. **6 APRIL**
    'Whose dog is that? I will knock him down!' shouted Montgomery – to which Captain MacNamara replied, 'Have you the impudence to say that you will knock my dog down? You must first knock me down.' At a duel fixed for the evening, MacNamara shot Montgomery through the right side, just above the hip; the bullet flew through his body, forcing the cloth of his coat and waistcoat into his body, and out the other side, taking a button with it. The wounded colonel was carried, spitting blood and trying hopelessly to speak,

to his bed, where he died soon afterwards with a gentle sigh. The Prince of Wales burst into tears when he heard the news. The judge told the jury to find his opponent guilty of manslaughter, but, after excellent references by the likes of Admiral Nelson, they found him not guilty and set him free. The handsome Montgomery was buried in a vault in St James's Church.

7 APRIL 1725 Smithfield lodger Vincent Davis of St James's, Clerkenwell, murdered his wife Elizabeth today. The day before, he had called drunkenly up the stairs: 'Is my bitch above? If she is, send her down with a candle.' When the wife reluctantly appeared she received a savage beating, and was forced to run for her life. The shocked landlady hid the battered woman underneath her bed. 'I am afraid he'll murder me,' the wife whispered to the landlady, 'for he has found his knife that I hid in my box; it lies by his bed-side with a bull's pizzle.' This he kept, he told the landlady, in order to 'pizzle his wife'. (A bull's pizzle, in case you need ask, is an archaic term for a flogging instrument made from a bull's penis.) The same scene was repeated on 7 April, but with three sad additions: the wife was heartily pizzled, had to flee for the landlady's room with a bleeding hand, and returned a final time, with the brutish husband hard upon her heels, to receive the knife in her chest. She managed to flee to the next-door neighbour's house, a tobacco shop, where she perished half an hour later on a pile of leaf tobacco.

'He has killed me; for God's sake, call somebody to seize him, and don't let my blood lie at your doors!' were her last words.

'For God's sake, don't let me be anatomised!' were his, as he was led away to Newgate. The prisoner turned in the dock when sentence of death was announced to solemnly declare, 'God damn ye all together.'

8 APRIL 1750 An earthquake struck London today. Houses shook, dishes rattled, and chimneys fell. Exactly four weeks later, a stronger earthquake struck, and the open ground in St James's Park visibly moved; lightning flashed in all directions, the fish leapt out of the water in the park, and all the dogs of London howled. Bells shook and rang across the city, and stones fell from Westminster Abbey. Rumours began to spread that an enormous earthquake was coming which would wipe out all of London. On that day, people began to flee. One source said:

> The whole of the City of London, the City of Westminster, the Borough, the suburbs, the West End, were out in the streets, or out in the fields, during that awful night. Many thousands lay in boats on the river, all the boats were engaged for the purpose; many thousands lay in the fields outside the town ... great ladies sat in their coaches, crowding the roads; all night long they sat thus, waiting in terror and suspense, expecting every moment the thunder and rumblings and the agitation of the world, when the proud pinnacles and spires of London should topple and fall and lie levelled in one common ruin.

When midday arrived, nothing at all happened and everyone returned home.

Stones fell from Westminster Abbey, seen here in around 1808, during the famous earthquakes.

1747 On this day, Simon 'the Fox' Fraser, 11th Lord Lovat (80), was beheaded on Tower Hill – the last man to be beheaded in the country. It was his second death penalty: the first was for kidnapping Lady Amelia Murray and forcing her to marry him. He was pardoned for supporting the government in their fight against the first Jacobite rebellion – and, ironically,

9 APRIL

The famously malign portrait of Lord Lovat.

he was beheaded on this day for his part in the '45 Rebellion.

As he was going to his trial, a woman looked into his coach and said, 'You ugly old dog, don't you think you'll have that frightful head cut off?'

He replied, 'You ugly old ——, I believe I shall!"

On the way to his death, the coach was held up by the crowd. He remarked to the Lieutenant of the Tower, sitting opposite, that they 'need not be in a hurry, for there would certainly be no sport' until he arrived. He rested in a chair on the scaffold, chatting to people in the crowd, before he lay down and his head was taken off. Scaffolds were erected so that paying guests could get a good view; one of the largest, with more than 1,000 people on it, collapsed on the heads of those beneath: twelve people were killed, and many more horribly injured. For their parts in the rebellion, Kilmarnock, Balmerino and Lovat were buried in the Tower; their coffin plates were uncovered in the 1840s and thrown to one side – before they were saved and put on display.

10 APRIL   1829   Three women – Esther Hibner snr, Esther Hibner (her daughter) and Ann Robinson – were indicted on this day for the murder of Frances Colpitt (10). Frances was a pauper who had been apprenticed to the family at Platt Terrace, Pancras Road, by the overseers of St Martin's parish. All of the children in the house – there were several others – suffered under the cruellest of regimes: they were starved, forced to work until the early hours (and sometimes all night) and sleep on the floor under a dirty old rug. Sometimes, in order to survive, they ate the raw scraps of meat brought to feed the dogs. Three children died under this regime. Frances was so unwell before her death that her feet had mortified, and her toes were actually falling off; her lungs became abscessed, and she died shortly afterwards. On Sundays, the children were locked into a small room. Frances had been struck until she fell repeatedly; when she could move no more, the cruel matriarch merely said, 'Let her lie there.' Though she could only crawl by this stage, the child was set to cleaning, and beaten with a cane when she could not do it.

Sentence of death was instantly passed on the oldest woman; the others were charged with assault. A little before 8 a.m. on Monday 13 April, the wretched malefactor was led to the press room. She exhibited a dreadful appearance. Her dress, a black gown, over which was a white bedgown, and the white cap on her head, contributed – together with the sallow complexion – to give her a most unearthly aspect. She refused to walk to the gallows, and so two men picked her up and carried her to the scaffold. The roar of the crowd as she was hanged defied belief. The two vile women who had helped in her vicious regime were sent to prison for just twelve and four months respectively.

1758 Today, between the hours of 10 p.m. and 11 p.m., a temporary wooden bridge (built for carts and passengers to use whilst London Bridge was being repaired) burst into flames. It was entirely consumed by fire. 11 APRIL

London's temporary wooden bridge proved even more temporary than planned: it caught fire, and was burnt to a crisp.

12 APRIL 1815   After the defeat of Bonaparte, the streets of the metropolis were brightly illuminated for three days of celebration. The streets were crowded to excess, and thousands of carriages passed back and forth, many covered with French and British colours. A large scroll was placed outside Revd Roland Hill's chapel in Blackfriars: 'A tyrant has fallen,' it said.

13 APRIL 1715   Moses Pierce died on this day. Pierce was a journeyman carpenter who was so proud of his fighting ability that he took to wearing a small sword wherever he went, and to boasting loudly of his skills with it. One day he was with a friend, Robert Trimble of St Marylebone, and the pair fell out over the correct way to hold a sword; Trimble told his friend that he 'knew nothing of it', which made Pierce so angry that, a few days later, he marched up to his friend and demanded a duel.

'You say,' he declared, 'I have no skill in small sword, but I have, and I am ready to answer you; and if you don't fight me, I'll beat you.'

They accordingly met at a specified place, whereupon Mr Trimble instantly stabbed his boastful friend to death. When the witnesses arrived, they saw the mortally wounded man swaying back and forth, crying out that he would fight Trimble again, and that he would 'have his blood'. Pierce then fell down dead. Robert Trimble was accordingly found guilty of manslaughter on 17 May 1716.

14 APRIL 1716   Today, as Mildred Saunders was proceeding along Shoe Lane, two boys ran up, pinned her hands and rifled her 'band box', taking away a 'suit of lac'd headcloths' and 40 yards of 'thread laces'. William Watts dropped the lace as he ran, but was caught with the headcloths in his 'bosom'. He was sentenced to death.

15 APRIL 1795   Daniel Mendoza was a world-champion boxer, whose style was scientific and included many defensive manoeuvres. This incorporated side-stepping, moving around, ducking, blocking and avoiding punches. At the time, this was revolutionary; as a result of this new style, although he was only 5ft 7in and 160lb, Mendoza was able to overcome much heavier opponents. He is the only middleweight ever to win the heavyweight championship of the world. However, on this day, Mendoza lost his title to John Jackson, who employed a tactic that would be considered ungentlemanly at least: he grabbed a handful of Mendoza's long hair, held him, and beat him unconscious in the ninth round. Jackson's own head was shaved, so other boxers could not play this dirty trick on him.

16 APRIL 1730   Schoolmaster Isaac Broderick, of the Company of Coopers School, assaulted Edward Caley (10) and William Ham (10) on this day. Broderick, shortly after taking over the school, began making the boys take down their breeches and then 'feeling about their bodies'. Ham told the court that the master 'strok'd all over his naked Body' and then sexually assaulted him. Other boys at the school confessed he had done the same to them. Caley was found to have a blister between his thighs when he eventually confessed the abuse to his grandfather. The grandfather went straight to the master – who told him he did it to 'improve him in his Studies'. Broderick was ordered to stand twice in the pillory, serve three months in Newgate, and pay a fine of 20 nobles.

1776 In 1765, Lord Byron was tried in Westminster Hall for stabbing Mr Chaworth in the gut in the Star & Garter Tavern, in Pall Mall, after an argument about the best way to keep game. Lord Byron was escorted from the Tower by the executioner, who carried a glinting axe. He was found guilty of manslaughter, but pleaded 'benefit of the clergy' – with the extra benefit that, as a Peer of the Realm, he would not be burnt upon the hand, or indeed face any penalty whatsoever. He was hence set free. **17 APRIL**

Eleven years later, ship's cook Christopher Saunders was sentenced to death for 'a venereal affair with a certain beast called a cow' at Limehouse Marsh. It was said that he had 'perpetrate[d] the detestable and abominable crime, not to be named among Christians, called Buggery'. The cow keeper, Abraham Denning, testified to seeing the prisoner 'stroking and patting' the cow: 'I saw him put his hands upon the cow's back, and wriggle himself about; he was about ten minutes in that posture, I believe it might be more.' Denning watched throughout, and then seized the cook and took him to the law. Saunders tried to explain that 'it was the first time', and claimed he would not do it again, but it cut little ice: he was sent to the gallows on 9 June.

1719 William Gibbs of Marylebone was indicted for the murder of an unnamed man at the fencing school. The dead man was the fencing master, and had told Gibbs that he was 'not fit to teach a gentleman'. Unless Gibbs drew his sword, he said, he would kill him. They fought, and Gibbs killed his attacker. As Gibbs had a very good character, and the fencing master a very bad one, Gibbs was found guilty only of manslaughter and burnt on the hand. **18 APRIL**

1779 A man came to Tyburn today for the murder of Martha Ray (34), the daughter of a stay-maker in Holywell Street, London, and the mistress of the 4th Earl of Sandwich, on 7 April 1779. As Martha was coming out of the Drury Lane playhouse, the echo of a shot was heard. Something struck the arm of John McNamara – it was a bullet, and it had just gone through the body of Miss Ray, who was on his arm. He stooped, thinking his companion had simply fainted from shock, and realised that his hands were covered with blood. She was carried into the Shakespeare Tavern, and her escort, realising the sight of so much blood had made him feel sick, went home. Miss Ray died. A fruit-seller saw the shooter: Revd James Hackman. Hackman had approached the victim as she waited for her carriage, grasped her gown and shot her in the forehead. He had then shot himself with a second pistol, falling 'feet to feet' with his victim. Alas, this second shot took no effect – so he started to beat himself over the head with the gun, asking the horrified onlookers to kill him. He had been trying to court Miss Ray for years, but had been repeatedly rejected. Eventually, her refusal had 'driven him to madness'. He was hanged on 19 April, saying, 'Oh! The sight of this **19 APRIL**

Revd Hackman shooting Miss Ray and himself at the same moment, an event acted out in the Old Bailey by the witness: bang, bang, 'like so!'

shocks me more than the thought of its intended operation!' when he saw the rope that was to go around his neck. He cried a little, and spent a horrible thirty seconds waiting after he dropped his handkerchief – the signal to end his life – whilst the executioner retrieved it, just in case a member of the crowd took this valuable souvenir.

20 APRIL 1785   In 1785, in consequence of a very high wind, some stones were blown through the skylight of the King's Bench, hurling fragments of glass all over the judges below. Parts of the ceiling fell down too, and the entire courtroom was forced to run. Mr Stebbing was thrown onto a bench and then trampled over by the other lawyers as they ran, bruising him severely.

Also on this day, in 1804, Joanna Southcott was paying visits to true believers in London. Next to the Elephant & Castle in Duke Street was her 'House of God' (labelled as such in enormous letters), where her dreams and visions were painted all over the walls. Joanna was first visited by 'an invisible spirit' in 1792. She thereafter decided that her family history was in fact 'a warning to the nations, that the end of all things is at hand'. She declared that she was the woman referred to in Revelations, i.e. 'the Bride, the Lamb's wife, and the Woman clothed with the Sun'. She was to warn the world of the coming Millennium, and make special pieces of paper for the names of the 144,000 people destined for heaven – which she personally sealed with an impression she found whilst sweeping the house. She lived a quiet life in a secret chamber shared with Christ, when he came for a visit. She had many benefactors – one alone left her £250 a year – and lived quite comfortably.

When Joanna was 65, she announced that she was pregnant by divine influence, and would bring forth the Messiah in due course. On 7 August 1814, Dr Richard Reece of the Royal Colleges visited Miss Southcott and declared that she was indeed pregnant, as he could feel 'a motion resembling that of a foetus' in the uterus. Alas, the baby did not appear at the time she specified. Joanna died in 1814 in Manchester Square, Islington – and was dissected by Dr Reece! Her body was kept warm for four days before she was dissected, just in case she should revive; eventually, putrefaction rendered her 'extremely offensive'. She is buried in the same cemetery – St John's Wood Chapel – as her arch rival, Richard Brothers. She was not pregnant. A deathbed scene was recorded, where she wept very much, and where her followers promised to bind up her prophecies for the future. These were opened in 1927 and found to contain a lottery ticket and a horse-pistol, but her followers insist that this was not the real box of prophecies. This will be opened when enough Church of England bishops agree to appear at the event.

1813 Warren Hastings was finally cleared of all charges of corruption today in 1795, after a trial lasting seven years. The charges alone took two days to read out.

21 APRIL

Eighteen years later, on this day, the following was written in a manuscript in the British Museum: 'The head of Oliver Cromwell ... has been brought forth in the City, and is exhibited as a favour to such curious persons as the proprietor chooses to oblige.' The head was originally buried – with its body – in Westminster Abbey, before it was dug up at the Restoration and hung from the gallows. The head was then chopped off and fixed on top of Westminster Hall – where it blew down, and afterwards vanished. The skull supposed to be Cromwell's had been embalmed and spiked; it was compared to pictures and declared a match.

The British Museum in 1827.

Alice Jones of King Street, Westminster, committed a hilarious theft on this day in 1720, in St Michael's Cornhill, taking 'a Bermudas hat' from the shop of Edward Hillior. After looking at lots of different ones, she left – and the shopkeeper noticed that 'she could hardly walk'. He called her back, and the hat 'fell from between her legs'. She was transported to the colonies.

22 APRIL **1809**   On this day, Jemima Ambrose (19) pinched a cloak, a gown, a great coat, two pillow cases and a few other items, including a baby's frock. Susannah Baldwin returned to her house at St Leonard's, Shoreditch, to find Jemima, her neighbour, in tears, saying she had been robbed; Susannah's door had been broken open too. The watchman came and searched the crying neighbour's home, where he found a chisel and a broken knife, which matched the marks on the Baldwins' door exactly. Under Jemima's arm, tucked in her armpit, she was hiding a tiny box filled with pawnshop tickets. Here is the prisoner's defence: 'The prosecutrix said if I would make the things good she would not hurt a hair of my head.' She was sent for six months' hard labour and fined 1s.

23 APRIL **1718**   Today, London's hangman appeared in court – facing a murder charge which saw him hanged. Hardened drunk John Price (41) had fallen upon cake-seller Elizabeth White in Bunhill Fields at about 10 p.m. He was overheard shouting, 'Damn you for a Bitch, why don't you take it in your field and put it in? If you won't put it in I'll rip you up.' He also demanded her money. Two passers-by had armed themselves and rushed to her aid – and, according to Old Bailey records, found her...

> ...in a very odd Posture, and a very bad Condition, with her Coats up to her Belly, Streams of Blood issuing out of her Eyes and Mouth ... she could not speak, but made a gagling [sic] Noise as if she had something in her Mouth, which appeared to be Blood.

One of her eyes had been beaten out. Several teeth had gone too, and her arm was broken. The witnesses took Price (who was covered in blood) to the watchhouse, where the watchmen told him that if he did not sit down and shut up they would throw him in the fire. Then they went back for the woman, who was found in the dark by a barking dog. She too was carried – but much more gently – to the watchhouse, where some women were tasked to hold her forwards, 'for she was choak'd with Clots of Blood in her Mouth and Throat, and could not speak'. She died four days later. Price was hanged on 31 May 1718. The next year, his replacement, William Marvell – who cut off Derwentwater's head in 1716 – was transported for stealing ten silk handkerchiefs from a shop in Coleman Street. He was unfortunately rather a famous figure, so as soon as the shopkeeper described the thief he was identified. He begged to be whipped, but was sent abroad instead.

On a lighter note, today in 1737, two footmen were tried for rioting in the Drury Lane Theatre after the management had decided to charge servants who came along with the ladies and gentlemen – previously they had got in for free, but were notorious for whooping and riotous behaviour during the play. A gang of 300 footmen got weapons, broke onto the stage, and attacked everyone in sight. The Prince and Princess of Wales, and other members of the royal family, were in the theatre at the time. Thirty footmen were arrested and taken to Newgate. The two who came to trial got six months' imprisonment each.

1805   At the Old Bailey, Esther Murray (9) was indicted for putting a pair   **24 APRIL** of shoes under her apron in a shop. The court recommended her to mercy on account of her age; she was whipped and returned to her mother.

1720   Zephaniah Martin, of St-Botolph-without-Aldgate, stole a periwig   **25 APRIL** from the house of Thomas Limes today. Martin came into Limes' shop, a hairdresser's, and claimed he was to meet someone there. He strolled about, read the newspapers, and handed over his own wig to comb – and then stole another wig the moment the shopkeeper's back was turned, and put it up the back of his coat. Limes' assistant had seen everything, and Martin was seized the second he was out of the door. 'For God's sake, do not to prosecute!' the wig thief cried. He came to the Old Bailey nonetheless, where he was quickly transported.

1716   Thomas Hurd (26) and his wife Anne, of Clerkenwell, stole three   **26 APRIL** sheep today. The owner saw three pelts hanging up in a 'boyling Cook's' shop with the head and feet chopped off, and found a pile of wool in the cellar. At the Hurds' he found 8 stones of fat, and some bags of wool. Hurd had a reputation for sheep stealing, and he was found guilty (though Anne was acquitted). He was hanged on 19 December 1716, confessing at the gallows that he also 'stole several Geese from a poor Woman, who made them a Livelihood for her and her Children'.

1720   Elizabeth Cranbery of Twittenham added a healthy dose of 'White   **27 APRIL** Arsenick, and other Poyson' to the breakfast of her father-in-law, Thomas Biggs, on 9 April. He died at 4 p.m., and the case came to court on this day. A woman who shared Elizabeth's room had discovered a neat little package of yellow silk in their room a few days before, filled with what looked like sugar: however, when she tasted the substance it burnt her tongue. Thomas and Elizabeth had recently fallen out, and he had threatened to throw her out. A few days later, the meal was served – a meal which tasted so strange that Biggs was forced to stop eating it. The bowl swam with odd flecks like lime or starch, and when the remainder was given to the dog it was promptly sick. Biggs cried out, 'What! Have you poisoned me? I'll search all your boxes.' He immediately did so, and caught Elizabeth trying to hide a packet of the powder in her hand. He sent his wife running to the doctor's with the powder, but it was too late – he died shortly afterwards. His stomach was found to be corroded and black. The prisoner claimed that the powder was to wash her gloves in, but the jury did not believe her, and she was found guilty, dying in prison before she could reach the gallows.

28 APRIL

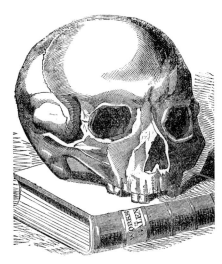

1718 William Pearse and Mary Jones of Holborn stole books on this day. Charles Stamper was lying on the grass, sleeping, when Mary Jones came up and asked him if he was single. When he said yes, she asked if he might like to live with her, so long as he could afford to buy her some nice clothes. The new friends decided to rob books from Mr Hawk's nearby chambers. They sold what they had taken and the profits were shared. The pardon for giving evidence went to Stamper and both other parties went to a new life abroad for seven years.

29 APRIL **1715** At 5 a.m. on this day, two watchmen at the warehouse of Benjamin Longuet & Partners heard a noise. They saw the door creak open and watched as a man crept in. It was John Smith, better known as 'Half-hanged Smith', one of London's most famous criminals. Ten years before, he had been hanged at Tyburn; after spinning in the air for fifteen agonising minutes, however, a great cry of 'reprieve' had gone up and he was immediately cut down. After some efforts he was revived, and the following description, repeated in many Georgian accounts, was given of his experiences:

> he, for some time, was sensible of a very great pain, occasioned by the weight of his body, and felt his spirits in a strange commotion, violently pressing upwards; that, having forced their way to his head, he, as it were, saw a great blaze or glaring light, which seemed to go out at his eyes with a flash, and then he lost all sense of pain; that, after he was cut down, and began to recover himself, the blood and spirits ... forcing themselves into their former channels, put him, by a sort of pricking or shooting, into so intolerable a pain, that he could have wished those hanged, that had cut him down.

No one appeared against Smith for this latest robbery, and he once again walked free from justice.

30 APRIL **1784** An alarming riot happened in White Hart Yard, Drury Lane, after a young prostitute – of no more than 13 – accidentally propositioned her own uncle in the street. He made her say where she lived, and then stormed the house, accompanied by a mob, and demolished it. The girl was rescued and returned to her family, and the mistress of the house was forced to escape out of the back door.

Today in 1805, Richard Haywood was hanged for stealing two pillows and two bolsters. When fellow prisoners said they were sorry to hear he was to die, he replied, 'I want none of your pity. Keep your snivelling till it be your own turn.'

MAY

Philip Nicholson beats his employers to death with a poker. (*See* 30 May)

Arthur Thistlewood and a Georgian engraving of his death. The Georgian era was the age of the broadside, and this example describes the events of 1 May. (With kind permission of Neil R. Storey)

Execution of the Cato Street gang: five coffins wait for their grisly load, whilst the executioner holds up the head, and the butcher waits behind.

1 MAY   1820 A scaffold was erected over the gate of Newgate today, and, at just before 8 a.m., five men were led out. They were shoemaker John Brunt of Gray's Inn Lane, cabinet-maker William Davidson, butcher James Ings (40), Arthur Thistlewood and bootmaker Richard Tidd (50) – the Cato Street Conspirators. 'We shall soon know the great secret,' said Thistlewood, as he stepped onto the boards. Tidd actually tried a little dance on the way to the rope, 'but they were all evidently under the influence of great terror'. Ropes went around their necks. An hour later a coffin was wheeled out, next to a block. A man holding a large butcher's knife, with his face covered, then arrived. The first body was put into the coffin, the head poking out onto the block. The head was cut off, and the butcher handed it to the executioner, who held it aloft, saying, 'This is the head of a traitor.' The head went into a box, and the others soon followed. A loud and deep groan of horror went up in the crowd each time a head appeared. (*See* 22 Feb)

2 MAY   1813 The Queen was attacked on this day by a domestic servant called Miss Davenport (30). Miss Davenport slept in the tower above the Queen's bedroom. 'At about five o'clock,' ran the royal report, 'the Queen was awoke by a violent noise at her bed-room door, accompanied by a voice calling violently for redress [for] her wrongs &c, and with the most distressing shrieks, screams and other noises possible to be conceived.' Davenport was carrying a letter, which she insisted on delivering to the Queen herself. Eventually she was carried up to her own bedroom, straight-jacketed, and then bundled into a coach headed for an asylum at Hoxton, dressed in nothing but her underwear and a man's greatcoat.

1810   Today in 1715 saw a total solar eclipse.

Ninety-five years later, Eleanor Williams (38) 'sideled [*sic*] towards the counter, put her hands behind her, and pulled the muslin off the counter' at the shop of Emanuel Thornley in Red Lion Street, Holborn. She put the muslin up the back of her coat. She tried to claim that it 'came there of itself', but the shopkeeper was unconvinced. Her defence in court was that:

> When the lady turned round, I told her I was very willing to strip, to see whether I had anything. I pulled off my old coat that I had on, and by pulling the coat off it throwed the muslin down.

The Old Bailey disagreed, and she was transported for seven years.

1767   On this day, one Francis Gorman was hanged at Tyburn for murder.
While he was hanging, a young woman with an unsightly facial tumour upon her was lifted up and had the tumour rubbed with the dead man's fingers, as a certain cure for the growth. Whether the cure worked or not is not recorded.

The application of the corpse's hand, thought to be a curative – though how it will help cure the face from there is anyone's guess.

Mansion House,
scene of an
attempted fraud.

Also today, but in 1799, the 'Tipu Sultan', the Tiger of Mysore, died (killed by Richard Sharpe, as all fans of the series know). The abilities of his executioners – who were able to drive nails into the heads of prisoners with just their hands – were legendary.

5 MAY **1803**   Today in 1803, the Stock Exchange was forced to close after a clever and unscrupulous stock manipulator delivered a letter to the Lord Mayor, at Mansion House, claiming that the war with France was over. All of the trade embargoes were instantly lifted, and stock prices rose sharply before the fraud was discovered.

6 MAY **1731**   On this day, infamous bawd 'Mother' Needham passed away. Exciting incidents in her life included the time her Conduit Street brothel burnt to the ground, leaving nothing but the skeleton of a French customer called Captain Barbute in the ruins. After some time in prison at the Gatehouse, she was convicted of 'keeping a lewd and disorderly house' in Park Place, St James's; she was fined 1s and ordered to stand twice in the pillory near her brothel. This was a terrifying prospect, and she hired a gang of men to screen her as she lay trapped there. She had also bribed officers to allow her to cover her face as she lay. However, she was still severely pelted with stones, dung and all manner of foul items. The crowd was so enormous that people were climbing onto things to get a look at her – and to take aim. One little boy climbed up a lamppost to see her, but slipped off and speared himself in the gut on some sharp railings. He died. Mother Needham followed shortly afterwards: apparently, the terror of facing the crowds again was too much for her.

1721   On this day, Mary Wilson of Chiswick, the servant of Mr Barker, was
found by another servant, Mrs Pepper, looking distinctly unwell – and, in fact,
as though she had just given birth. Mary eventually directed the suspicious
woman to the washhouse, where the latter found a dead baby girl lying on
the cheese press. Mary told a friend that her infant had been stillborn, and
that it was so limber that one might 'wrap it around one's hand like a cloth'.
The child's hands were open, and a surgeon later discovered that both of
its arms were broken. It had died before it was born, and the jury therefore
acquitted Mary.

1760   The body of Lawrence, Earl Ferrers, was finally taken off display
and allowed home on this day, after he had been executed for the murder
of his steward and hanged. Earl Ferrers had been escorted to his death on
5 May, with a coach behind him to take his dead body to Surgeons' Hall.

He was the very first man to experience the
'new drop' – falling through a trapdoor,
rather than being pushed out of a cart to
slowly strangle. The whole apparatus was
cloaked in black. Hundreds of thousands
of Londoners watched him fall to his death;
'I suppose,' he said, 'because they never saw
a lord hanged before.' In fact, the crowds
were so enormous that it took more than two
hours to get to the gallows – his Lordship said
that, 'passing through such crowds of people
[was] ten times worse than death itself.'
When he got to the gallows, he accidentally
handed the executioner's payment to his
assistant, and started a squabble. He was
hooded, and stepped under the beam: 'Is
this right?' he asked. Then the floor fell from
under him, and his body began its journey to
the anatomisers.

Earl Ferrers on
display in Surgeons'
Hall after he was
hanged.

Execution of Earl
Ferrers on the 'new
drop'.

Also on this day, but in 1792, an attempt was made to set the House of Commons on fire. As the smell of burning spread, a vigilant watchman found that the ceiling of a water closet had been broken and a pair of trousers, filled with flammable materials, had been pushed in and set on fire. If this hadn't been discovered, it is likely that the whole building would have burnt to the ground.

9 MAY   1729   On this day, London writer Thomas Woolston was fined £100, plus one whole year's imprisonment, for comparing Jesus to a wizard. He suggested that the voice from heaven had been achieved via the medium of ventriloquism, and that Jesus had cured disabilities by 'shaming [the cripple] out of his pretended illness'. One of the judges declared the booklets the most blasphemous thing he had ever read, and added a £2,000 fine, with £2,000 in sureties, to ensure Thomas's good behaviour for life.

Three years earlier, three patrons of 'Mother Clap's Molly House' – milkman Gabriel Lawrence (43), woolcomber Thomas Wright (32), and furniture upholster William Griffin (43) – appeared at the gallows. Mother Clap's coffee house for gay men was by the Bunch of Grapes in Field Lane, Holborn, and had thirty or forty customers a night. The secret underworld was first uncovered after a falling out with 'treacherous, blowing-up Mollying Bitch' Mark Partridge: a row with his lover had spiralled into police raids. At Thomas Wright's trial, treacherous rent-boy Newton deposed:

> There were 8 or 9 of them in a large Room, one was playing upon a Fiddle, and others were one while dancing in obscene Postures, and other while Singing baudy Songs, and talking leudly, and Acting a great many Indecencies.

Another witness said (as recorded by the Old Bailey):

> Sometimes, they'd sit in one anothers Laps, use their Hands indecently, Dance and make Curtsies and mimick the Language of Women – O Sir! – Pray Sir! – Dear Sir! Lord how can ye serve me so! – Ah ye little dear Toad! Then they'd go by Couples, into a Room on the same Floor to be marry'd as they call'd it ... When they came out, they used to brag in plain Terms, of what they had been doing.

The three men were hanged, and Mother Clap faced the pillory and a prison sentence. However, it is not thought that she survived the first part of her punishment.

10 MAY   1768   This day saw, in 1735, one actor kill another in a fight over a stock wig. However, a more famous disaster occurred today in 1768, when the magnificent John Wilkes, Mayor of London, MP, journalist, Radical and Hellfire Club raconteur was held in the King's Bench Prison on a charge of seditious libel, after criticising a speech given by the King (within which the peace with the French was praised) in No. 45 of his publication *The North Briton*. The number forty-five began to appear everywhere: chalked on houses and coaches, inn signs, on tribute items such as coins, pots, snuffboxes, wigs (with forty-five curls), buttons, dresses and badges. Getting the enormously popular man of the people to the prison was a feat in itself: the London mob caught hold of the carriage taking him there and wheeled it all the way to the Three Tuns Tavern in Spitalfields, where they all went for a drink. Wilkes eventually managed to slip out and hand himself in. Time went on and Wilkes remained in prison – and the crowds started to gather. Then, on this day, a riot began that spread across London.

An 'overzealous Justice', Mr Gilliam, decided to read the Riot Act to the crowd (which included a body of sailors who climbed up the prison's walls and offered to let the astonished Wilkes out). He then sent in the constables – and all hell broke loose. The 'lobsters' seized several passers-by, causing the crowd to break out into loud hisses and abuse of the soldiers, and to throw a few stones. One hit Gilliam on the head, whereupon the blockhead ordered the guards to fire...

> ...which the infernal scoundrels instantly did, with ball, whereby several persons lost their lives, some of them not being in the mob at all, for the vile assassins fired in all directions, and even across the public high road. One poor woman was killed seated upon a cart-load of hay going by at the time.
>
> (*The Memoirs of William Hickey*)

One rioter, in a scarlet waistcoat, was chased into the yard of an inn near the borough, kept by a Mr Allen. Unfortunately, at this very instant the son of the innkeeper appeared – and, unluckily for him, he was also wearing a red waistcoat. He was shot.

A large body of Horse Guards then galloped into the fray, slashing left and right with their broadswords. The innkeeper's murdered son was paraded on a board through the streets of the capital, and rioting groups pulled down buildings, demanded pay-rises with menaces, and dunked unfortunate Londoners in the Thames. At last, days later, the rioting died down – just in time for Wilkes to be sentenced, to two years in prison and a £1,000 fine. Three soldiers and the justice appeared in court, charged with murder, but were acquitted.

1812 Today, as Mr Perceval was entering the Lobby of the House of Commons, he was shot. The only words he uttered were, 'Oh! I am murdered!' Spencer Perceval died shortly afterwards, the only prime minister in British history to be assassinated. Someone then exclaimed, 'Where is the rascal that fired?' **11 MAY**

Mr Bellingham coolly replied, 'I am the unfortunate man.'

He did not make any attempt to escape. Bellingham, 'a raw-boned man ... about forty-two years of age, with a thin, long visage, aquiline nose, and short brown hair', had spent years in a Russian prison, and wanted some redress from the government. He shot Perceval through the heart before any

Spencer Perceval
murdered by
Bellingham,
sighing, 'Oh! I am
murdered!'

member had time to react. On 18 May, a few minutes before 8 o'clock, this wretched man appeared on the scaffold, perfectly resigned to his fate, and, in about two minutes, was launched into eternity.

12 MAY **1719**   On this day, Samuel Harrison of St Giles', Cripplegate accidentally stabbed his daughter Hannah Harrison in her left cheek with a tobacco pipe, near the eye; the wound was 3in deep, and killed her nine days later. The two were business partners, and they had fallen out over money one evening in the Eagle & Tree in Moor Lane. Samuel began waving his pipe in the air as they argued; eventually, his daughter used such 'provoking language' that he thrust the pipe forward – and into her cheek, upon which she instantly swooned away. A tiny fragment of the pipe snapped off in the wound, causing the malignant fever that eventually carried her off. The jury found the broken-hearted father guilty of manslaughter; he was burnt on the hand and set free.

13 MAY **1718**   On Ludgate Hill, Robert Ferryman ran up to Lydia Ashley and ripped off her pocket with two sharp tugs. Inside were three handkerchiefs, a snuff box and 7s. A passer-by gave chase, shouting, 'Stop! Thief!' The prisoner, rather cleverly, joined in, shouting, 'Stop thief!' This led to some quick mental calculations, before the vigilante Londoner amended his cry to, 'Stop him who cryes stop Thief!' Ferryman was caught right at the corner of the Old Bailey. He tried to claim that the thief had already run past, but his captor was having none of it. He was transported for seven years.

14 MAY **1828**   One morning, at the garden entrance of St James's Palace, as King George III was stepping out of his chariot, a woman pushed forward and

handed a piece of paper to him. At that instant, she struck the King's breast with a concealed knife. As she was making a second thrust, one of the yeomen caught her arm, and, at the same instant, one of the King's footmen wrenched the knife out of the woman's hand.

'I have received no injury; do not hurt the woman, the poor creature appears insane,' said the King. The knife had cut the King's waistcoat, and would have killed him if he hadn't been bent over making his bow. Margaret Nicholson was committed to Bethlehem Hospital as a criminal lunatic. She was moved, with the other inmates, from the old hospital in Moorfields to the new hospital in Lambeth, where she died on 14 May 1828, in her 99th year, having been confined for forty-two years.

Left Margaret Nicholson attacks the King.

Below New Bethlem Hospital at its site in St George's Fields; it moved here from Moorfields in 1815. The old site, where the Bedlam of *Rake's Progress* fame was witnessed, is now Finsbury Circus. The new site, pictured here, is now the Imperial War Museum.

15 MAY **1800**   A horrid case of treason and attempted murder took place in the Drury Lane Theatre on this day, when a man stood up and fired at the royal box. The audience screamed out, 'Seize the villain!', and some hardy members of the orchestra seized the gunman, one James Hadfield, and dragged him into the music-room. The crowd then sang a hearty chorus of 'God Save the King'. A piece of shot was later found embedded in the box, about 14in above where the King's head would have been, and another in Lady Milner's box below. When the King's son, the Duke of York, went to examine the would-be assassin, the criminal said, 'God bless your Royal Highness. I like you very well; you are a good fellow.'

James Hadfield, it transpired, had been one of the Duke's orderlies. He told him that he was tired of life, and thought that he would certainly be killed if he were to make an attempt upon His Majesty's life. The man who had been sitting next to Hadfield (and who had grabbed him the moment he opened fire) noticed that the gunman had a severe wound on his cheek and also on his temple, and thought him 'a pitiable object'. The injury had been caused by French cavalrymen running their swords into Hadfield's brain (once above the eye, and twice through the back of the skull, with a deep wound on the temple to boot). They had then chopped at his hand, run him through with a bayonet, and 'left him in a ditch amongst the slain'.

This dreadful treatment, it seems, had deranged Hadfield: one man, who met him in a POW hospital in Brussels, had made the mistake of asking him where he was from, to which Hadfield had rejoined, 'I came from London; I am King George.' This reply obviously took the soldier aback – and he was further surprised when Hadfield asked to borrow his mirror and took to stroking his face and head. When the man asked him what he was feeling for, he said, 'I am feeling for my crown of gold; I am King George, and I live in Red Lion Street, Clerkenwell.'

Hadfield's brother David told the court that, since his injury, the prisoner had been in the habit of 'hallooing out', and otherwise raving, when the weather grew hot; he was also in the habit of informing people that he was a member of the royal family, God, or Jesus Christ. Other strange acts he committed that day included hurling a kettle of water onto the floor and declaring that it was to be his new bed, making a second bed in the kitchen cupboard, and threatening to kill his sister's child. He also mentioned that he had been to dine with the King in his sleep. The jury, understandably, found him not guilty by reason of insanity.

16 MAY **1719**   John Frost of St Andrew's, Holborn, saw hackney coachman John Jones fall – stone drunk – from his cab today. Frost told another cabdriver, who proposed to drive the drunken cabbie home, that he also lived where the coach was going, and the driver let him in. During the journey, unbeknownst to the new driver, Frost ripped out and stole all of the seats. When he was arrested, he was still carrying them. He claimed – probably truthfully – that he was 'in drink', but was transported nonetheless.

1716 Three dreadful highwaymen – William White, Thomas Thurland and John Chapman, all from St Andrew's, Holborn – were arraigned on this day for robbing John Knapp and John Gough. William White was further charged with the wicked murder of widow Mary Knapp. White and Thurland stood silently in the dock and refused to plead, so two men, appointed by the court, attempted to force the matter by tying whipcord around the criminals' thumbs and pulling as hard as they could on the rope. This went on for more than fifteen minutes, but without success. Eventually, however, when they were taken into the press yard (where rocks and other heavy weights would be placed on their bodies until they were crushed to death), the men relented, and entered a plea of 'not guilty'.

17 MAY

Widow Knapp had been travelling home from Sadler's Wells Theatre with her son when their light was blown out. Her son's hat and wig had then been removed and he was knocked to the ground. His mother had screamed, at which a pistol was fired, and she roared out, 'Lord, help me, help me!' in the darkness. When a light was fetched, it was discovered that she was dead, with a weeping bullet wound in her left cheek just under the eye. All three men were hanged.

1827 One of the most bizarre episodes in the history of the London press took place in Leadenhall Street, when William Corder advertised for a new wife: he had just murdered his fiancée. A lady who ran Grove House Academy, Brentford Lane, Ealing, replied, and they were soon married. On 19 April, horrified searchers found the corpse of Maria Marten – a woman Corder had promised to elope with – buried under a grain bin. Corder was swiftly tracked down and arrested. He was tried, found guilty and executed, confessing:

18 MAY

William Corder.

> I acknowledge being guilty of the death of poor Maria Marten, by shooting her with a pistol. The particulars are as follows: When we left her father's house, we began quarrelling ... A scuffle ensued, and during the scuffle, and at the time I think she had hold of me, I took the pistol from the side-pocket of my velveteen jacket and fired. She fell, and died in an instant.

More than 7,000 people attended Corder's execution on 11 August 1828. When Corder said goodbye to his London wife for the last time, he said, 'I hope you will not marry again; and, above all, not marry in a similar way; *it is a most dangerous way of getting a husband.*'

William Corder
throws Maria into
her shallow grave.

19 MAY **1720** At Lambeth, John Thompson, Joseph Brown, Mary Dunford, Mark Travilian and Elizabeth Campbell of Stepney allegedly kidnapped widow Rachel Rogers (aged between 60 and 70), who was worth £20-30,000 – with 'Intent to Marry and ravage the said Rachel Rogers against her Will'. After marrying Mrs Rogers, Thompson took her for dinner – where she started to feel sleepy, and took a nap. The group then carried her upstairs, undressed her and put her to bed. Brown tied her legs to the bedposts. Afterwards, he went to Lambeth, and took possession of all her treasure.

To prove the case in court, the prosecution tried to call Mrs Rogers – but the council for the prisoners objected, saying that she could not give evidence against Thompson because she was married to him. The prisoner then presented the clergyman who had married the pair, who said that he had married them quietly, at home, to avoid the woman becoming 'a town talk'. Since no one else had been in the room at the time of the marriage, it looked like a genuine match – or, at least, the prosecutors could not prove it was not – and the prisoners were released.

20 MAY **1715** John Smith, 'alias Mackentosh', of St Martin in the Fields, broke into Randall Lee's house at midnight. The owner came home and found his house broken open – and Smith in the cellar, clutching a dark lantern, a chisel and a bundle of matches. Smith claimed that he was 'very much in Drink and coming by, fell into the Cellar'. The jury found this hard to believe. Finding him guilty of burglary, they sent him to the gallows.

1717   The proprietors of the Boarded House, Soho advertised a savage entertainment today: an African tiger was to be tied to a stake and attacked by six dogs. A mad bull and a bear, both covered with fireworks, were also exhibited, along with six fighters.

1725   As Thomas Ball, watchman, was proceeding along the street at midnight, he heard a mysterious 'jumbling' from behind a closed door at Richard and Elizabeth Swithin's place in Dover Court. An even louder rumbling commenced, punctuated by the man crying out, 'Lord! Lord! Lord!' Richard Swithin was found bleeding on the floor, stabbed through the coat, waistcoat and shirt, blood gushing out underneath him. Elizabeth claimed that Richard, whose house often resounded with cries of murder, had 'given it to her [a hearty whipping] to her heart's content' when he got into the house that evening – and then stabbed himself, just to frighten her. The jury found this unlikely, and Elizabeth was found guilty of murder and sentenced to death.

1785   The *London Magazine* reported that at 5 a.m., as the mail cart was driving over Blackheath, the driver noticed a horrible sight: a half-naked woman was twisting and struggling on the floor, a rope tied around her neck. The rope was wrapped so tightly that it was difficult to remove it without cutting her. Her shift and her stockings were cut to pieces. She wore satin shoes with silver buckles and appeared to be about 17 years old. When she could speak, she said her name was Bonner. She claimed that she was an orphan who had been attacked by her wicked guardian and his wife so they could steal her fortune; they had then abandoned her to die, alone, on the heath. She described the wicked pair, and a hunt began. Whether the couple were ever caught is not known – and nor is the veracity of her story.

1725   On this day in 1736, the magnificent Daniel Malden (23) made the first of his two escapes from the condemned hold of Newgate, after lifting up a loose floorboard in his cell and digging through the floor into a cell below (which had no bars).

However, there was to be no such escape eleven years earlier, when the famous Jonathan Wild visited the gallows. Wild presented himself, from his offices at No. 68 (marked with the sign of Charles I's head) in the Old Bailey, as a man who could recover anything stolen, and catch any criminal. Hundreds of Londoners visited his offices in Newgate to seek his help. In reality, however, he was responsible

Perhaps London's first 'master criminal' – the marvellous and horrible Jonathan Wild.

for most of the thefts: every thief and criminal in London had become a part of his corporation. Any criminal who refused his terms would be arrested and hanged. He divided the town into districts, and appointed gang leaders for each, who would report all thefts to him; gangs specialising in all sorts of thefts were formed and set to work. They would tell him what they had stolen – or he would ask them to steal a specific item – and when the owner came to ask for his help he would pretend to discover the thief and persuade him to return the items. The grateful owners would then give Wild a 'present' of money and cover all the expenses he had outlaid during the search. His agents were all felons who had illegally returned to the country before the length of their transportation had elapsed – so none of them could inform on him. In court, it was proved that he had actually

Jonathan Wild pelted by the mob on his way to execution – though, given that Londoners specialised in throwing offal and dead cats as well as stones, he may have escaped quite lightly. He is lying down because of the effects of a massive overdose of laudanum.

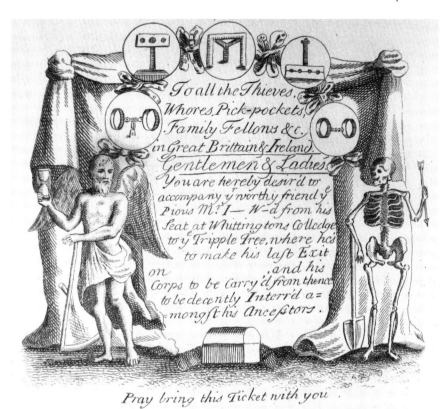

Ticket to the execution of Jonathan Wild, with the London underworld's version of 'Friends, Romans, Countrymen'.

hidden convicts on the run in his own house so they could escape justice. He had also ordered or committed several robberies himself, and had built giant warehouses to hide stolen goods. An enormous army of 'artists' worked day and night upon stolen items such as watches, seals, snuff-boxes and rings so that they could never be recognised by the original owners. Wild routinely bought false witness statements so that he could hang whoever he liked and claim the reward. He told the ordinary of Newgate that he had wounds and scars all over his body from his career capturing criminals such as Jack Sheppard and Joseph 'Blueskin' Blake – who cut Wild's throat after he refused to save him from hanging, and, but for his rusty knife, would have cut it clean off – and that he had two silver plates in his skull where it had been cracked during these arrests. Wild refused to attend Newgate chapel because he was lame, and because his enemies would attack him the moment he appeared. The night before he was hanged, he tried to kill himself with a vast draught of laudanum, but alas without success: it meant that when he appeared to die, in front of an enormous crowd, he was white-faced and delirious. His skeleton is still on display in the Hunterian Museum.

1715   Richard Marston of St James's, Westminster, stole from the wardrobe at Whitehall and took the 'crimson velvet carpet' from the ballroom at St James's Palace on this day. He worked at the Palace, and had been given the key to fetch a chair. Instead, he fetched goods worth £28. He was sentenced to death, but was later respited.   25 MAY

26 MAY **1720** John Wilson, of St Dunstan in the West, stole a leg of veal today from the larder of Joseph Foulk. A passer-by saw the prisoner running along holding the leg at arm's length, heard the cry of 'Stop thief!', and grabbed him. Wilson was whipped.

27 MAY **1817** Miss Mary Ashford (20) was murdered at Erdington; her body was found on this day. It looked like Abraham Thornton was the killer, but it could not be proved. However, Mary's brother refused to let the case drop, and used an ancient law, 'appeal of murder', to demand that Thornton be tried again at the Court of the King's Bench. However, this charge could be defended against under the same ancient law by 'wager of battle' – the last time this defence was used in an English courtroom. Thornton picked up a pair of gauntlets, put one on and threw the other on the floor. As Thornton was a strapping chap, and his rival was a young and weedy man, Mary's brother had to refuse the challenge. Thornton therefore went free.

28 MAY **1715** Two Londoners were lucky to escape with just a fine today, after rioting in Basinghall Street at about 11 p.m. A great mob, including Bolton Freeman and Thomas Page, swept down the street, smashing windows and 'hollowing'. When Constable Thomas Morten arrived, they attacked him and 'abus'd him in a barbarous Manner, by giving him a Blow upon the Forehead, which laid it open to the Skull'. Freeman admitted 'hollowing', and Page was caught with the constable's blood on his clothes. As they had fallen in with the mob 'by chance', they were fined 10 marks each and released.

29 MAY **1732** John Cooper fell into a conversation with 'leather breeches maker' Thomas Gordon in a pub in the Strand on this day, over three pints of 'huckle and buss' (gin and ale). As he was leaving, according to Cooper, Gordon suggested a walk in Chelsea Fields – where, 'in a private Place among some Trees', he pulled a knife and demanded John Cooper's ring, coat, breeches and waistcoat (kindly offering his own as a replacement, so his victim would not be naked).

However, a very different tale emerged in court: it appeared that Cooper had in fact handed over his fancy clothes in return for sex. He had then decided he wanted them back again, but Gordon refused to comply – so Cooper trumped up the charge of robbery. Margaret Holder, the woman who ran the Strand pub where the two had met, informed the court that Cooper was by trade a 'milly cull' – a man paid for 'going of sodomiting Errands'. It turned out that Cooper was also extremely well known in the Drury Lane neighbourhood, but not by the name of John Cooper. He usually went by a much more inventive cognomen: Princess Seraphina. A whole wonderful underworld of transvestite Londoners was revealed to the Old Bailey: Mary Poplet of the Two Sugar Loaves, Drury Lane, described how the Princess and the prisoner argued over the clothes on the night of the 'theft'. 'I have known her Highness a pretty while,' she said, as the Princess used to enquire at her pub 'after some Gentlemen of no very good Character'. Poplet helpfully added:

I have seen her several times in Women's Cloaths. She commonly us'd to wear a white Gown, and a scarlet Cloak, with her Hair frizzled and curl'd all round her Forehead; and then she would so flutter her Fan, and make such fine Curtsies, that you would not have known her from a Woman.

The Princess was a great fan of masquerades, especially at Vauxhall, 'and always chuses to appear at them in a Female Dress, that she may have the Satisfaction of dancing with fine Gentlemen.'

Mary Robinson told the court that, as she was trying on 'a Suit of Red Damask at my Mantua-makers in the Strand', the Princess came up, told her she looked 'mighty pretty', and asked to borrow the suit for a date with 'some fine gentlemen' in the Seven Dials. One 'gentlewoman' had a hilarious tale of dating woe to share: he had been to a ball in 'a Velvet Domine, and pick'd up an old Gentleman, and went to Bed with him, but as soon as the old Fellow found that he had got a Man by his Side, he cry'd out, Murder!'

The case finished with the testimony of Andrew Monford, who said that Gordon had said to Cooper, 'Did not you put your Hand in my Breeches, to pull out what I had?' As several Drury Lane residents gave Mr Gordon the character of 'an honest working Man', the jury acquitted him.

Vauxhall Gardens, haunt of Princess Seraphina, in 1785: the Prince of Wales is pictured on the left, with Johnson, Goldsmith and Boswell. He is whispering into the ear of Mrs Robinson, his first publicly acknowledged mistress. He promised her £20,000 if she would consent, but never paid up. (Courtesy of the Library of Congress, LC-DIG-pga-03193)

30 MAY   1813   On this morning, footman Philip Nicholson went to fetch a surgeon – his master and mistress had been murdered! They lived in what was to be Napoleon III's English residence at Camden Place, Chislehurst. They were found in their room: Mr Bonar (70) on the floor, and Mrs Bonar, covered with blood, dying in her bed. A bent poker was on the floor. She whispered her last words – 'Oh dear!' – and breathed no more.

First Nicholson galloped to the house of Mr Astley Cooper, who rushed off to Camden Place. Next Nicholson went to the Red Lion near Bedlam for a calming drink. Suspicion then fell on the footman because of his strange conduct. He was found deep in his cups at the Three Nuns, in Whitechapel, where 'a smart scuffle ensued, in which Nicholson received some bruises, but he was secured, and conveyed to Giltspur Street Compter. He was now in a state of intoxication approaching to insanity.' A verdict of 'wilful murder' was eventually passed against the wicked footman. However, Nicholson tried to cheat the hangman: he had smuggled a razor into the prison, and with it cut his throat. He was discovered in a water-closet, with a gash in his neck so deep that his head was almost severed from his body. The surgeon quickly sewed up his wound. On 7 June, his wound tore open. Bursting into tears, and on the point of death, he confessed:

> I took the poker from the hall grate, and a lighted candle in my hand from the hall ... I gave my mistress two blows; she never moved. I left her, and went round to master, and gave him two or three blows; and he said 'Come to bed, my love,' and then he sprung from the bed and seized hold of me. I hit him in the struggle about the arms and legs; we struggled fifteen minutes or better, he was very near getting the better of me; I got him down by force, and left him groaning ... I did not know what provoked me to do it, more than you do.

On the gallows, he blamed 'a temporary fury from excessive drinking'.

31 MAY   1787   Servant Henrietta Radbourne (or Gibbons) bayoneted her mistress, Hannah Morgan, through the top of her head on this day at her house in George Street. Morgan died on 11 July. A great cry of 'murder!' and 'fire!' went up at 3 a.m. Watchmen's rattles sounded in the fog, followed by heavy rapping on the Morgans' shuttered door. Eventually a neighbour clambered through the window, and met Henrietta, in nothing but her petticoat, upon the stairs. 'For God's sake, come, and help my mistress, she is murdered!' she said. Morgan was found in a bolted room with her throat cut 'in a most terrible manner, the blood running all down her cap, down on the floor, and all trickling down her face'. Blood covered the window – it had spouted out of the woman's head onto the cobbles below as she cried for help from the window. The house was firmly locked up, and a search in all the cupboards revealed no intruders inside. A bayonet attached to a stick was found propped up in the fireplace. Grey hairs were found on the end. Luckily for the servant, as there was only one witness she was cleared of petit treason, which would have seen her burnt; unluckily for her, she was hanged for murder instead.

JUNE

Branding on the hand.

1 JUNE   **1827**   At about 11 p.m. on this night, Chinaman Edward Hudson Tredway (47) of Chelsea appeared at the house of Sarah Tredway and confessed that he feared he had killed her sister, Ann, known as 'Nance'. He had dabbed her face with vinegar in an effort to restore her, but to no avail. When he returned to the scene with Sarah, Ann was dead. Edward admitted that he had elbowed his wife twice in the side after a jealous quarrel. After the first blow, she had said, 'You have hurt me very much.' Five pints of blood were found in her chest: her spleen was ruptured, and one rib was cracked.

Edward kissed his children, said 'goodbye', and went off to the watchhouse, arm-in-arm with the constable, Samuel Vorley. At Edward's trial, Vorley told the court:

> He wished me not to put him into a cell alone, and I allowed him to sit up with me all night; he was agitated during the night, and frequently said, 'Oh! My soul! Oh! My Nance!'

Edward told the Old Bailey, 'I would have given my soul to have called her back to life.' He was found guilty of 'slaying', and sentenced to three months only.

2 JUNE   **1715**   On this day, William Painter was acquitted of a charge of murdering a 7-year-old boy. He had run over the child's chest with the wheel of his cart. However, it transpired that the boy had run into the road and fallen underneath the wheel, so that the prisoner could not possibly have stopped.

3 JUNE   **1786**   Christchurch spinster Catherine Hughes attacked her sister Elizabeth Ham with a large butcher's knife at her house in Spitalfields. Catherine had been increasingly distracted over the last few months, becoming more and more frightening and looking 'very wild indeed'. One witness said that 'her eyes [were] just ready to burst out of her head'. Catherine had told her servant, Ann Good, that she planned to haunt her; she had also begun to say that the servant was 'pelting her' when she wasn't even in the room. Furthermore, she had picked all the skin off her lips until the blood ran down her chin.

On this day, a neighbour heard something fall in the shop, which he thought was 'a sheep or a lamb', and a woman cry out; he then heard the clatter of the door knocker falling. Puzzled, he crossed the road and saw a third sister, Mrs Hawkins, roving back and forth inside, distractedly. He kicked the door open, and saw a black petticoat and a woman's chest, covered with gore. A woman was seen climbing out of a window and over the roof: it was Hughes. She was found sitting under the steps of a nearby slaughterhouse, 'all a tremble and a twitter'. She said that she did not know how or why she had committed the crime, but that 'the Devil had been very busy with her, and they had had a great many words'. She was found not guilty of murder and sent straight to Mr Mendez's asylum at St Luke's.

4 JUNE   **1773**   'Signor Torre' let off a spectacular show of fireworks in Marylebone Gardens in honour of George III's birthday, with two portraits of the King

and Queen surrounding a huge model of Mount Etna. When the fireworks had finished, the curtain covering the mountain was lifted, and, as the crowds watched, 'lava' rushed down its sides. A terrible tragedy happened on this day three years later, at the Tower Hill fireworks, when a railing collapsed: many Londoners were thrown 30ft into a ditch. Twenty people died, and many more were injured.

1739   Razor and penknife-maker Thomas Bridge (53) of St Andrew's, Holborn, confessed to his friend today that he had murdered his wife Elizabeth with a sharp-pointed, ivory-handled butcher's knife – all whilst eating a piece of bread and cheese. He was rambling, and appeared to be drunk; there was a large bloodstain on his back, and another on his leg, and his face had patches of missing skin. He had lost his house key, so a little boy was sent up a ladder to peer in, and confirmed that there was indeed a dead body lying on the floor. Blood covered the corpse's fingers. Before confessing to his friend, Bridge had visited Sarah Mauden's clothes shop to buy himself a new shirt – to be hanged in. (She noticed blood on the cuffs of the shirt after he tried it on.) Hannah Coles lived above the Bridges, and had heard a 'thumping about' on the night of the murder: it had shaken her bed and the things on her shelves. Bridge told the court that, during a drunken argument, his wife 'fell like a Lump of Lead' onto the knife. He was hanged on 3 August 1739. *5 JUNE*

1780   On this day in 1736, Daniel Malden made his second escape from Newgate, despite being chained to the floor. He borrowed a knife, sawed off his chains, sawed through the iron bars inside the hole that the condemned prisoners used for a toilet – tearing his nails off in the process – and squeezed through the small hole he had made – though he spent half an hour hanging head-first in the sewer after the irons on his feet caught on the bars. He then fell 30ft to the floor of the sewer – which meant, rather horribly, that he was too stunned to move when another prisoner used the hole, a calamity which covered his face and 'almost poisoned him'. He then made his way, ripping his flesh horribly on the narrow sides, along a tunnel and into the common sewer. 'I was then,' he told the ordinary, 'in a sad nasty pickle.' Eventually he reached an old privy, where he climbed out of the seat of the toilet – and by now he must have been in the most revolting state – and found himself by Christ's Hospital. Here he took a needle and thread, turned his waistcoat into a pair of trousers to cover his irons, and walked free – well, until he was caught and hanged in October, anyway. *6 JUNE*

Forty-four years later, the convicts were to have an easier time of it – the London mob pulled the walls down for them. Unhappiness over the Papists Act (which allowed Catholics to inherit and purchase land, amongst other things) came to a head when Lord George Gordon led a mob of 50,000 men over London Bridge and through Westminster to call for a repeal of the Bill. It failed, and violence spread across the city. Catholic chapels in Lincoln's Inn Fields and Duke Street were burnt; Catholic homes were looted. Houses were sacked – and then the mob turned towards Newgate. They started to throw blazing firebrands towards the buildings, and the fire soon took hold. The walls were ripped open, and all 300 prisoners were released. Londoners who failed to chalk 'No Popery' on the outside of their houses soon found them in ruins. Two attempts were made to destroy the Bank of England, Mansion House and the Guildhall, but they were fought off. The King's Bench and the fleet were also fired at, and the whole of the city went up in flames. Troops shot people dead in the street, and spirits mingled with blood where distilleries had been broken open. Bodies lay amidst the wreckage – Londoners who had drunk themselves to death on stolen liquor. In total, 285 Londoners died. When order was finally restored, the city was in ruins – as was the reputation of John Wilkes, who had defended the Bank by ordering the troops under his command to open fire.

7 JUNE   **1753**   Jacobite Archibald Cameron (46), who escaped from Scotland after the Battle of Culloden, was arrested in 1753 and taken down to Tower Hill. On this day, he was led from the Tower at 10 a.m. by a party of Horse Guards, who delivered him to the Sheriffs of London outside Traitors Gate. He was tied to a hurdle and dragged through the city to Tyburn, dressed in a light-coloured coat, red waistcoat and breeches and a brand new wig. He looked around all the way there, and thousands of eyes from the streets, windows and balconies watched him pass. Two hours later, he reached the gallows. As a kindness, the officers there agreed to wait until he was dead before he was cut open. He told the executioner that he could help himself to any money that was in his pockets. After forty-five minutes, his head was cut off and his bowels pulled out. Both head and body were stuffed in a coffin and taken to Mr Stephenson's; his remains were then buried at the Savoy Chapel. He has the distinction of being the last Jacobite executed.

8 JUNE   **1786**   A rather comic duel was fought on this day in Hyde Park, between Lord Macartney of Charles Street, Berkeley Square, and Major-General Stuart of Lower Grosvenor Street. Macartney had suspended Stuart from his command in Madras, which had provoked the duel. The men arrived at 4.30 p.m. and stood twelve paces apart. Stuart asked whether his rival would be able to see him with his weak eyesight; Macartney replied that he 'did perfectly well'. The major-general then informed Macartney that his gun, which he was aiming at him as best he could, was not cocked. His Lordship thanked his opponent, and cocked it. Stuart had only one leg thanks to an unlucky hit by a cannonball in Mysore, and could not stand without support. They both said 'ready', and fired. Macartney was wounded, and the surgeons helped him to take off his coat, and eased him to the ground. He was faint with the loss of blood. A short while later, both men took a carriage home. This was not the first time his Lordship had been wounded in a duel: he had been shot in the ribs the year before, but again gamely continued with the fight until the seconds had called a close to the affair.

9 JUNE   **1792**   Another duel was fought on this day, between the Earl of Lonsdale and Captain Cuthbert, of the Guards. Captain Cuthbert had been ordered to stop the traffic in Mount Street, and had halted his Lordship's coach. Lonsdale leaned out of the window and said, 'You rascal, do you know that I am a Peer of the Realm?' The captain immediately replied, 'I don't know that you are a Peer, but I know you are a scoundrel for applying such a term to an officer on duty, and I will make you answer for it.' They met and fired at each other, but luckily no one was hurt – although the captain would have been killed if the bullet had not bounced off one of his buttons. The seconds then interfered, and matters were settled amicably.

1762   A cat fight today between Mary, wife of John Cooper, and Lydia, wife of William Fletcher, ended with Fletcher's wife being brought home with blood 'over her handkerchief and into her shoes'. Mary had thrown Lydia to the floor after she had refused to leave the Coopers' inn: Lydia claimed she was too frightened of her husband to leave. Lydia held on to the doorframe whilst Mary pulled her arm. Eventually Mary cried out, 'If you do not get out, I will knock you down, and kill you!' They continued struggling in the street, until Lydia fell over and hit her head, cracking her skull. Her opponent was found guilty of manslaughter and burnt on the hand. **10 JUNE**

1764   Shoemaker John Turtle (60) came to the gallows on this day. One evening in May, Samuel Roaper of Periwinkle Street, Ratcliffe Square left rope-maker Joseph Chambers talking to Turtle. A few minutes later, he heard Chambers calling out, 'Roaper, Roaper, my guts are coming out!' He found his friend with his bowels poking out of his side, 'as much as would fill a hat', and four more stab wounds on his chest and thighs. It turned out that Chambers had been sleeping with Turtle's wife Peg, 'everybody's whore', and refused to give the man a pot of beer by way of apology. He paid for it with his life, and Turtle followed shortly afterwards. In Newgate, Turtle was much annoyed by do-gooders: one offered to read to him as he went to the **11 JUNE**

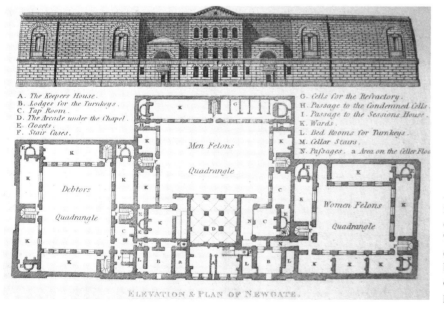

A plan of Newgate from the late eighteenth century. The condemned cells were accessed by a passage shown on the top left of the plan.

gallows, but 'when he began to represent to him how terrible it must be to go out of the world unprepared and impenitent, Turtle told him, if he had nothing else to talk of, he might go about his business'. He was faint and weak with terror on the platform, and kissed the executioner's hand; The ordinary's report states that 'he appeared in tears just before he went off'.

12 JUNE **1742** Two cheats called Thomas Lyell and Lawrence Sydney, who won more than £4,000 at a masquerade using nine sets of loaded dice, were pilloried on this day. They were marched from Newgate to a pillory opposite the Opera House, where they faced the wrath of the London populace. They were pelted with sticks and stones until they bled.

13 JUNE **1732** John Waller, a man who gave false evidence so he could claim the reward, met one of the grimmest fates in London's history today. As he was standing in the pillory for his crime at the Seven Dials, in London, two men in the crowd made a vicious and disgusting decision. After William Belt had locked Waller into the pillory, Edward Dalton (26), an itinerant shoe-black, and Richard 'Sergeant' Griffith (39), a butcher's carrier, pushed their way to the front and stood up on the pillory board. Griffith grabbed the man's coat, and Dalton the waistband of his trousers, and they ripped his trousers down; they then pulled Waller out of the boards. As Belt struggled to put him back in, and as Waller hung by just one hand, the other two men ripped off all of the poor man's clothes. They then beat him with 'collyflower stalks', which had already been flying through the air so thickly that anyone else on the platform had been forced to step down.

They forced soot down his throat, with more of the rotten old vegetables, and then started to jump and stamp upon his naked body and head, kicking him all the time. This went on for more than fifteen minutes. The crowd then grew so violent that it surged forward and threw the entire wooden structure to the ground. Waller's body lay in the dust, whilst countless Londoners surged over him. Dalton then stamped upon the man's privy parts, upon which the poor man gave a soft and dismal groan and moved no more.

'Well played!' said Griffith as he stamped.

'Damn him, I'll never leave him while he has a bit of life in him!' replied his friend.

After nearly an hour, with his body dragged one way and then the other in the dirt, the corpse of the perjurer was manhandled into a coach and driven to Newgate. The dead man's mother, Martha Smith, was waiting there. The prison refused to take Waller in as he was dead, and so his mother, wailing, climbed into the coach with the ruined body of her son. As the two men saw her get in, they cried out, 'Here's the old bitch his mother! Damn her, let's kill her too.' They leapt to the coach door, swearing and cheering, and began a grim game of tug-of-war with their victim's body. 'We have sent his soul halfway to Hell,' said Dalton. 'Now we'll have his body to sell to the surgeons for money to pay the Devil for his thorow passage.' Martha described the horrid scene she found in the coach:

My son had neither Eyes, nor Ears, nor Nose to be seen; they had squeezed his Head flat. Griffith pull'd open the Coach-door, and struck me, pull'd my Son's Head out of my Lap, and his Brains fell into my Hand.

The motive was very simple: Waller's lies had hanged Dalton's brother. Dalton's fate was simple too: he was hanged by the neck until dead at Tyburn in October. He 'own'd that he had been a great Swearer, Drinker, a Whoring Fellow and Sabbath-breaker', 'cried very much in Chappel', and died, along with Griffith, 'penitent, in Hopes of Salvation through Christ, and in Peace with all Men'.

1719 On this day, four unlucky weavers of a mob of nearly 4,000 were committed to Newgate. The previous day, they had torn around Spitalfields attacking any woman whom they could find wearing Indian calicoes or linens, and sousing them with ink, acids and other fluids. Indian fabrics were taking over from home-grown materials, destroying the weavers' livelihood. Two more men were captured, and the troops were forced to fire into the crowd to drive the mob back, wounding three persons. On Sunday night, two more were sent to the prison for tearing the gown off the back of one Mrs Becket, leaving her in the street in a difficult situation. **14 JUNE**

Also today, but in 1821, the following incident occurred (as reported in *Edinburgh Magazine*):

A dreadful and melancholy accident happened to Mr Hadland, who kept a shop in Fetter Lane, Holborn, London, for the making of sausages. As he was feeding the steam engine, used for chopping the meat, his apron caught by accident in one of the cogs of the machine, which drew him in; and before the engine could be stopped he got entangled in the wheels, and was crushed to pieces; he had his arms, legs, and thighs broken, and his flesh shockingly mangled. In this dreadful state he lived until Thursday morning, when death put a period to his misery.

1737 On this day, Hans Mac-Connel (or Connel) of St Ann's, Middlesex, received a subpoena that saved his life – it provided an alibi, suggesting that he could not have committed a most hideous crime. On 16 June, at about noon, Robert Long of Limehouse went out. When he returned in the evening, he found his wife's throat cut and his child's neck bone 'disjointed', its head hanging to the body only by a bit of skin. Two hammer blows marked their skulls. Because Hans had appeared in court at 4 p.m., he was cleared of the crime. **15 JUNE**

1727 Nurse Catherine Banfield, of St Sepulchre's, dropped John Cornish (1) into a fire on this day, burning him 'in a surprising manner' from his waist to his toes, of which he instantly died. She did not tell the parents for four days, and then she lied and claimed that John had suffered a fit. She told the court that the death was a tragic accident, caused when flames had leapt onto the child's clothes whilst she was out of the room. **16 JUNE**

17 JUNE **1760** Soldier William Odell strangled his wife Elizabeth on this day. Elizabeth's son – also a William (15) – last saw his mother alive heading towards the Black Lion near Hangar Lane, Acton; she was going to show a woman the way home for a small fee. At 10 p.m., Elizabeth began the walk home from the lady's house. Meanwhile, William snr, who treated Elizabeth and William jnr very badly, and beat his wife 'almost blind', was seen to go in search of Elizabeth, claiming he would kill both women if he found them. Elizabeth never reached her home.

A week later, when asked where she was by local temptress Mary Middleton ('a naughty woman before her husband marry'd her'), William declared 'he knew she never would come back no more'. He refused to reveal her whereabouts, though he claimed to know them. Then Elizabeth was discovered 'barbarously murdered' in a pond. At first her body was thought to be a pile of weeds, then a dead sheep – and then they realised it was the corpse of a woman. Her body was bruised, her nose broken. Her tongue poked out of her mouth, and her eyes, nose, mouth, and ears were full of blood. Her body was as 'red as fire' at first, then quickly went black. She had been strangled with a very thin piece of string. Odell quickly signed his own death warrant. Mary said that she'd heard the wife's arms had been cut with a knife. 'They were not, by God,' he replied, 'they were cut with a sword.' M. Maria Enamure, who had been sleeping on a nearby pile of hay on the night of the murder, had heard 'a dismal scream', followed by a cry of, 'For God's sake, for Christ's sake, will nobody come to assist me, but let my husband murder me?' Odell was hanged on 15 September 1760. He asked the executioners to take his body past the house of Mary and make her touch his chest or shake his dead hand, to bring home what he insisted was her false testimony with the greatest effect.

18 JUNE **1814** On this day in 1814, whilst the Battle of Waterloo raged, Mayor Sir William Domville entertained the Prince Regent, the Emperor of Russia and the King of Prussia to a dinner so sumptuous that the bill came to £25,000.

Waterloo Bridge, which opened on 18 June 1817 and was named in memory of Wellington's famous victory.

Also on this day, but in 1741, James Hall (37) of St Clement Danes, crushed the skull of his master, John Penny, with a club in his chambers at Clement's Inn. He then cut his master's throat, and carefully drained every drop of blood into the pots and pans in the house. The blood was mixed with water and poured through a grate by the door; he then stripped quite naked, and threw the body – also naked – over his shoulder, trooped down the stairs with it, carried it out into the garden and dumped it in the 'bog house'. When Penny's body was found, Hall was instantly arrested. Hall was an 'obstreperous, ill natur'd, sullen Man; inclined to Women, Drinking, and Gaming'. When the day of execution came, his wife was waiting in the press yard. As he stepped out into the light, she gave a strange cry and hurled the hood she was wearing into the dust. He was executed on 14 September 1741, at the end of Catherine Street, in the Strand, after being drawn all the way on a hurdle. His body hung for three quarters of an hour, after which he was taken down, and carried to Shepherd's Bush, in order to be hung in chains.

1821   On this day, George IV was crowned, and the out-of-favour Queen Caroline brazened it out and decided to attend. Some of the houses nearby made as much as £1,000 renting out viewing space. Therefore, the maximum number of people watched today as she was rudely, and most firmly, turned away. She had written to the King beforehand to inform him that she planned to attend, and asked what dress she should appear in; 'A white sheet, in the middle aisle of the Abbey,' was one wag's reply. **19 JUNE**

'Immense shouts, clapping of hands, and waving of hats and handkerchiefs, announced the approach of the Queen,' reported *The Trial at Large of Her Majesty Caroline Amelia, Queen of Great Britain*. Soon a 'pin-drop silence' fell, as she approached the abbey – broken by a cry from inside of 'Shut the gates!' All the soldiers formed ranks, with their bayonets fixed. First Caroline tried the Dean's Court entrance, where she was refused. She then, humiliatingly, had to wait for her carriage to return, to take her to Palace Yard. All the while, the crowds shouted out, 'The Queen! The Queen!' She spotted a second entrance and opened the door of her carriage to try it – so that parts of the crowd started to shout 'Shame! Shame!' at her boldness. The second set of doors was shut in her face. She finally spied the Peers' platform, and talked her way in and along to Poets' Corner – where she was turned away because she did not have a ticket. This made several people waiting nearby start laughing. Caroline was forced to get into her carriage and go home. She languished as soon as she returned home, and a string of announcements followed, such as:

Brandenburgh House, Aug 2, 1821, half past 10, p.m., Her Majesty has an obstruction of the bowels, attended with inflammation.

She was blooded to the astonishing sum of 66 ounces of blood. She died on the 7th, causing all her domestics to 'shriek'. Blinds were pulled across London as a mark of respect. Her coffin was made in Mount Street. Her last words were, 'Well, my dear Doctor, what do you think now?'

20 JUNE 1715 A fight broke out in a public house, near St James's, between Daniel Jones and his female companion. Words led to blows, and eventually the quarrel rose to such heights that the man drew his sword and ran at the woman. She managed to slip out of the door, but unfortunately the blade ran into the body of a poor boy standing nearby, who worked at the house, and killed him. The 'violent tongue' of the woman was accepted as the cause of the quarrel, and Jones was charged with manslaughter, branded and set free.

21 JUNE 1815 Patrick Cushion, alias Kishon, was indicted for stabbing labourer Owen Gilliss of Queen Street, Chelsea, on this day. Cushion said that he was a poor old Irish soldier who had been teased all day by the men for his nationality. When he had offered to buy them a drink if they would stop, they had happily agreed – before drinking away every penny he had and then returning to their taunts. He was very much afraid of them, and so picked up a rusty old piece of razor wrapped in a stocking, and took up a stand against the wall, ready to defend himself. When he would not go to bed, some of the men got up and began to stalk him. He struck out, and was bundled from the room. 'If I hurt anyone, it was not with any malice, but merely in my own defence.' He was acquitted of all charges.

22 JUNE 1752 Thomas Wilford (17), a Bishopsgate Street Workhouse cripple from Fulham with only one arm, was indicted on this day for murdering his wife, Sarah Williams (22). He claimed the dubious honour of being the first man to be hanged and anatomised under the new Statute (which said that no murderer was to be buried unless he had first been anatomised). Wilford had fallen in love with Sarah whilst seeking treatment for a venereal disease in Fulham Workhouse (though they had been friends since they were young). One day, he told a fellow-lodger that he had almost cut off Sarah's head. After a panicked moment, the woman managed to stop a watchman and borrow a stub of candle. She struck a match, and the horrified onlookers saw blood light up from Wilford's reddened elbow to his breeches. The couple had fallen into a vicious row when she had stayed out late and would not tell him why, until eventually he had pinned her down with his stump and sawed at her throat with a clasp knife. He wept when the death sentence was passed, prayed at the gallows and pitched out of the cart a penitent man.

23 JUNE 1819 The *Gentleman's Magazine* recorded:

> During a severe storm on this day, three men (haymakers) were in the fields between Clapton and the river Lea, eating their dinner under a tree, when one of them, finding the rain penetrating through the leaves, left his companions and sheltered under another tree a short distance away. He had no sooner got under the alternative tree when he was struck senseless on the ground by lightning. After some time he recovered and looking around discovered the lifeless corpses of his companions, both having been struck dead.

1720   Mad doctor Theodore Christopher Fabritius, of St Leonard's in
Shoreditch, was witnessed perpetrating a horrible attack on this day. His next-
door neighbour, Elizabeth Wilson, was familiar with his violent methods: she
usually heard a woman in his house, Grace Shaw, shrieking several times a
day (even on Sundays). Sometimes Grace would be ceremoniously marched
into the garden to be beaten with a horsewhip. On this day, the doctor was
seen beating the woman until her ear bled. Countless visitors had found her
with black eyes, running through the house with blood upon her, or locked
into various rooms. They had seen her kicked off ladders and attacked in the
garden (once with a broomstick, which had knocked off her hat – the doctor
had then picked up the hat, which had trailing strings attached to it, and
had attempted to choke her with them). The gardener, William Hobbs, often
saw Grace beaten with a cane, and sometimes punched in the face. Once a
thick stick was used, whilst the doctor shrieked, 'Damn you, do you cry out?'
He had then rammed the other end of the stick into her mouth, cutting her.
Another time he said, 'Damn you, can't you kneel?' and pushed her to the
floor before stamping on her. She gave herself up to death at last on 26 June.
The woman who came to lay out her body found she had 'black places on
her head, face, arms, neck, shoulders, back and legs, a sad ear, and her cap
bloody'. Her nose was broken, and a front tooth had been knocked out.

The doctor claimed that Grace was a 'lunatick' whom he was curing.
Grace's mother had sent her to him, though he admitted that she had asked
him not to hit her in the face any more. He called witnesses to say that his
whip, cane and stick were not of a particularly thick nature, and others
to describe how his methods had previously worked. He was acquitted of
murder, and found guilty only of manslaughter. His hand was burnt, and
he was set free.

1790   Captain Harvey Aston met Lieutenant Fitzgerald at Chalk Farm
Lodge this day after a quarrel in the Mess. Fitzgerald was offered the first
shot. Carefully balancing the barrel of the pistol on his arm, he fired: the
bullet struck his opponent on the wrist and rebounded up into his opponent's
face, smashing through his right cheekbone and tearing out through the
back of his neck. However, the horrible wound was not fatal, and the slight
rebound may even have saved the captain's life. On receiving this wound,
Captain Aston called out to his antagonist, 'Are you satisfied?' to which the
lieutenant – unsurprisingly – replied, 'I am satisfied.' The men then went
home. Sadly, the brave captain was later killed in another duel.

Also today, in 1810, a coach from Brighton, rattling along at full speed
down the Brixton Causeway, caused a calamity when the wheel fell off.
Sixteen people were horribly injured, including one gentleman whose thighs
were both broken.

1786   Today, porter John Hogan of Marylebone murdered servant Ann
Hunt with a broom and a razor. Prior to this, Hogan had delivered some
furniture to Ann's house and had been entranced by the woman when she
opened the door; the two had started a secret relationship. Then, one Sunday,

Mr and Mrs Orell, the girl's employers, went out for a walk. When they returned, the house was shut up and silent. They eventually managed to break in, only to see 'a spectacle' in the kitchen 'as dreadful as ever presented itself to the human eye': Ann was crouched in a corner, on a floor covered with blood, her throat cut from ear to ear; her breast was cut in many places, and one of her arms was broken above and below her shattered elbow. Her dress had been torn off, and seemed to have been 'rolled in blood'. Her skull was fractured – but she was still alive! Mr Orell's reaction was not the most helpful: he said, 'Good God, Nanny, what have you been doing?' He then rushed her to Middlesex Hospital, where her eye was declared to be standing out 'in a manner that was shocking'. Her cheekbones were shattered, and her neck, throat and windpipe were slashed. Her face was also deeply cut. She died on 27 June.

A few days later, in one of the 'cakes' of blood on the floor, a nosegay of cabbage flowers was found. It formed the final part of a description so exact that Mr Orell was able to issue a handbill that led him straight to the porter. Orell dragged Hogan into the room where Ann's body lay, and forced him to touch her. Hogan seemed unconcerned by the spectacle – though it was so horrible to look at that one of the police guards burst into tears and had to leave the room. The prisoner's partner of more than a year described washing a bloody shirt on the night of the murder. She also told the court that her lover had confessed to murdering Ann after she refused his advances, and had thrown some stolen spoons off London Bridge. Hogan was hanged in Charlotte Street, Marylebone, and anatomised.

27 JUNE   **1777**   Dr Dodd, who forged a bill for £4,200 in the name of Lord Chesterfield, went to his death today. An eye-witness said:

> The Doctor, to all appearances, was rendered perfectly stupid with despair. His hat was flapped all around, and pulled over his eyes ... He came in a coach and a heavy shower of rain fell just upon his entering the cart, and another just upon his putting up his umbrella.

The witness thought the umbrella was a bit unnecessary, as 'he was going to a place where he might be dried'. Then a game ensued: he took his wig off – then he put it on again – then he took it off again. Then he put on a nightcap, but it was too small, forcing him to take it off again. He refused to move in the cart, and died very quickly. He was buried in Goodge Street, Tottenham Court Road – after being given a warm bath first, just in case he revived. Dr Dodd's publications included *The Frequency of Capital Punishment inconsistent with Justice, Sound Policy, and Religion.*

28 JUNE   **1718**   On this day, as Stephen Awdley was walking by Whitechapel church, his brother William approached him and said that he knew where they could find a man who had been 'murdered by a bitch' – a woman they both knew. They walked to the site and found there, curled up in a ditch,

the torn body of Nathaniel Asser, which they transported to a nearby house. William Awdley was shortly thereafter suspected in the case and arrested. He told the court that he had stumbled, after a long night of drinking, across an acquaintance called Sarah Brown. Brown had said she'd found a gentleman sleeping in a nearby ditch with gold rings on his hands, so they had gone and pulled off the rings – and then William had hefted two large bricks at the recumbent man, striking his head and side. Surgeons found pools of congealed blood in Nathaniel's brain, and bruises covering his body. William initially tried to claim that he was asleep in a neighbouring field during the attack, and Sarah claimed that she was at a nearby house, but the jury found them both guilty, and sent them to the gallows.

The Newgate cart waiting underneath the gallows. This image shows the execution of Dr Dodd, hanged on the 27th and 'perfectly stupid with despair'.

1821 On this day, hairdresser John Hone was walking through fields by Gray's Inn Lane when he observed 'a lad', William Dawson, lift up his carbine, aim carefully at the fence, and fire. Unfortunately for Dawson, Dennis Butler was standing behind the wooden boards he was shooting at: the bullet flew straight through and killed him. 'He said he was extremely sorry for it, but that he did not see any body when he fired,' the arresting constable told the court, and Dawson was acquitted. **29 JUNE**

1742 On this day, prostitute Mary Terry, of the parish of St Catherine's, was accused of cutting the throat of Tower Hill stick-seller John Hussey. Mary was 'seen' holding an old hat under Hussey's chin – into which he was bleeding profusely from a wide, jagged cut to his throat. The court found the story of the witness, Rebecca Holder, deeply suspicious – and more so when it was revealed that Terry was vital to several pending legal cases against Holder's associates. William Wintrx, the coroner's deputy, came to view the body – lying in the pub with its head near cut off and a hat full of blood next to it – and decided that there was not enough blood in the room. This suggested that the man had probably been murdered somewhere else, and had been dragged there to incriminate Mary Terry. The court declared, 'It is an unreasonable Thing to suppose, that you should see a Man standing up, and bleeding into a Hat, with his Throat cut, and not cry out murder, and give an account of it directly.' Terry was therefore acquitted. **30 JUNE**

JULY

In July 1804, Richard Patch (38) embezzled the money of his master, Isaac Blight. The next year, in order to keep Blight from discovering and revealing this wicked crime, Richard took off his shoes (so that he could walk silently) and sneaked into Blight's house at Rotherhithe, where he shot Isaac dead. Patch's alibi, that he was 'indisposed with bowel troubles' at the time of the shooting, did not protect him for long – especially after a pistol's ramrod was found in the outhouse. He went to the gallows, where he was so annoyed by constant demands to confess that he attempted to throw himself off the platform. Thievery was rife in July, and other Londoners were involuntarily separated from their property on 1, 9, 11, 15 and 20 July.

1749   An enormous body of more than 400 sailors gathered outside a
house in the Strand on this evening, armed with cutlasses and bludgeons,
after rumours had spread that some sailors had been ill-treated by the
women within. Peter Wood's house, the Star, which had a reputation as a
bawdy house, was destroyed in an attack the next day. First, the lamp at his
door was shattered; then all the windows followed. Shutters and sashes were
forced out, and eight or ten sailors forced their way through the windows
and into the house, where everything inside was smashed. All the while
they cried out things such as 'Down with the bawdy-houses! Where are
your whores?' The sailors' hands went 'all over' Mrs Jane Wood, and she
was 'shoved about like anything'. Everything that could be moved was
stolen. Two of the rioters were sentenced to death. A large number of sailors
attended the gallows, as they had heard that the men were to be dissected;
however, when they heard it was
not true, they let the event carry
on peaceably.

Today, in 1810, a storm blew
off a brick parapet in Rupert
Street – straight onto the head
of Mrs Lemaire underneath,
crushing her skull dreadfully. In
addition, Mr Byfell's daughter
was crushed by a falling chimney
in Park Street – even though her
mother and brother, walking
either side, were unharmed;
a coach in Sloane Street was
blown over, breaking the arm
of the servant travelling with
it; a woman in Duke Street
was crushed by a chimney pot;
and a woman in Westminster
was struck blind by lightning
– though her sight, amazingly,
recovered a few days later.

The mob attacking
the house of Peter
Wood, at the sign
of the Star: 'Down
with bawdy houses!
Where are your
whores?!'

1809   Elizabeth Pike (68) was sent to prison for six months for stealing
a pewter jug from the Gun public house, Union Street, on this day. The
landlord found it tucked under her cloak. When she was caught, she begged
the landlord to forgive her; he sent her to the Old Bailey, where her defence
was: 'I only beg for mercy, I would not hurt any person living.' Mercy was
not forthcoming.

1809   Henry White and James Smith were tried today for breaking into
the house of Francis Sitwell, Esq., of Durweston Street, St Marylebone. They
had drilled a hole in the door under the lock, reached in and opened it. Lock-
picks, a dark lantern, an iron crowbar and a pistol were found scattered

along the road the two men had tried to escape by. They were found guilty and sentenced to death.

Also on this day, surgeon Joseph Savage examined 'a great spectacle indeed': the body of Reuben Main jnr (10) at some brick fields. One worker at the fields had awoken to find that his shirt sleeve was on fire; he had pulled it off, and run out naked into the night. Outside, he heard a great cry from Reuben snr: 'My boy is burnt!' The boy was trapped inside one of the burning huts. He was eventually dragged out with a hand rake, 'dead, with his little entrails out'. Reuben said, 'If I had known the child had been in at the time, I would have saved him or lost my own life if I had a thousand.'

4 JULY 1820 On this day, the Secret Committee of Lords, Earls and Bishops reported on...

> ...allegations supported by the concurrent testimony of a great number of different persons ... which deeply affect the honour of the Queen, charging her with an adulterous connexion with a foreigner originally in her service in a menial capacity.

The Queen of England was about to appear in court on a charge of adultery – rather an interesting charge when one considers that George IV was already married to Maria Fitzherbert when he wed Queen Caroline. The man in question was one Bartholomew Bergami or Pergami, a married footman from Milan. The next day, in the House of Lords, a 'Bill to deprive her Majesty, Caroline-Amelia-Elizabeth, of the title, prerogatives, rights, privileges, and pretensions, of Queen Consort of the realm, and dissolve the marriage between his Majesty and the said Queen' appeared. It alleged that the Queen had bestowed on him 'indecent and offensive familiarity and freedom, and carried on with him a scandalous and adulterous intercourse; by which great scandal and dishonour were brought upon her Royal Highness, as well as on this Kingdom'.

The 'trial' described how the Queen had moved Bergami into a room attached to hers by a corridor. On 9 November 1814, allegedly, great use was made of this convenience after a late night at the opera. According to the maidservant, the royal bed was not slept in that night, though the dent of two sleepers was allegedly found in Bergami's. A few days later, the Queen was changing costume at a masked ball – into a very 'indecent' replacement – and asked for a servant to help her change: she sent for Bergami. Bergami's own servant, Theodore Majocci, testified to seeing HRH creeping along the corridor to his room, and to the 'sound of kissing' echoing from within. A long catalogue of close or attached rooms across the Continent was then listed, including one room in Sicily where the Queen had been observed coming out of Bergami's room undressed and carrying her pillow. Tents in Africa, beds in Europe – out of all manner of places, Bergami was seen stumbling, undressed. He was also witnessed embracing her as he lay in bed; she was seen sitting on his lap in a carriage; and they were spotted canoeing together on Lake Como. Luckily for the Queen, the magnificent Henry, Lord

Brougham was the lawyer for the defence. As his biography has it, 'Day after day, for three weeks, the Queen sat at the bar, while her Italian servants, and English officers who had observed her conduct, narrated foolish or disgusting tales.' In forty-nine days, Brougham tore these stories to shreds, ending with a speech where he declared the evidence:

> ...inadequate to prove a debt, impotent to deprive of any civil right – ridiculous to the lowest offence – scandalous if brought forward to support a charge of the highest nature which the law knows – monstrous to ruin the honour of an English Queen!

One-hundred-and-nine found her guilty; eight-one innocent. However, enough support had gone from the Bill that it was abandoned. All the while, the streets were filled with Londoners expressing their support for the Queen, and well-wishers crowded around her house, Brandenburgh, at Hammersmith. Thousands of cries of 'God Bless your Majesty' were heard each day as she left for the court, and almost a million people signed a petition in her favour. Her popularity was enormous, but she died soon after a scandalous event (*see* 19 June), amidst rumours that she had been poisoned. When an attempt was made to avoid taking her funeral procession through London, the mob blocked the route to force it through the city. The Horse Guards charged, and two Londoners were killed. She was buried in Brunswick with a tomb marked, 'Here lies Caroline, the Injured Queen of England.'

Perhaps history's handsomest lawyer: Henry Brougham, later a founder of University College, London and of the Central Criminal Court, and Lord Chancellor during the reign of William IV. His defence of Caroline was one of the most famous speeches of the day.

Queen Caroline, in a hat that even Lady Catherine de Bourgh might be ashamed to be seen in.

5 JULY **1721** Apprentice mantua-maker Barbara Spencer (24) of St Giles', Cripplegate, who had a naturally furious temper after a youth spent running wild, was burnt for the crime of coining this day. A Mrs Bunn claimed she saw the woman pull some shillings – coins which 'she perceived to be bad' – out of her bosom and hand them over to another prisoner in the exercise yard of a London prison; Spencer was in this prison after being stopped in the company of an acquaintance, who was carrying 28s in bad coins and a set of moulds. The hideous nature of the punishment was made more horrible in this case by the London crowd: Spencer 'was very desirous of praying, and complained of the dirt and stones thrown by the mob behind her.'

6 JULY **1737** Fisherman John Daffon threw a knife into the back of his own son, Richard Daffon, in the Hat & Feather in Milford Lane on this day, after a petty fight over a net which had been confiscated. When they found they could not get it back, John had suggested they have a drink to cheer themselves up.

'Damn you, you want to get drunk all day – you shall have no more!' his son had replied.

John, in a temper, shouted, 'Must I be rul'd by the children, and be afraid of having a pint of beer!' and dashed the blade onto the table. It skittered off, and flew into Richard's back. He died. The court decided that a fever he had recently suffered was to blame for his death, and set the heartbroken father free.

Thirty-eight years later, across 'the pond', the Continental Army 'resolved to die like freemen rather than live like slaves'. Stephen Sayre, a friend of John Wilkes, was arrested in October for plotting to kidnap George III, the colonies were declared in uprising – and, at the very end of the year, one Jane Austen was born.

George III, who narrowly avoided kidnap several times during his reign.

1783 The *London Magazine* reported:

7 JULY

> This day, a gentleman from Hackney was returning from Chigwell with his wife and daughter, a fine girl of three years of age, the latter leaning against the coach door. It unfortunately burst open, by which accident the young lady fell with great force against a tree stump and her skull was fractured. She died soon after she was conveyed home.

Also today, Mrs Christian Davies, more commonly known as 'Mother Ross', was buried. When Mrs Davies' first husband, Thomas Welch, was kidnapped and forced to turn sailor, Mother Ross had decided to disguise herself as a man

to find him. However, she enjoyed being 'Christopher Welch, soldier' so much that she had abandoned the search in favour of reliving the 'masculine habits' of her youth – 'romping' with every woman she came across and performing 'the most desperate acts' of valour on the battlefield. She was shot in the ankle, shot in the hip – imperilling her disguise – and finally suffered a fractured skull, whereupon she came clean about her true identity. She then found her husband and stayed with the army as a sutler. Her first husband later died at Taisnieres

Queen Anne, who granted Christian a pension.

(she found his corpse after 'turning over near two hundred bodies in search of him'); a second husband, a grenadier, died of a gangrenous wound at St Venant. Her third husband, a soldier from whom she took the name Davies, retired into the Chelsea Hospital, and she, living nearby, went to court twice a week. As Queen Anne had already granted her £50 plus a pension of a shilling a day for her achievements, to which the courtiers added more, she lived extremely comfortably, and, when she died on 7 July 1739, she was interred in the burying ground of the hospital with full military honours.

8 JULY   **1732**   On this day, Francis Walford and Thomas Darby killed black Londoner William Stanley with a shovel. At 9 p.m. in Elmstreet, Gray's Inn, Stanley was talking to his wife as the two men, both labourers, were working nearby. They put up a screen to hide the bricks and dust they had so far pulled down, and Stanley said, 'I hope you won't screen your rubbish upon my ground.'

'Damn you for a son of a bitch, but we will,' was the reply.

Stanley went inside, but the wife – fatally – added her two cents' worth as they tidied up: 'It's hard that we can't stand at our own door to take a mouthful of air, but we must be choaked [*sic*] with your dust,' she added, tartly.

'Damn you, you bitch – send your buck out and we'll thrash him!' The men said. The husband, hearing this, ran straight across the street and kicked down their screen door. They retaliated by setting it up even nearer his door, and then stirring up a simply enormous cloud of dirt, which boiled through the Stanleys' open windows. Words came to blows, and Stanley was struck. 'Fetch a constable, for he has cut me down the head!' he said as he collapsed. When his skull was opened after death, 'faetid corrupted Matter' poured out. The jury heard that Stanley had punched one of the builders before he was hit, and so acquitted both the prisoners.

9 JULY   **1718**   Long-Acre servant Mary Price (21), alias 'Purry Moll', of the parish of St Martin in the Fields, was indicted this day for wrapping a leather belt around the neck of a 3-year-old girl and choking her to death. She pleaded guilty, which surprised the court so much that they stopped to ask if she was sure. She replied that if she did confess it, she 'confess'd nothing but the truth'. The court delayed her judgment so that they could assess whether she was insane, but when she returned to the court she again cheerfully declared that she was guilty, and that she 'did it out of revenge' against the father of the child, who she would have choked instead had he been within her reach. 'Blood required blood,' she said, and she required the due sentence of death. The child was the daughter of a soldier who had taken away a small, plain tobacco box, a trinket given to Mary by a man she loved, who had since gone away to sea. She told the ordinary of Newgate that the child had stolen it and given it to the soldier. In revenge, Mary had taken away his daughter with the grip of one of his own leather garters. He had been a friend of the family. She was sentenced to death.

1720 Elizabeth Catlin of St James's, Westminster, placed her newborn baby under a pile of coals this day, but may or may not have strangled it to death. Catlin had just started a new job as a cleaner. Her employer noticed she looked rather peaky, and asked her if she was perhaps pregnant: Catlin retorted that she was merely suffering from a bout of collick caused by eating cabbage. The lady then went out. When she returned, she found her new servant lying in bed with a suspicious puddle on the floor (which Catlin said had been caused by the cat knocking over the chamber pot). The body of a baby was found hidden in the coal vault. No marks of violence were found on it, and, as the prisoner told the court that labour had come on much earlier than expected, and that the baby had died at birth, she was acquitted.

10 JULY

1721 Mary Johnson of St James's, Westminster, was caught on this day wheeling a suspicious-looking handcart filled with a pair of boots, seven pairs of shoes and a pair of slippers. She claimed that she had purchased them from 'a man' in Islington, but when she was taken to Newgate she confessed that she had stolen them. She was transported.

11 JULY

In 1726, William Brown was prevented from escaping the scene of his crime by the simple method of his 'victim', Thomas Newton, grabbing tightly on to his family jewels and calling for the watch. Newton was on the hunt, with a couple of constables, for homosexuals, after the infamous Vere Street Coterie had been dispersed. Newton had gone to a notorious haunt in Upper Moorfields, and it was there that Brown sidled up to him: 'Tis a fine Night,' he said.

'Aye,' Newton replied.

Brown then took Newton's hand and guided it to his breeches, and 'put his Privities into it'. Newton gripped tight. Brown told the court, 'I think there's no Crime in making what use I please of my own Body,' but the court sentenced him to the pillory.

1722 A case of shoplifting was heard on this day when Sir Charles Burton, Baronet, was found guilty of stealing a seal set in gold from a London shopkeeper. Sir Charles was browsing the stock when the keeper noticed that the seal was missing. She demanded that her aristocratic client shake out his handkerchief, which she noticed he was gripping rather tightly. Weakly, he wafted the offending item. She demanded he do it again with more vigour. 'What?' he said. 'Do you charge a gentleman with theft?' She took the handkerchief from him, and found the seal tucked inside it. The Baronet's mother had left him £500, but he had lately fallen on hard times. He was sentenced to transportation, but in light of this story his sentence was reduced to a private whipping.

12 JULY

1715 Thomas Harvey, of St James's parish, Westminster, was sentenced to death on this day for causing the death of John Jones, a gambler who made an unfortunate remark at the Phoenix gambling den in the Haymarket. Harvey had lost some money and refused to pay; Jones remarked, 'Tis but just that every gentleman should have his own,' whereupon Harvey,

13 JULY

aggrieved, struck him with his cane, and then thrust it into his eye. Jones instantly dropped, fell into violent and 'dismal' convulsions, and died the following day.

Today in 1810, Miss Tandy strangled herself at her uncle's house in Titchbourne Place, after tying a noose to her bedpost. She had been sent there to stop her seeing a suitor whom her parents considered unsuitable.

14 JULY   **1739**   On this day – the day the Bastille was stormed in 1789 – parish beadle John Thackery received a message from an Isleworth farmer, Mr Ions, telling him that he had found a baby lying dead in his field, covered over with a little grass. A blow to its head had left the 'scull' so soft that he 'could have thrust [his] finger into it'. A woman told him that she suspected local fruit-gatherer Elizabeth Harrard (32). Harrard was arrested and then immediately put to bed, for she looked very ill. She told the midwife who examined her that she had suddenly gone into labour whilst climbing over a stile, and, as some men had come along at that very moment, she had run away and left the child behind. When the midwife said she found this tale rather unlikely, Harrard changed it, claiming that the newborn had accidentally rolled from her lap into the river. Then she claimed it had died and so she had thrown it in. She added that she had been wandering for days, being refused by parish after parish. The Newgate chaplain was very sorry for her hard life, and comforted her when she was sentenced to death.

15 JULY   **1734**   William Newell, alias Black-head, and Thomas Martin, alias Paps-Nose, stole a whole host of clothes from a ship called the *Happy Return* today. The captain of the ship went to buy a replacement hat – and found his very own staring back at him in Benjamin Green's shop in Rosemary Lane. 'Why, this is one of the hats that I have lost!' said the captain.

'Is it?' said Green. 'Then I can help you to the man I had it from.'

Both thieves were quickly arrested. Black-head was acquitted, and Paps-Nose was transported.

16 JULY   **1757**   Fulham man James Wales (16) was indicted on this day after being caught in a compromising situation in a stable. Mr Peter Garry had ridden to the Peterborough Arms at Parsons Green to meet some friends, and put his horse in the stable. He ordered that she be made comfortable. When his friends did not show, he wandered over to the stable, pipe in hand, seeking some company, and found the stable door shut. Surprised, he strolled past the window – and was horrified to see Wales in the act of making violent love to his horse. He ran for help, hailing a surprised fellow customer called Mr Campbell with the line, 'You'll see something that will surprise you: there is a little fellow buggering my mare in the stable!' Garry brought his whip down with a crack on the startled groom, and whipped him all around the stables as the man struggled to pull up his breeches. Wales claimed he was merely 'putting a blanket' over the animal, and Garry thought about letting the matter drop. However, Wales foolishly waved his fist at the customer and threatened to take him to the courts for his assault. Outraged, Garry had the man arrested. Wales then claimed he had merely been relieving himself between the two horses, but he was sentenced to death. The mare had since died.

1742 A horrible case occurred in the early hours of today, after a general round-up of Covent Garden prostitutes began: William Bird, keeper of St Martin's Roundhouse (near where the National Gallery now stands), suffocated Mary Maurice and three other women by thrusting them into 'the hole' with twenty-three other unfortunate Londoners. The heat was intense, and the one window was shut and padlocked. As the supplies of air dwindled, everyone in the hole began to shriek out 'Murder!' Some of the prisoners started to have fits; a pregnant woman went into labour pangs, and then died. She had simply been walking home from her job as a servant. Another had not been in London above an hour, and was walking to see her sister. Many were homeless beggars. One prisoner pushed her pipe into a hole in the shutter over the window, and the prisoners took turns to suck in air – until someone grew so impatient that they pushed forward, and snapped the pipe. 'Die and be damned,' was the response. At about 5 a.m., Mary grew light-headed and said, 'Let me die, for God's sake.' She was as good as her word. The keeper was tried – and acquitted! Since his job was putting people in the roundhouse, which task he had done, a charge of murder could not be upheld. *17 JULY*

1722 John Molony and James Carrick met their date with destiny at Tyburn this day after taking a watch, crystal snuff box, silver-hilted sword and £42 from William Young in Covent Garden, saying they would shoot him in the face if he moved. His hands shaking, the robber said, 'Sir, I am in haste,' and demanded Young's cash. As the coins spilled to the floor, the robber saw that they were only silver. 'Damn you, Sir, do you trifle?' he shouted. They then told the coachmen carrying Young to run on with their customer. This they did for a short while – but then they turned around and ran after the robbers. Others took up the chase, dogs were loosed, and around Lincoln's Fields they brought Molony to the ground, making him scream out 'like a hare'. Carrick was captured trying to spend his illegal gains, and his pockets were filled with Young's property. Both robbers went to the gallows. *18 JULY*

1791 Mr Graham, of the Temple, and Mr Julius, a pupil in the office of Messrs Graham, attorneys, of Lincoln's Inn, fought a duel today at Blackheath. One of them, after too much to drink, had offended the other's religious principles. Mr Graham fell by a shot which passed almost through the lower part of the belly, ripping open his femoral artery as it went. He died the next day. *19 JULY*

Also on this day, but in 1727, Samuel Hammond of Bishopsgate stabbed his master to death after he called him a 'blockhead' for using the wrong tools. Hammond died of a fever in the condemned hold before he could reach the gallows.

20 JULY   **1770**   The Chichester mail was stolen from the post boy between Newington and Clapham on this day; the straps which tied it to the cart had been cut while the boy was asleep. It was found in a ditch with most of the letters opened and some of the bags missing.

On this day in 1739, the throat of Poplar shorewoman Mary Goynes was 'maliciously' and 'feloniously' squeezed by her husband, Gardner Edward (47), until she breathed her last. Neighbour Mary Cadmore had been walking past their shop and heard a noise. She found Mrs Goynes sitting in the corner rubbing her arm and muttering, 'O that wicked villain! That wicked villain has wrung my arm to pieces!' Her husband was present, and retorted, 'Did I do it, you old toad? I only flung a pint of beer at you.' Two hours later, an even louder shout was heard – and Mrs Goynes' face was seen to be 'all over gore blood'. She whispered, 'Now he has done my business!' and fell into a fit. Goynes' step-daughter told the Old Bailey that the wicked husband would 'heave stones, brick-bats, pans, pipkins, and iron bars at her, and bruise her in a gross manner'. On the day of the murder, he had 'buffeted her in the face with his hat, till her eyes ran down with blood'. The prisoner promised to 'be as good as I can to [his step-daughter] now', but was sentenced to death. 'He wept often in his cell when alone by himself,' said the ordinary of Newgate, 'and hoped to obtain the mercy of God through Christ.'

21 JULY   **1747**   At 3 p.m., a woman ran out of Anne Williams' house carrying a bloody shoemaker's knife. Someone had just stabbed Anne's husband, Fleet Market fruit-seller Thomas, in the back. Anne was found sitting next to him, muttering, 'I did it, I did it, I did it.' Her husband's eyes 'twirled' and he breathed slower and slower – and then he whispered that he had fallen on the knife and killed himself. Anne told the court that her husband had come in, attacked her (as usual) about her 'eyes and nose' and had then bitten her on the finger 'very much'. In the struggle to get free, Thomas had been pushed onto the knife blade. He had cried directly, 'Lord, Lord!' and then ran into the back room, where he pitched over the bed and fell. 'Mr Williams, don't frighten your wife,' said the neighbours who came in, but he was not jesting: he was dying. The court took Anne's ill-use into account and charged her with manslaughter only – had she been found guilty of murder, she would have been burnt.

22 JULY   **1722**   When Thomas Bullock (23) found that his income was insufficient to support his taste in clothes, he accepted a position with Mr Claude Langley, a Frenchman who lived in the same lodging house. When the family were out, he broke open the drawers and took 27 guineas and some French coins. He was executed for the crime on this day.

Also on this day, in 1728, 'a silly, ignorant, and timorous creature', Eleanor Redden of Stepney (38), let her lover into her mistress's house so he could steal five silver cups and a punch ladle. She was sentenced to death.

23 JULY   **1779**   At about 3 p.m., the children of Mary Robinson came out of the 'vault' and said they could hear something in there – it sounded like crying.

All of the lodgers crowded into the wooden shed with a candle and started poking about; one, Miss Watkins, said that a kitten must have rolled in. When they pulled up the boards, however, they saw a child's foot sticking out – and pulled out a baby. Upon this, Mary fainted. When she came to, the child was being cleaned on the carpet, wrapped in a colourful apron, whilst its stomach was rubbed with a soft flannel. It was fed and opened its eyes, and looked very hearty – but it started fitting half an hour later, and passed away. The child turned out to be Miss Watkins'; she told her fellow lodgers that it had slipped out all of a sudden and fallen into the hole whilst she was using the vault. She was acquitted of any crime.

1721   At the boarding house in Marylebone Fields on this day, a panther was set to fight twelve dogs for a prize of £300, one dog at a time. Tickets cost 2s 6d or 2s. Other attractions on the day included a baited bear, a baited ass, and a mad bull with fireworks attached all over its body and bulldogs set to chasing him.   **24 JULY**

Also on this day, in 1789, the turnkey of the Fleet Prison assaulted a prisoner, Charles Hart, and threw him into a 'cold, damp, and unwholesome' cellar under the ground for sixteen days. He died. However, another prisoner described the room as 'as big as fourteen rooms above', with a fireplace and a four-poster bed. The jury cleared him of all charges.

1737   A false rumour of the Queen's death caused a run on black cloth throughout the city, with some sellers even sending out to Norwich. The price of cloth rose by 20 per cent before the King ended the rumour by sending a runner to Hampton Court. He returned with the news that all was well.   **25 JULY**

In 1727, Mary Davis of St Margaret's, Westminister, attacked Elisha Lynes (80) with a broomstick behind the New Church, Westminster after the latter cheated her out of some cinders they planned to sell. Elisha died afterwards, but the jury decided, to Mary's relief, that old age was the cause.

1813   On this day, William Broughton noticed a shoe poking out of a pond at Mr Adam's brick-field in Gray's Inn Lane. A battered hat was lying abandoned nearby, with a bit of human hair on it. Three holes nearby marked the turf – they looked like hammer blows. A few drops of brain were scattered on the leaves nearby. The shoe was attached to the body of a man in a brown coat, a yellow waistcoat and corduroy breeches. The body was taken to the Prince Regent public house – along with his brains (later identified by the surgeon as merely 'coagulated blood'), which were scooped up by the labourer. The dead man was identified as Edward Clifford. Clifford's partner told the court that she had met brick-maker James Leary (30) and his wife in the street as she and Edward had climbed off the wagon that first took them to London. The couples had fallen to talking, and the Learys offered them a room. They had stayed there for a few days, during which time the wife foolishly mentioned that they had quite a sum of money with them with which to start their new life in the city. After that, though the Cliffords moved into a new lodging house, it proved quite hard to shake the   **26 JULY**

Irish couple. The pair then took Mr Clifford out for drink, and he was next seen being dragged from the pond. The money had not even been with the husband: it was sewn into the wife's petticoat. She was forced to spend some of it buying the men who had carried home her husband's corpse a drink. Leary was hanged at Newgate.

27 JULY   1790   After an argument on Waltham Bridge, unemployed Robert Natcot cracked the skull of Jewish Londoner Moses Davis with an iron key taken from the tollgate. Natcot was an old inmate of Bedlam, a mad old soldier who had escaped from several different incarcerations. He started to rave on the bridge, telling the stranger he had just hit in the face with the key that, 'if he got at him, he would run him through with a bayonet'. The poor old man was escorted home, crying out that he had lost his eyesight, and asking what would become of his wife and family. He was put to bed, which quickly filled up with blood. Then he perished. The prisoner's defence gave him little hope of acquittal: 'I have nothing at all to say.' He was found not guilty of murder and sent straight off to the madhouse.

28 JULY   1761   On this evening, in the appropriately named Ball Alley, Lombard Street, butcher Giles Cooper was walking home from Leadenhall Market through a dark passageway and saw two men whispering in the darkness. He told the court that he had frequently 'run up against men there', and collared one of the two men. He dragged him into the light by the fencing school nearby and swore at him, saying, 'What the Devil do you stand lurking about here for?' He then went into his house – but heard, as he was waiting for the door to open, the sound of renewed whispering. As soon as he got inside, he fetched a servant and a lit candle (which he hid beneath his cupped hands), and sneaked back out into the night – where he found William Bailey and footman Robert Stimpson 'in a very indecent posture' in the alleyway. Both of their breeches were down, and their pose left little to the imagination. 'They made no resistance in the world,' he told the Old Bailey, 'but begg'd and pray'd I would let them go, for it would be the ruin of them.' The two men tried to claim that they were on their way to the post office – which was hard to believe, given that it was the middle of the night. Bailey was sent to the pillory, and sentenced to six months in Newgate; Stimpson managed to run away.

29 JULY   1785   A much darker case occurred on this day, when Richard Read awoke to find his temporary roommate, Roger Sweetman, with his arms 'clenched round' him:

> ...he had turned me on my face, and he had got his instrument between my thighs, and I twisted myself and made him break his hold, I got my breast on the bedstead, and I took hold of him with my left hand, and gave him two or three good pelts over the head, I laid hold of him by his breast, the fleshy part; then I asked what he thought of himself, and what he deserved, he said, do not tell, do not tell, my dear, do not tell, several times over.

Richard did not tell – until Roger was taken up for another similar offence. Poor Roger suffered two public whippings and three years in Newgate.

1733 Mary Wood of Nicholas Alley, Chick Lane, opened her door at midnight – and in ran her neighbour, Christian Lamb. 'Save me, Woody, or I shall be kill'd tonight!' she called. Her husband Richard (42) was hard at her heels and knocked her down. The inhabitants of the house tried to push him out, but then – realising that he would be harassing them all night – they pushed the wife out instead, and slammed the door on the quarrelling pair. Christian was found dead the next day, beaten to death in her own kitchen with a 'nasty, ragged, rough' stick and the heel of a shoe. Her husband had knelt upon her – leaving a perfect impression of the house key, which was tucked in her bosom, carved into her chest. As she was breathing her last, the husband came in to talk to her surgeon: 'Damn her, is not the old bitch dead yet?' he said. He had previously hanged her himself – the neighbours had had to come and cut her down to save her life. Richard went to the gallows in October.   30 JULY

1816 This afternoon, the remains of Miss Burrowes of Red Lion Street, Clerkenwell were taken to St James's Church, Clerkenwell Green, for interment. Tragically, the sides of the 20ft grave gave way and buried the gravedigger and his assistant under its weight. Several men immediately set about shovelling away the earth, which kept falling in. In about an hour, the body of one of the men was recovered, apparently dead. He was eventually restored to life. The body of the other workman was not discovered until nearly 10 p.m.   31 JULY

AUGUST

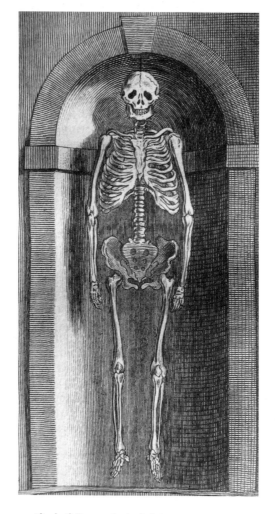

Elizabeth Brownrigg's skeleton on permanent
display in Surgeons' Hall, in its own little niche.

George I.

1714 Today George I became King, when Queen Anne died after suffering from gout.

1 AUGUST

Five years later, the mistress of Mary Gough, of St Margaret's, Westminster, came up the stairs and found Mary's bed covered in blood. A dead baby was wrapped in the bed sheets. Mary had been suffering from what she claimed was 'the chollick' for several days. The poor servant had recently suffered a bad fall, slipping from a chair, and had lost the baby; she proved in court that her room contained a chest full of linen ready for the baby's arrival, and she was acquitted.

1738 In 1738, the whole city was alarmed by the sight of two eagles – or possibly cormorants – perching on the top of St Paul's, one on the pineapple and one on the cross. They remained there until a man went up to the

2 AUGUST

gallery and fired a gun at them, at which they flew away. When London's pressgangs realised what a great draw this had been, one of them placed an unfortunate live turkey on the roof, and helped themselves to many of the sturdy men who turned up to see it.

3 AUGUST   **1811**   Ships at Shadwell Dock were vulnerable to London's thieves, as John Bull of the *Mars* discovered when he noticed his shoes, jacket and waistcoats were missing. Luckily, he noticed William Bramley (30) on the gangway – and found the items hidden up his shirt. Bramley was sent to the house of correction for one year.

4 AUGUST   **1781**   Bartholomew Fair this year exhibited Mr Thomas Allen, 'the most surprising small man that ever appeared before the Public'. On this day, at Queen's Lodge, Windsor, Miss 'Lady' Morgan, 'the Windsor Fairy' (35), met the King and Queen. She weighed only 18lb, and admittance to see her cost 1*s* (children, half price).

On this day in 1722, Katherine Ward (or Priest) of St Martin's, Ludgate, hailed a cab on Ludgate Hill. When one pulled up, she threw her arms around the driver's neck and hugged him close; she then 'grew familiar with his breeches'. This he wouldn't have minded, but when he realised that she had run off with his money, he called for the watchman. Katherine was stopped, but no money could be found on her – until the watch looked in her mouth, where 3*s* 6*d* was found hidden. She was transported.

5 AUGUST   **1726**   The magnificently named Sarah Hatchet was sitting on a bench in St Martin's Lane on this day, swaying and much the worse for wear, when a stranger called Thomas Jones sat down next to her.

'Give me a little water, and I'll tell you a secret,' she slurred.

'What secret?' he replied.

'Why,' said she, 'Don't ye know a man was murdered two nights ago? Well, I held his head, whilst his throat was cut.' Luckily, several witnesses appeared in the court to say that 'she would say anything when she got drunk', and that 'a halfpennyworth of Geneva would make her speak all the Extravagancies of a Person in Bedlam.' She had been seen lying unconscious next to her basket of guinea pigs on the night of the crime, and was acquitted.

6 AUGUST   **1815**   On this day, the Duke of York slipped on his way out of the bath at Oaklands and broke 'the large bone of his left arm, half way between the shoulder and the elbow-joint'.

7 AUGUST   **1746**   In 1746, Jacobite Captain James Dawson was hanged, drawn, and quartered on Kennington Common. On the very day of Dawson's execution, he was to have been married to his sweetheart. The *Whitehall Evening Post* of 7 August 1746 contains the following account of the execution and the fate of the unfortunate lady:

[she] followed the sledge in a hackney coach ... Having arrived at the place of execution, she got near enough to see the fire kindled that was to consume him, and all the other dreadful preparations, without betraying any of those emotions her friends apprehended. But when all was over, and she found he was no more, she threw her head back in the coach, and ejaculating, 'My dear, I follow thee! Lord Jesus, receive our souls together,' fell on the neck of her companion, and expired the very moment she had done speaking. Most excessive grief, which the force of her resolution had kept smothered within her breast, is thought to have put a stop to the vital motion, and suffocated at once all the animal spirits.

Also today, but in 1794, London witnessed one of the worst storms ever. Lightning hit the pavement by Temple Bar, and produced 'an effect similar to an explosion of gunpowder'. Houses on both sides were shaken, and doors were thrown open by the blast. The central beam of Lloyd's Coffee House was cracked, bringing the whole ceiling down – and allowing inches of rain in. Ball lightning fell in the streets, and one Londoner was actually killed by it.

8 AUGUST

1776 Wagon thief and highway robber 'Jumping' Joe Lorrison – the name came from his skill at jumping into moving wagons and throwing out the goods to his accomplices before leaping off again – stole a watch from musician John Edwards. Edwards worked at No. 66 in the Old Bailey, and was walking from Islington on a winter evening, by starlight, when Jumping Joe and three other men leapt out and stopped the group he was with. They levelled large horse pistols, waved cutlasses, and robbed the men, pushing pistols into their mouths and generally terrifying the group. When Edwards gave them a 'stern' look – trying to memorise their faces – one of the men started to bluster. 'Who are you looking at?' he shouted. 'I'll cut you down if you look at me.' Suddenly, one of the women in Edwards' party managed to break free and run for help. The robbers made it less than 50 yards before they were stopped. Lorrison had thrown his gun down, and begged to be allowed to escape, but it was no good; however, the evidence against Lorrison was very weak, and he was released.

9 AUGUST

1767 One of the most famous victims in London's criminal history perished on this day, when Mary Clifford (14) finally gave herself up to death after more than a year's worth of abuse. She had been whipped, caned and struck with a stick; her neck had been held with ropes and iron chains. A space under the stairs had become Mary's dungeon, at the Flower-de-Luce Street, Fetter Lane house of James Brownrigg, midwife Elizabeth and their son John.

As soon as Mary was bound as an apprentice, the ill-usage began. First, she was beaten on the head and shoulders with a walking stick and a brush. Then, when Mary began wetting the bed, she was moved into the cupboard-sized coalhole-cum-cellar under the stairs. Her food supply was restricted – but when she was caught foraging for food, a new cruelty emerged. She was forced to wash her naked body in front of Elizabeth, whilst being beaten

Elizabeth Brownrigg at work: whipping her naked servant girl, waiting in her cell at Newgate, and, finally, a depiction of the dungeon where her two teenage employees were imprisoned.

with a riding whip or a leather belt – 'all the day'. After that she was often thrown naked into the cellar, with nothing but a pile of straw to sleep on – though there was a bed in every room. She was locked in (with the other female apprentice, Mary Mitchell) for hours – and days – at a time. Both girls were invariably naked, and invariably covered with welts and cuts from their ill-treatment. A 'teaspoon full' of blood also splashed about the floor each time. Elizabeth Brownrigg then discovered a new variation: tying the girl – naked again – to the water pipe for ease of access. The pipe went over the girl's head, so her arms were in the air. A hook was attached to the pipe and Mary was tied to it to be beaten once a week. Then a heavy 'jack chain' was dragged in, and bolted to the yard door. The other end was wrapped tight around the teenager's neck. She was chained to the door all day, and tied up in the cellar all night – with her hands behind her, and the heavy chain around her neck. Her neck started to swell as the heavy iron chafed at it. The male apprentice, Benham, had once been told to lock her in. He refused to look at her as he did so, for, 'I thought she might have some cuts by being beat, and my heart ached.'

Then Mr Brownrigg bought a hog to live in the yard. Eventually, the smell grew so offensive that they were forced to open the skylight. A boy who lived next door peered through, and spotted 'something lying upon the ground bloody'. He threw a small piece of mortar down, and as it moved he realised it was a person:

She looked up in my face, I saw her eyes black, and her face very much swelled; she made a noise something like a long Oh; and then drew herself backwards; I heard Mrs Brownrigg speak to her in a very sharp manner, and asked what was the matter with her.

He went for help – and Elizabeth Brownrigg ran. Mr Brownrigg was forced to fetch the girl, who shuffled out into the light…

> …in a sad condition indeed. Her face was swelled as big as two, her mouth was so swelled she could not shut it, and she was cut all under her throat, as if it had been with a cane. She could not speak … Her shoulders were all cut to pieces.

Her head was wounded, and her legs were cut 'cross and cross' with many thin blows. All three Brownriggs were caught and carried off to prison; Mary went to the workhouse, where the apothecary found her 'from the bottom of her feet to the top of her head almost one continued sore … I never saw such an object in my life'. James and John were acquitted; Elizabeth was hanged and dissected on 14 September 1767. 'Do you think that God can forgive such a wicked creature as I am?' she asked before she died. As she passed through the streets on the way to her death, thousands of Londoners shrieked at her, shouting that they 'hoped she would go to hell, and … the Devil would fetch her soul'. She acknowledged the justice of her sentence before she died, and her last words were, 'Lord Jesus, receive my spirit!'

1759   Today, 'an astonishing sea-monster' caught 'on a float of ice in the north of Siberia' (a sea-lion) was brought to England, and could be seen near the foot of Westminster Bridge, along with a large eagle captured at the siege of Quebec, a 'half and half' made up of half wolf and half bear (the 'Egyptian night wolf'), great apes from all around the world, and a 'curious and suprizing collection of uncommon beasts and birds' to boot.   **10 AUGUST**

1813   Two young boys were working in a field near Finchley Common on this day, and paused to examine some slugs. One then stood up – and pitched forward dead, with blood spouting from his ribs. He had been shot right through the chest by a soldier standing on the road. The soldier, Thomas Moon (20), declined to give any reason for opening fire, and was found guilty of manslaughter.   **11 AUGUST**

Two years earlier, in 1811, a watchman in Golden Square discovered a man – one Joseph Harvey – suspended by the leg from the top of an iron-railing; he immediately gave the alarm, and the unfortunate sufferer was conveyed to the Middlesex Hospital in a state of insensibility. When the man recovered, he explained that his wife had run off with another man whilst he was away in India, which had made him so depressed that he had started to suffer from nightmares. He imagined that his rival stood at his bedside, with a pistol in his hand. In a paroxysm of terror, he had started up from his bed, thrown up the sash, and jumped out of the window. The railing had caught his leg, and his face hit the pavement. He went quite mad as a result.

1719   On this day, James Tucker, of St Giles', Cripplegate, turned around to adjust his cart-load of bricks by the 'Sun Dyal' in Goswell Street, and his lead horse galloped over Samuel Mabus (4), killing him instantly. The wheel   **12 AUGUST**

of the cart ran over his head, cracking it like a melon. A passer-by gave a great cry of alarm and ran to catch the little boy, but he could not get to the cart fast enough. Tucker jumped down from his cart and cradled the child's body; then, seeing that the boy was dead, he ran. However, he was eventually captured, tried, found guilty of manslaughter and burnt upon the hand.

13 AUGUST **1726** Mark Shovat of Covent Garden sent for apothecary Mr Disney on this day, claiming he was suffering from a cold and feeling sick. Disney advised taking some rhubarb, and said that the patient might drink another concoction he had been sent by a local apothecary. Unfortunately, it turned out that the drink had been sent not by the doctor but by a kindly neighbour, and that what she had taken for 'an innocent cool thing' was in fact a decoction of 'white Arsnick': Mark started to retch blood, suffered 'violent purging, the Gripes, Cramps, and Fainting Fits', and died on the 20th. His guts were found to be 'lined with blood' and 'bylous Juices'. Luckily for the neighbour, the death was laid to natural causes, after several people testified that they had tried the potion without ill effect; the neighbour was acquitted.

14 AUGUST **1718** Francis Bolanson of St Andrew's, Holborn, was indicted for murdering her baby by throwing it into a privy. The baby's body was discovered, but it was so decomposed that it was impossible to tell whether the child had been living or dead when entombed, or whether it had been carried to full term. The prisoner told the court that she had been extremely frightened by an extraordinary outbreak of thunder and lightning a few weeks before, and that she had shortly afterwards caught a fever and the measles – after which she had lost the baby, six weeks short of her due date. She could prove that she had made provisions for the child, and that she had been very ill at the time; she was acquitted.

15 AUGUST **1759** Today, Napoleon Bonaparte's birthday, William Tipton, landlord of the Fox & Birdcage in Goswell Street and ex-servant to a Chelsea madhouse, allegedly threw 'weakly' bandy-legged William Walker out of the window because he cheated at a pub game. William's skull cracked, and he talked incoherently at St Bart's until he died. The landlord was given a very peaceable character in court, and as he insisted that the man had climbed out of the window himself – you could walk along a thin board to the next house – he was acquitted.

Another Londoner leapt from a roof today in Johnson's court, Charing Cross. In 1794, George Howe appeared on the roof of a London bagnio 'in his shirt, in apparent great agony, as if he was closely pursued from within'. He threw himself from the roof, and smashed to pieces on the tiles. A massive mob gathered, and the premises were searched – a man was found, 'smothering in the height of small-pox, in a loathsome cellar'. The next day the mob was back, and pulled the house to the ground, along with several others. An inquest declared that Howe had suffered 'accident death in endeavouring to escape from illegal confinement in a house of ill-fame'.

In 1800, it was prisoners of the state who were disturbing the peace: as the bell rang for lockup at the Coldbath Fields Prison, the prisoners began to complain. They were pushed into their cells, but all of them began to shout things such as 'Murder!' and 'Starving!' A huge mob gathered outside the prison at this, and began pulling down the walls. Order was only restored with great difficulty.

1756   On this day, John Girle (26) shuffled into a Holborn pet shop and attempted to sell some birds he had captured. The disabled owner, Thomas Roberts, shouted out a refusal from the cellar – and got a mouthful for his trouble: 'Damn you, you hump-back son of a bitch, if you was up stairs I'd punch both your eyes out!' Girle then left the shop – but appeared creepily at the window with a stick, which he poked into the shop. He smashed a birdcage. Thomas' wife Sarah, two babies in her arms, tried to push him away as her husband ran up the stairs, but the disgruntled would-be bird-dealer thrust his stick over her shoulder – and speared out Thomas' left eye. 'Stop the rogue, my eye is out!' cried the husband. The wife turned, 'and saw the blood and jelly of his eye running down his cheek'. As they were extremely poor, Sarah was forced to treat the eye herself with egg whites and rose water. Girle was sent to Newgate for a year for the assault. Thomas remained in pain for months afterwards, and was subject to violent fits. He died six months later. The jury found the deceased's defence for the new charge of murder so unconvincing that they actually charged his witness with perjury. Girle was sent to the gallows at Tyburn. | 16 AUGUST

1791   Just as the King reached the rails in the Green Park on this day, James Sutherland Esq. drew forth a paper, stuck it on the rails, threw off his hat and discharged a pistol into his bosom. He instantly fell dead. A green silk purse containing 2*d*, a snuff box and a white pocket handkerchief were all that was found in his pockets. The paper was a suicide note, but the coroner brought in a verdict of lunacy on his death. | 17 AUGUST

1745   As news of the Rebellion in the North began to spread, treasonable papers, called 'Pretender's declarations', were pushed under people's doors, or dropped on the parade in St James's Park. A camp of defenders was formed to defend London on Finchley Common, with the King himself in command. Then, on 16 April 1746, the Battle of Culloden finally crushed the '45 uprising. Two of the rebel Peers captured at the battle came to their deaths today: Earl Kilmarnock and Earl Balmerino. Balmerino kept his spirits up in the Tower, on 18 August, by showing Kilmarnock how to lay his head on the block, advising him to bite his lips as the axe fell. He volunteered to have the axe in his coach, though he warned the executioner, 'Take care, or you'll break my shins on this damned axe.' Balmerino was so popular that the guards at the Tower were forced to cover up his windows to stop him talking to the crowds. When his death warrant came down at dinner, his wife fainted: 'Lieutenant,' he said, 'with your damned warrant you have spoiled my lady's stomach.' The two earls walked to the black-draped block, | 18 AUGUST one in black, one in his shroud with rebel colours over the top. Sir Walter Scott has it so:

> When he [Kilmarnock] beheld the fatal scaffold covered with black cloth, the executioner with his axe and his assistants, the sawdust, which was soon to be drenched with his blood, the coffin prepared to receive the limbs which were yet warm with life – above all, the immense display of human countenances which surrounded the scaffold like a sea … his natural feelings broke forth in a whisper to the friend on whose arm he leaned, 'Home, this is terrible!' He then tried the block a few times, and at last gave the signal – dropping his handkerchief – and his 'head was cut off at once, only hanging by a bit of skin'. It went into his coffin. New sawdust was then strewn onto the platform, and a new axe brought. Balmerino told the crowd that if he had 1,000 lives, he would lay them down for the same cause. He had shouted 'God save King James!' as he came through the gates to Tower Hill. Balmerino died in three blows, 'tossing up his arm [for the blow] as if he were giving the signal for battle'. As they walked there, seeing the sea of London faces looking from every window, Balmerino said 'Look, look, how they are all piled up like rotten oranges.'

19 AUGUST   1774   Patrick Madan, a convicted footpad, was standing at Tyburn on this day, with a noose around his neck and the swaying cart beneath his feet, when suddenly a man called out from the crowd that Madan was innocent. A brief respite was ordered. For almost an hour, the men at the gallows stood with the ropes around their necks. Then Madan was taken back to prison, and the other men were hanged. Mr Merritt told Justice Aldington at Bow Street that he had in fact committed the robbery himself. Madan was pardoned; Merritt was tried – and acquitted! However, one Amos Merritt was later hanged for theft.

20 AUGUST   1745   Today, pipe-maker Thomas Morgan (40), of Covent Garden, knifed his wife Elizabeth to death after bailing himself out of the Gatehouse Prison, where he had languished since his wife had had him committed for assaulting her (attacking her until 'her breasts they were as black as any woman's breasts could be'). The day after his release, all was quiet – no one appeared to open the pipe shop. Eventually, an employee bored a hole in the wall of the Morgans' bedroom, and saw a puddle of blood on the floor. He pushed open the door, and saw 'two naked legs lying on the floor'. It was Elizabeth, and she had been stabbed twenty times, 'three on the side of her belly, six along her throat, and … a great many behind her ear'. Someone had tried to slit her throat, cutting her hands as she fought for life. Her shift was as red 'as if it had been dipped in blood'. Two of the stabs had hit the heart and lungs. A stream, 'as if a person had been killing an ox', ran from the body to the bed. Thomas was hanged at Tyburn on 4 April 1746.

21 AUGUST   1762   On this day, Peter Dove was taken to the London Hospital after shoe-seller Esther Levingston ran riot on the night of the 20th: first, Mrs Ashby

was whipped, stabbed in the face and left lying 'for dead' with her petticoats pulled over her head; next, Esther declared that 'she would set all the bitches on fire, and make a rare bonfire'; and finally, when the law came to tell her to be quiet, watchman Peter Dove was stabbed in the gut. His bowels were seen to be poking out of the wound, 'about as big as a little apple'. He died on the 23rd, and Esther was hanged at Tyburn the next year. Her two children, aged 13 and 9, wept in the press yard on her last day of life; she spent the night in prayer, the early morning in tears and in pacing the press yard waiting for the death cart and, a little after 10 a.m., as the executioner tied her up, the mid-morning asking for more prayers. She left the cart – and this world – at 10.30 a.m.

1717   On this day, the *Flying Post* reported that...   22 AUGUST

> ...several lewd and disorderly persons, and players of interludes, had erected booths and sheds at Tottenham-Court ... wherein were used a great deal of profane cursing and swearing, together with many lewd and blasphemous expressions, also several rude, riotous, and disorderly actions committed.

The booths were pulled down.

1800   John Bickerstaff helped himself to 4lb of tea from the East India Co.'s   23 AUGUST
offices in Haydon Square on this day, tucking the tea down his breeches and into the crown of his hat as he walked amongst the auction. He was quickly arrested – and whipped 100 yards across the square as his punishment.

East India House.

24 AUGUST   1736   Today, a remarkably fat boar was captured coming out of Fleet Ditch into the Thames. It proved to belong to a butcher's, near Smithfield Bars. He had missed the hog for five months – all the time, it seems, the pig had been in the common sewer. It improved in price from 10s to 2 guineas.

25 AUGUST   1719   As Mr Whitworth was making candles in the cellar of his master's shop in Arlington Street, Piccadilly, he heard a noise outside. He discovered Robert Eden arguing with another man, beadle James Barber of St Martin in the Fields. As he watched, Barber struck the other man on the head with his staff, hitting him repeatedly as Eden tried to raise his sword. Eventually Eden, stunned, dropped to his knees. A great crack then rent the night.

'Would you stab me?' cried out Barber. 'Get up, you dog, or I'll knock your brains out!'

Eden lay in the watchhouse he was dragged to all night, speechless and edging towards death. He died soon after the doctors reached him. The inside of his skull was found to be fractured, and filled with a large quantity of congealed blood. Barber claimed that Eden had attempted to stab him in the street; however, he could produce no witnesses to this effect, and he was therefore sentenced to death.

26 AUGUST   1718   William Townsend, a publican in the Artillery Ground, Spitalfields, attacked his wife Catherine, bruising her on her head, back, stomach – and even on her toes. She died on this day. Drinkers in the house saw him push his wife up the stairs, where he threw her onto the floor, struck her, kicked her several times on the side – and then kicked her straight in the face. One of the men, alarmed, said he feared the man would kick her brains out. Crying, 'Will you kill me?' the poor woman was then dragged bodily from the room. Catherine was pregnant at the time she was attacked, and she miscarried two days later. The print of a bruise could be seen on the dead baby's forehead. She followed her child to the grave the following day. Catherine had allegedly hurled two pint pots at her husband the night she was attacked; a heavy drinker, she had fallen in and out of bars throughout the neighbourhood in recent weeks. The court weighed this against the prisoner's character, which was given as a very quiet one, and decided to acquit him.

27 AUGUST   1752   A horrible attack came to an end when 'little woman' Elizabeth Saunders of Three Crowns Court, Whitechapel, died. She had tried to stop her partner, weaver Abraham Ward (48), beating her son – ripping the tail of his coat in the process. This was a terrible mistake, and in response she was kicked up and down the court. Then she was told to get out.

'You rogue,' she cried, 'I have nowhere to go. You have sold my things – where must I go? And besides, I am not able to move: you have beat me till I am not able to stir.'

A few days later, he was seen beating her with a lump of wood as she tried to hide a bag – full of her last few possessions. He took the clothing and pushed her down the stairs. She was left covered in blood, with a ragged wound on her head. Taken to a surgeon in Petticoat Lane, she found she could not pay for help.

'You must go home and pull off that gown and pawn it,' suggested the neighbour who had taken her.

She looked on it sadly, and said, 'It is all bloody: who will take it in?'

The gown was in fact the reason she had been beaten – her husband wanted her to pawn it. She shuffled home, feeling very sick. Her brain mortified, and she died at the London Hospital. The husband was captured by a plucky neighbour, who grabbed him by the arms in the street and shrilled out, 'A murderer! A murderer!' He was executed on 11 December.

1730   Gilder Gilbert Laurence of St Brides was indicted on this day for committing 'the detestable crime of sodomy' upon his apprentice, Paul Oliver (14). On the night of the crime, when the two men had gone to bed, the older man had suddenly leapt upon the boy, pinned him to the bed (nearly stifling him) and assaulted him. 'He hurt [me] so much,' Oliver said in court, '[I] thought he would have killed [me].' Laurence had made several advances on the previous nights, but 'none like this'. The boy had told his mother that Laurence had used him 'barbarously', and she sent for a surgeon. He discovered the boy's fundament 'much lacerated', and the wicked employer was sentenced to death.

28 AUGUST

1783   Fugitive master forger William Wynne Ryland, of St James's, was caught on this day after his wife accidentally took one of his shoes to a cobbler – with his real name written inside. When the law burst in, they heard 'something like a spewing, or noise in the throat', and found Ryland stretched out, a basin under his throat and blood pooling onto the floor. He had slashed his throat with a razor. He was bound up, rescued and sentenced to death.

29 AUGUST

Ryland cutting his throat after a mix-up with a shoe destroyed his false identity.

30 AUGUST   **1731**   A gruesome accident occurred on this day in Whitechapel, as wounded 'lame old man' and ex-prize-fighter William Metcalf crossed the street in the evening. A rattling dray filled with barrels swept past, and then a great crack went up – William's stick had caught in the wheel and snapped, pitching him under the cart. His left thigh was shattered and he died in September. The driver was found guilty of 'chance medley' (partly to blame, but not at fault) and set free.

31 AUGUST   **1730**   An advertisement for a display at Bartholomew Fair in Hosier Lane, Smithfield, was printed in the *Daily Post* for the last day of August, advertising 'two rattle snakes, one a very large size, and rattles that you may hear at a quarter of a mile distant...'. A burrowing snake, 'the teeth of a dead rattlesnake to be seen and handled', 'a sea snail taken on the coast of India', and 'a curious collection of animals and insects from all parts of the world', also went on display.

SEPTEMBER

Fire! This rather Quentin Blake-esque image from *Real Life in London* shows the London fire crews at work (left) in the chaos of an inferno. Blazes broke out on 8, 15 and 20 September.

1 SEPTEMBER   **1767**   James Woodman ran over Elizabeth Ayres (2) today in King Edward's Street while trying to avoid a pothole. A passer-by picked up the child, but 'its head fell down'. It was too late: the wheel had passed over her jaw, killing her instantly. Blood spouted out of her right ear. The driver, 'when he was about two houses beyond the child, turned round and wrung his hands, and seemed very sorry'.

'How shall I face that infant in another world?' he said. 'If my life would pay for it, I would freely give it.' He was burnt on the hand and released.

2 SEPTEMBER   **1826**   Bartholomew Fair commenced on this day. Shows included trick riders, 'four lively little crocodiles about twelve inches long, hatched from the eggs at Peckham, by steam', two larger crocodiles, four cages of fierce rattlesnakes and 'a dwarf lady'. A glass blower (in a cleverly constructed glass wig) also made teacups and glass tobacco pipes for 3d, whilst his companion, a female sword swallower, performed tricks such as licking a red-hot poker.

Fire caused more of a problem in 1803, when someone forgot to put out the lights at Astley's Amphitheatre near Westminster Bridge, and the whole building was destroyed – along with forty houses nearby.

3 SEPTEMBER   **1719**   Mary Tame of Harrow on the Hill appeared at the Old Bailey today charged with hurling her 2-year-old sister into a pond, choking and drowning her. It transpired in court that Mary was an 'ideot' who had been left to look after the little girl; when her sister, Elizabeth, had gone to wash her face in the water, she had let her fall in, and, unaware of any dangers involved, left her until she drowned.

4 SEPTEMBER   **1825**   In the middle of the night, Eleanor Hunt's mother Mary Ann stumbled drunkenly into the dark room in George Yard, Whitechapel, which they shared with two others. She nearly climbed into the wrong bed in the gloom, annoying the sleeping occupant, John Rankin (26), intensely. He sat up in his bed and they began to trade insults. When Mary Ann called him a 'damned dirty thief', he could take no more, and leapt at her with the headboard of his bed. As her daughter shrieked for help from the window, John struck the old woman several times. When the room's shocked occupants lit a candle, they illuminated the old woman, spread-eagled on the bed, with a piece cut out of the bridge of her nose and bruises on her face. She was dead. John's defence was that he was sorry, but that 'he had to rise early ... and required rest'; her abusive and drunken behaviour had prevented this. He was sentenced to six weeks in prison.

Today in 1731, Sir John Gordon of Westminster ordered the arrest of several disabled vagrants, with 'stump hands, sore arms, legs and faces', who had been leaping out in front of pregnant women at the church doors and frightening them.

5 SEPTEMBER   **1762**   Mrs Hawley was thrown into Mr King's Chelsea madhouse by her relatives on this day – even though she was not mad. She was kept under lock and key until, by good fortune, a doctor acquaintance happened to see her at the window and got her released.

At just past midnight in 1810, watchman Edward Watkins heard a cry of murder at No. 5 Onslow Street. Ann Griffith was found, by the swinging light of a lantern, on a bloody bed in a 'filthy' room upstairs: her throat was slashed, but she was still alive. Outside, a dark figure was knocked flat by a passer-by, and taken to New Prison, Clerkenwell. It was Ann's own husband, Richard – jealous because his wife, he claimed, had let two young men take 'indecent liberties' with her, and had said another lover, called Jem, was going to give him a 'wapping'. The wounded woman was rushed to hospital, but died between her house and Holborn Bridge. The husband – who must have charmed the court – was found guilty of manslaughter only, and released.

1769   A horrible case came to court after the landlady of the Lamb **6 SEPTEMBER** Inn at Stanwell was found with a great ragged hole cut into her face. The landlady's daughter, Margaret, had left her mother, Sarah Phipps, and gone to eat breakfast. When she returned, she had found her mother lying on her left side, with her head upon her arm, seemingly asleep. Her skull had been beaten in with the head of an axe, which was found in the next room. Her common-law husband, William Taunton, was quickly arrested. He had attempted to kill her four days before with the poker, after she had asked him whether he would or would not like his cucumber peeled for supper. His defence – that his wife had told lies of him, claiming he was 'not a man sufficient for a woman' (which had made the women present laugh at him), and that he was not in his right mind after twice attempting to do away with himself – failed to influence the jury. He was hanged, dissected and anatomised on 11 September.

1720   A fatal fight broke out over a small haymaking rake on this day. **7 SEPTEMBER** John Mayling of Middlesex was at work bringing in the hay in the fields surrounding London. As he walked to dinner, he spotted the dainty-looking tool lying on the floor. He picked it up and offered it to his wife. Thomas Corral angrily called out, 'That's my wife's rake. You shan't have it!' He snatched the tool back, and bashed Mayling with it. The other man retaliated, kicking Corral's feet from under him and then kicking him again. Corral died as a result: a large bruise by the groin was given as the cause of death. But, since Corral had attacked first, and was known to be in sickly health anyway, the jury acquitted Mr Mayling of all charges.

In 1715, another haymaking crime took place, with one of the strangest names in criminal history. Trolly Lolly (30) of the parish of St Mary, 'Whitechappel', was tried for stealing a pair of sheets from Christopher Hurt. Christopher heard a noise, looked out the window, and saw Trolly departing with his sheets. He ran out and caught her. Her defence was that she was going haymaking, and saw the door was open. Her poverty had driven her to it. She was hanged on 21 September 1715.

8 SEPTEMBER 1725 One of the last fires to occur on London Bridge took place on this date. *Mist's Weekly Journal* reports:

> On Wednesday night, between eleven and twelve o'clock, a fire broke out at a Haberdasher's of Hats, on the Bridge foot in Southwark, which burned on both sides of the way with great violence for four or five hours. We hear that about sixty houses are consumed, some upon the first and second arch of the Bridge; and had it not been for the stone gate which stopped the fire very much, the rest of the houses on the Bridge had in all likelihood been [burnt] down.

9 SEPTEMBER 1811 At Union Hall, Southwark, on this day, chimneysweep James Dale was charged with an enterprising sideline: climbing down chimneys, into the house, and along to any riches that were kept inside. One Mr Stewartson, a haberdasher, awoke to find all his bread and cheese had been eaten in the night; a gown pattern (which would have felt in the dark exactly like a banknote) had also gone. Next door, Mr Freeman found he was missing four silver spoons and a silver vegetable fork. Rival haberdasher Mr Bishop found his chimney pot had been taken off – though the burglar had obviously been interrupted – and the World Turned Upside Down public house had lost a bag of half-pence. Sadly for Dale, he had accidentally dropped his pocket knife in one of the houses, with his initials carved on the handle – next to a picture of a chimney sweep. He had also left a sooty impression of his foot on a clean rug. He was sent to prison.

10 SEPTEMBER 1787 A tremendous storm of rain, thunder and lightning struck in 1739, wrecking many ships on the Thames.

Forty-eight years later, Major Browne challenged Sir John MacPherson to a duel in Hyde Park. They met near Grosvenor Gate at 11 a.m. and retired to a quiet spot, where a bullet flew through MacPherson's coat; the next shot hit his wallet. They then shook hands and left the field.

11 SEPTEMBER 1739 Today, rag-seller and 'illiterate, obstinate, ill-natur'd creature' Susannah Broom (67) of Shadwell, who had been married for more than forty years and had seven children, attacked her husband John (60), killing him. She slashed his thighs and stomach with a double-bladed penknife, carefully washed the blood from his corpse, tucked him in and went away without a care in the world. A neighbour had previously heard the old man crying out, 'For God's sake don't murder me! For Christ's sake don't murder me!' John was frequently chased with the poker: 'I have saved him from her a great many times,' the neighbour added. John was found, cold and stiff, 'cut in a very vile manner'. There was gore all over the floorboards – and on the prisoner's hat. A neighbour saw Susannah leaving the house, and said, 'Lord, how bloody Mother Broom is!' A final witness heard John's last words: 'Broom! Broom! For Christ's Sake! For God's Sake! Don't kill me – don't murder me in this manner!' Susannah was burnt in December; a horrible punishment for a horrible crime.

1755   The sanguinary tale of 'hard-hearted, barbarous woman' Mabell Hughes (77) was published by the Old Bailey on this day, after she stamped and beat a child to death in Aldgate Workhouse. Alexander Knipe (11), a silk-winder, was struck with a stick as he played with his friends; Mabell then proceeded to trample on his groin. She said not a word during the savage assault. Alexander groaned throughout the night – and when his roommates awoke the next day, it was to find a corpse staring back at them. His arm was 'green' and his swollen 'cod' was dented with the clear print of a toe. His last words, to a maternal sort in the workhouse, were: 'O Mamma, I cannot stand ... I am a dying, I shall die.' Mabell's job was to oversee the silk production, and the boy was said to be 'a very mild temper'd child [who] would not hurt a worm'. The surgeon found that 'the gut had been forc'd down violently into the scrotum ... and occasioned a strangulation by the tightness of the part'. The prisoner's defence was that the boys had been making a 'sad noise' and sometimes threw her silkwork into 'the vault'. She claimed that a chest in the room had struck the boy's crotch as he fell, rather than her foot. Unfortunately, the woman she called to defend her character declared: 'I beg to be excused in regard to her character, if you please; I can't say, but I have heard of her beating the children very much.' The ordinary's account of her was similarly uninspiring: 'She scarce escaped from being an ideot, [and was] as unfit to have management of children, as to tame lions.' She was hanged on 15 September, with 'some sense of hope after death'.

1756   On this day, John Lawley bit off the little finger of Constable Joseph Forest or Forrel. The trouble had started with drinks in a Cripplegate public house, which had turned into swearing and barracking, and degenerated into an all-out riot. The landlord was dubbed 'a mungrel and half mungrel', and his 'arse' was threatened with a whipping; the windows were shattered with a brick when Lawley was thrown out; two watchmen were bitten (on the leg and a chunk from a hand); the constable was beaten – and then, as the handcuffs came out, the unfortunate man's finger was seized upon and the teeth deployed.

   'Damn the son of a bitch!' cried the policeman. 'He has bit my finger off, I believe!'

   The wound was so sharp that the bone shone out, and 'the flesh was so clean bit away, it look'd as if it was shaved round'. The mangled digit had to be amputated; the victim died of a fever soon afterwards, but, as the wound was not thought to be the cause, Lawley was set free.

1730   On this day, servant Samuel Netherton was holding his master's horse in Fleet Street when he suddenly realised that his coat was moving. He discovered that his handkerchief was gone – and found it in the hand of Dennis Cormick, who he chased all the way down the street. Cormick tried to claim that he had just picked the handkerchief up from the ground, but the court disagreed and sent him off to the colonies.

   On this day in 1800, two letters were stuck on the London Monument, inviting readers, 'as they valued their rights as Englishmen, to attend to the

Corn-market on Monday'. The purpose was an enormous gathering to protest the price of bread, by menacing the corn dealers. Several were attacked, and many windows and lamps were broken. Bakeries in Whitechapel, Shoreditch and Blackfriars Road also received a visit from the mob.

15 SEPTEMBER   1791   On this day, at 10.30 p.m., a dreadful fire broke out near Cherry Garden Stairs, Rotherhithe. The fire burned for a considerable time with great fury. It began at a chandler's, and several barrels of tar caught fire before it was discovered. A number of engines attended, both on the river and on shore, but, due to a lack of water, the shore engines were of no use and the river engines could not be brought close enough to quell the flames. The fire spread, and it was 6 or 7 a.m. before it subsided in any way. By this time, fifty houses had been entirely burned down, many of them being warehouses containing property to a very considerable value. Numerous poor families were burnt out and their meagre possessions completely destroyed.

16 SEPTEMBER   1747   At between 5 p.m. and 6 p.m. this evening, drunken sailor Thomas Chapman returned to his East Smithfield home after a fortnight at sea, shouting out, 'Hollo! Are you all dead or alive?' He had a bottle in one hand – and a pistol in the other. In a sudden moment of confusion, which swept over him when he saw his wife Jane sitting in a chair nursing her baby, he lifted the gun to touch her breast – and pulled the trigger. She fell sideways from her chair, deep burn marks on her skin and a pistol ball in her throat. Then he declared, 'Lord Jesus Christ have mercy upon me. I have killed my wife accidentally!' He was found guilty of manslaughter.

Also on this day, but in 1795, John Lewis was sentenced to death for gathering a mob to pull down the house of William Ostliff at Charing Cross after he was refused a drink. The house had a pub sign outside, but no longer served drinks – unfortunately for them. The landlady watched in horror as her door was burst open, and she was forced to run upstairs and climb out of a window to safety. She could hear the sound of things breaking, and the mob spent three hours wrecking the house and 'halloing' that they would set it on fire. Lewis had spread a rumour that the house was full of kidnappers, and that 'there were people chained down in the cellar, and one nearly dead'. A group of 200 soldiers, saying 'damn your kidnapping eyes', had thus come to the rescue.

17 SEPTEMBER   1817   Today, in Sea Coal Lane, Mrs Redgrave took her little girl Eliza (2) for a stroll. As she was walking along, carrying the child, a cart swept past and brushed her arm – hurling the child onto the pavement, where the wheel crushed its neck. The mother ended up between the two wheels, and called out, 'Let me out!' as the wagon stopped. A resident then yanked the tiny legs next to her – and pulled a corpse from under the cart. The driver, Edward Cooke (36), was sent to Newgate for six months.

18 SEPTEMBER   1809   Today, a riot began at the Covent Garden Theatre's reopening; a fire in 1808 had destroyed most of the scenery and wardrobe, but a subscription

from many noble patrons had saved the day – until the theatre's doors once more opened for business, with a new – and very unpopular – ticket price. When the owner stepped onto the stage...

> ...he was greeted by a volley of hissing, whistling and shouting. This disrespectful behaviour continued throughout the performance of Macbeth, and every time Kemble or the leading actress stepped on stage there were cries of 'Old prices, Old prices'.

The crowd refused to file out at the end, even when the Riot Act was read, until at least 2 a.m. These 'Old Price' riots continued for an astonishing sixty-five days – with new twists such as insults thrown towards any ladies unlucky enough to step into a private box; customers playing on rattles, horns, bells and trombones during the play; insulting placards in the crowd; and armed spectators – until the management were forced to fold and change the prices.

1720   Today, Elizabeth Cole was sailing from Temple Stairs and joined two Londoners, Thomas Tompion and his wife Ann, in a boat. They obligingly moved over, and she felt a rustling about her petticoats – caused, she thought, by the hoops of the two skirts coming together. Then the pair suddenly remembered 'some writings' they needed to go back for – so they hailed a passing boat to shore, got into it and waved goodbye to their brief acquaintance. When Elizabeth reached Pepper Alley, however, she realised that the rustling had been caused by Ann gently reaching into her skirts and lifting her purse. She swiftly went for a thief-taker at the Old Bailey, and informed them that they should be on the lookout for 'a Fat Man with a Smiling Countenance, a Sword by his Side, and a Two Tail'd wig on' and a woman in 'a Red Damask Silk Gown and Petticoat [with] a Gold Chain and Locket about her Neck, and Bobs in her Ears'. Hiding under a cloak, the thief-taker escorted Elizabeth to a nearby house, where she saw the husband and wife. Ann was sentenced to death but was later reprieved, and her husband was acquitted.   19 SEPTEMBER

1761   Harmondsworth man Richard Parrott (50-70, according to his best estimates) cut out his wife's tongue on this day because she 'told a great many lies of him'. He was dragged off to the constable 'in a very bloody condition' – all over his shirt and fingers. The policeman then went to find the victim of this vile action: 20 SEPTEMBER

> She lay on the bed, leaning over one side, spitting blood, but could not speak. Her mouth was swelled, and battered in such a manner, there was no such thing as seeing her tongue. She was so swelled and black, she looked like a blackamoor; I should not have known her, though I had known her from a little girl, being born in the same parish.

Her chest was bruised where Parrott had knelt upon it; her nose and cheek were black. She made feeble gestures towards her mouth with her fingers to explain what had happened, and 'put her hand down, and crawled it up her belly' to show how he had offered to 'rip her up' if she did not stick out her tongue. Seven teeth had been knocked out; he had then 'pinched her on the nose until it was as black as a hat' and she was forced to comply. She died on 7 October, starved as she could no longer swallow properly. The prisoner's defence was that she had been attempting to kill him by putting 'brimstone' onto his clothes, but the court rejected this attempt at a lunacy defence, and he was sent to the gallows.

In 1808, the Covent Garden Theatre burnt to the ground. Horribly, the passageway into the theatre collapsed as the fire took hold, and many Londoners were crushed by burning debris. The corpses of fourteen Londoners were dug out, in a 'shocking' state, and sixteen others went to hospital with awful burns.

21 SEPTEMBER   **1723**   Humphrey Anger (29), of Hornsey, robbed one gentleman of the silver button from his breeches and then followed, on this day, by robbing John Sibley of 9s 6d between Knightsbridge and Hyde Park Corner. The robber apologised to the Old Bailey for not being able to give exact details of the times and dates of his crimes – sadly, he said, he had lost his pocketbook containing 'particular account of all the robberies he had committed'. This he kept so he could offer an excellent – and impossible to resist – testimony for King's Evidence should he ever be captured. Without it he was sentenced to death. 'From the time of Condemnation, to his Death,' said the ordinary, 'he extremely lamented his Condition, with a vast number of Tears.' His father had been a Chelsea pensioner.

22 SEPTEMBER   **1747**   On this day, Jane Ellis noticed that Elizabeth Best had gone into the cellar of her shop; Jane used this as an opportunity to put two cloaks and a hat into her apron. When the lady reappeared, Jane pretended to ask for the maid – but the woman kept her in the shop until her trick was discovered. Jane was transported.

Also on this day, but in 1761, George III was crowned – whereupon the diamond fell out of his crown between Westminster Abbey and Hall, and had to be found and returned.

23 SEPTEMBER   **1814**   James Dobbins (27), of Millfield Farm in Kentish Town, lived with washerwoman Elizabeth, his partner of twenty years. One day, he came home to find her sprawled on the floor, with her head cut open entirely, and 'the bones scattered about the place'. A bent and bloody poker lay nearby. A passing carpenter had seen a stranger lurking nearby that afternoon, with a black handkerchief about his neck. Another had seen the man actually in the cottage of death, calmly eating a sandwich. A last group had seen him walking through the fields, arms filled with stolen laundry. He was quickly arrested. A surgeon was not called in to take evidence, for when 'the pieces of the scull [sic] bones are found about the place, and the scull beat in, there is no occasion to call the surgeon to say that was the cause of her death.' The murderer was William Brunskill's last client at Newgate.

1720 On this day, William Ockendon (16) of Chiswick and John Haley (16) were out hunting birds together when, by a horrible accident, John managed to shoot himself under the left arm, burning his clothes and ripping an inch-wide hole in his body. He died on the spot. **24 SEPTEMBER**

1823 Another of London's interminable traffic accidents occurred on this day when two drays attempted to pass each other in Worship Street. A Londoner, John Tucker, tried to press himself against the wall, but the second cart caught him and ran over his head. His brains were observed to be glinting 'amongst the dirt'. The cart was 7ft wide – and the passageway 13ft. If the driver had been paying attention – he was retying his apron string at the time – the victim would have been fine. The driver was confined for six months. **25 SEPTEMBER**

1743 Three men – one a boy of 13 – jumped William Warwick in Bishopsgate Street after he came to the aid of a passing washerwoman whom they had accosted: his eye was almost knocked out, and they broke his leg so that the bone poked out through his stocking. He died as a result, and they were found guilty of manslaughter. **26 SEPTEMBER**

Today in 1817, Welshman David Owen (45) cut his own family to shreds in Prospect Place, St George's Fields. He knocked on the door of the house, owned by his brother-in-law, Mr John Jones (40), and then flew in with a knife the minute it was opened. 'You wretches,' he said, 'I am come to kill you all!' After kneeling on Jones and cutting his neck, head and stomach, and chopping off a piece of his ear, he was hustled out into the street by a passing shoe-seller. However, Owen ran back in with a second knife to attack his sister: he put his knife in her mouth and pulled it out again – straight through her cheek to the ear. A servant girl was also mangled before he was secured. Hundreds of people flocked around the door, but they were too frightened to enter for nearly an hour. Eventually, carrying pokers, clothes-props and bludgeons, the mob ran in. Owen had spent the hour sharpening his knives. By the time he was beaten and manhandled to Union Hall, he appeared 'more demon than a human being', and had blood from his shoes to his face. He was sent to Horsemonger Lane Gaol. The cause of the bloodshed was that the London family had sued Owen for payment of the care of his two sons, who lived in the capital. The shock of the suit had, Owen thought, killed his wife, and he had become determined upon revenge. He was sentenced to death.

1810 Six members of the 'Vere Street Coterie', a famous homosexual club, came to the pillory in the Haymarket on this day. They received one of the most severe assaults in London's history, when fifty women, at the head of an enormous crowd, 'assailed' them 'incessantly with mud, dead cats, rotten eggs, potatoes, and buckets filled with blood, offal and dung' in the pillory, **27 SEPTEMBER**

and with fish they had brought, stinking, to throw. All the way back they were attacked too: eventually, they were 'so thickly covered with filth, that a vestige of the human figure was scarcely discernible'. People even stood up to hit them with whips as they passed. They were all bleeding, but escaped with a lighter sentence than two other members of the 'coterie', who were hanged. Drummer boy Thomas White (16) and John Newbolt Hepburn (42) were executed outside Newgate on 7 March 1811.

28 SEPTEMBER

1736   Today another Gin Act was passed, adding a massive 20*s* tax to every gallon sold. The Acts attempted to reduce gin drinking in the capital, which was up to an estimated two pints per Londoner per day by this period. In fact, the era is known as the 'gin craze' for the enormous popularity of the drink – which was also thought to be the main cause of crime in the city. However, the Act annoyed London's drinkers so much that sixty soldiers had to be sent to protect the house of Sir Joseph Jekyll, Master of the Rolls at Chancery Lane and the main reason the Bill had been approved.

Covent Garden in 1720. Whilst a London child's parents were here, their daughter was accidentally poisoned with gin. (Courtesy of the Library of Congress, LC-DIG-ppmsca-12670)

Also on this day, a widow accidentally killed a 5-year-old child in Lascelles Court, St Giles' – by giving it gin whilst its parents were at Covent Garden Market. The little girl started to vomit, and died at 8 p.m.; she had consumed 'two glasses of gin, one of rum ... part of two pots of porter, and a small drop of wine' at the Rose & Crown in Broad Street. The widow, who 'did not think it would hurt' to let the child have a few, was sentenced to six months' imprisonment in Newgate.

COVENT GARDEN

1755   On this day, carpenter's apprentice Joseph Oliphant fought with his mistress, Mary Smith; the next day she stabbed him in the side with a 5in 'breast-wimble' gouge. He cried out 'Oh!', reeled, 'gave his foot a stamp, and gaz'd at her the space of a moment, and tumbled down into the yard'. A half-moon-shaped cut curved under his heart. When Mary was told that the man was dead, she replied, 'Pshaw, I don't believe it.' Someone in the house ran for the law – who turned up with an axe and smashed her door down to get in. Mary declared, 'I am a ruined creature!' and went off to Newgate. She had a very good character in general, and was found guilty of manslaughter, burnt on the hand and released.

1781   At Mr Wright's butcher's shed in Whitechapel this evening, two local watchmen – Joseph Driver and Robert Evans – came to blows after Evans strolled into his rival's territory. 'What business have you upon my beat?' demanded Driver – and they scuffled. Driver called for help, and his rival fled back across the road to his own stand – carrying a heavy stick, broken in two. 'Damn the old scoundrel, I have broke my stick over his skull!' he muttered as he went. Evans later told a colleague, 'I am sorry my stick was not shorter, I would have given him more; he has insulted me so often. Who is to put up with these affronts?' Driver, meanwhile, was complaining bitterly to his colleagues. 'Feel my head!' he told one. By the light of the lantern, the man saw a lump, topped with a small scratch. The surgeon at the London Hospital was similarly unimpressed with his wound, which he examined on 2 October. 'I could find nothing the matter,' he said. However, when the patient died a few days later, 'Mr Blizard took off the scalp, and examined the scull [*sic*], and found a fracture extending quite down to the hollow of the eyes.' It turned out that, during the night, a watchman's rattle had been heard. Evans had approached Driver to ask him what the matter was, only to receive a rude answer – followed by three pushes and three blows. Driver had then raised his staff threateningly, and received his death wound in return. Evans was branded on the hand, and imprisoned for one month.

OCTOBER

John Thurtell cutting the throat of Mr William Weare. Though other editions favoured finer quality copper engravings, Robins' edition, with its cheery woodcuts, sometimes succeeds in capturing the horror of a scene where its more delicate rivals fail. Weare is the man on top, while Thurtell presses a knife to his throat from underneath. This is based on the testimony given in court: so much blood, he claimed, fell onto his face as he was doing it that he was almost choked.

1736 In the evening, during the performance of *Dr Faustus* at the Covent Garden Theatre, actor James Todd fell from the upper stage 'in a flying machine' when the wires broke. He fractured his skull, and died miserably; three others were hurt, but recovered.

1722 The most almighty battle occurred in Westminster on this day over a badly behaved dog, ending in a woman's death. The dog bit Mr Thornton in Stretton Grounds, Westminster. Naturally, he was extremely angry at this, and followed it to the door of the house it had run out of. Mary Bolton then ran out of the house and pushed Mr Thornton's wife, Clementia, in the breast – whereupon she fell over and died. Mary next turned to the stunned Mr Thornton and said, 'Go ye dog, lye down by the bitch your wife, and I'll sprinkle water on ye both.' A witness elaborated on this, claiming that what she actually said was, 'Take a knife and stick yourself, ye nasty white-liver'd dog, and then you may lye down by that bitch, your wife.' Mary said in her defence that she had been called an ugly coarse bitch, a nasty draggle tail'd toad, ugly puss, and stinking punk, and told to go wash her smock. The court heard how, due to the deceased's poor health, it was possible that she might have been 'strangled purely by the violent emotion of the wind in scolding'. The jury agreed with this version of events, and Mary Bolton was acquitted.

1737 On this day, an amazing gelding belonging to Mr Richard Fendall of Southwark died after accidentally cutting its knee. Fendall was totally broken-hearted by this loss, as the horse had been in his possession for forty-four years, and had once taken him 50 miles in a single day.

Today in 1810, Mr Hussey's daughter, of Swallow Street, fell out of a second-storey window and was spiked on a railing. She died the next day.

1783 Eighty Newgate convicts, who were awaiting transportation, rioted today aboard a ship at Blackwell. When they got on board the ship that was to take them overseas, they somehow managed, en masse, to tear off the collars chaining them together and begin running amok. Three of them were shot (one through the neck) before the riot was brought under control and the men forced down into the hold of the ship.

1721 John Miller died on this day in the parish of St Martin's. A case appeared at the Old Bailey to decide if the cause of death was a 1in wound caused when William Palmer, of St Olave, Southwark, struck the deceased with a boat-hook near the left hip. Their boats had become entangled as they shot under the bridge. A brief but vicious fight had then broken out, and Miller managed to punch the other man and hit him with his oar before he was caught with the iron hook. Miller later found out where Palmer lived, in Pepper Alley, and showed him the hole in his front.

'Look what you have done,' he said.

'Look what YOU have done,' Palmer replied, showing the man the welt on his arm caused by the oar. Miller's wound was investigated by surgeons after he died and found to be trifling, and so Palmer was acquitted of murder and burnt on the hand instead.

6 OCTOBER   **1823**   On this day, apprentice butcher George Davis (16) was observed in Bridge Road, Lambeth, committing one of the most amazing acts of sleepwalking ever recorded. In the grip of the most profound sleep, he climbed onto his (saddleless) horse and attempted to gallop out of the stable, and was only wrestled from his mount and forced back indoors with a great deal of effort. He paced back and forth for fifteen minutes, and seemed to think that the hold-up was because he had reached a turnpike on his journey. Doctor Mr Benjamin Ridge was called, to whom the boy handed a sixpence to pay the toll. When it was handed back, the sleeping boy declared he had received the wrong change, angrily shouting, 'None of your nonsense! That is the sixpence again: give me my change.' He would not be contented until he had received what he felt was the correct change. His pulse was racing at 136 beats per minute, and he made great efforts to whip his horse onwards – even though it now stood contently in the nearby stable. His face was totally expressionless, and his eyes were shut. The doctor, Mr Hewson, told the onlookers about a Mr Harris in Holborn, whose son had once walked out onto the roof in his sleep. To the listeners' astonishment, George then joined in with the conversation, observing that the other sleepwalker lived at the corner of Brownlow Street. He then folded over, unlaced one of his boots and informed the astonished crowd that he wanted to go to bed. Three minutes after touching the sheets, he woke up and asked why his arm was bandaged, having absolutely no recollection of any of the night's amazing events.

7 OCTOBER   **1725**   Foster Snow stabbed Thomas Rawlins to death on this day at Snow's public house, the Feathers Alehouse in Holborn. Rawlins owed Snow money, and the tension had been building for some time; about a month before this tragic event, Snow informed a friend called John Rude that Rawlins was a villain and a rascal, and said that he would think no more of killing him than of killing a toad. When Rawlins stepped into the Feathers on the 7th, the atmosphere was therefore tense. Rawlins brought some rabbits with him. Whilst they were cooking, Snow stalked into the kitchen and declared, 'You are a sorry dog!'

'And you're another,' replied his enemy.

'What?' Snow roared, 'Must I be abused in my own house, and by a man who owes me money? Sirrah, you're a rogue!'

'Call me a rogue,' responded Rawlins coolly, 'and I'll lay you behind that fire.'

Snow's wife told them both to be quiet, and received a stinging slap in response. This caused Rawlins to leap to her defence; in a towering temper, Snow swept up a knife that lay near him and plunged it into Thomas's chest, killing him instantly. Snow was sentenced to death.

8 OCTOBER   **1728**   On this day, George II wrote a note to the chairman of the Westminster Sessions from Windsor Castle, authorising a reward of 40s for anyone who would hand over a convict who had sneaked back into the country before his

George II.

time of transportation was over. Such men (and women) were being blamed for all manner of thefts, loose and disorderly houses, drinking dens, gaming houses and the general corruption of London morals.

In 1770, on this day, schoolmaster John Barney was indicted for the wilful murder of William Poole (12) by beating his head into a wall in the schoolroom. Poole's skull cracked above the right ear, and he died the next day. Three other pupils told the court that William had been called on to read something out and did it badly. The schoolmaster had responded by slapping his head with an open palm, and his head was crushed into the chimney. William cried out that his head hurt, and then ran out of the room to be sick. He died during the night. Doctor Hunter scalped the boy, sawed open his skull, and found a shard of bone the size of a sixpence twisting into the brain. It had been chipped off by the sharp point of the chimney; given the thin nature of children's skulls, not much force would have been needed to inflict the injury. 'Had he been my own son,' Barney said, 'I could not have taken more pains with him ... I loved him.' He was acquitted, but his heart was as broken as William's skull.

9 OCTOBER **1777**   A gravedigger at St George the Martyr, Queen Street, Bloomsbury, was caught stealing the corpse of Mrs Jane Salisbury on this day for dissection – the first case of a London bodysnatcher. Gravedigger John Holmes (as well as his assistant, Robert Williams) was tried at the Guildhall before Sir John Hawkins. Mr Eustanston told the court that he had been walking home at about 8 p.m. with some friends when they met Williams and Holmes walking jauntily along; Williams was carrying a sack over his shoulder.

'What have you got there?' asked the man.

Williams, looking deeply suspicious, replied, 'I don't know.' It was not the best answer, and when they tried to pull the bag away from him he started to beg, and said he was just a poor man home from the harvest. Inside the bag was a very surprising harvest indeed: the gently wasting body of an old lady was found trussed up inside, with her hands tied behind her back and her heels twisted up so that they almost touched her ears. The cord around her neck had pulled her head back at a grotesque angle, so she was staring back at the astonished men. The court gave both men six months', and two severe whippings each, both to last all the way from Kingsgate Street to Dyott Street, St Giles' (almost half a mile) – though this part was later remitted.

10 OCTOBER **1807**   Moses Moses (14) was playing with an acquaintance, apprentice glass-cutter Alexander Hart (14), in Strype's Yard, Spitalfields. Their game took place amongst piles of bricks and ruins made where some houses had been pulled down. Suddenly, a man appeared and hefted a brick at the boys. He went into a house – from which he re-emerged, two minutes later, carrying a gun; he fired, and Alexander dropped on his face. The man, who turned out to be crippled caretaker George Houghton, was heard to mutter, 'Damn your eyes, you young rascals, I think I have shot some of them [the pieces of lead or 'swan shot'] into you.'

Henry Samuel, a passing coalman, happened to trip over the body of the boy. He turned the stricken child over; seeing blood, he asked if Hart had hurt his mouth: 'Oh, my mouth! My back!' the boy replied. He was paralysed, and bleeding from a hole in the back of his neck (with a slug lodged in his spine); another shot had gone through his coat and waistcoat. The prisoner had been hired to protect the property, and to fire off a gun every night to dissuade thieves. His defence was that the boys had been throwing bricks at him and his house, and he meant to disperse them. He was given six months' imprisonment and a 1s fine.

11 OCTOBER **1737**   Today, a letter arrived at a shop in Isleworth, together with a bundle of clothes (returned to their owner after a short loan). The letter was from Mary Chambers, and informed the recipient – Mary's landlady – that the writer had gone to live with a relative in 'the Wilds of Kent'. The day before, Mary had been quite excited: she was off to a reunion with her husband, George Price. However, the letter contained some strange news: Mary claimed that she was now on the run from her husband, whom she had 'driven into debt'. The letter had another strange feature: it appeared to be in the husband's own handwriting. Mary's body was found on Hounslow

Heath with a slit throat. Price's alibi was proved to be a lie as he'd claimed he was at a theatre on a day when there was no play. He was sentenced to death, but died in Newgate before he could reach the gallows.

1720   A strange case came to the Old Bailey on this day. As Josiah Wright   **12 OCTOBER**
was walking by Tower Hill at about 9 p.m. on 7 September, he heard a cry of distress. He found a woman crawling along the floor, and watched as a man kicked her in the small of the back, crying out, 'Get up, you bitch – you shall have a run for it!' Josiah recognised the man as Henry Membry, a dyer who lived in Tower Street. Membry then went for a drink in the Nag's Head and complained loudly of the 'loose cattle' on the Hill, before declaring that he had knocked one woman down on one side, another on the other and a third up the hill and down again. The third woman was one Ann Pooley, a prostitute dressed in a daring combination of yellow stomacher and black stockings. She was found lying battered and speechless in Thames Street a short while later – whereupon the constable promptly ordered her to be picked up and carried to Tower Hill so that his parish wouldn't have to pay for her upkeep and care. She was rediscovered, slumped on a pile of straw on Tower Hill the next morning, and was finally taken to a nurse. She died in the workhouse later that night; her body quickly turned 'as black as a shoe from ear to hip'. A friend told Membry that he was being accused of savagely assaulting a woman, and he found Ann before she died and had her washed and searched. No substantial pre-mortem bruising was discovered (though her post-mortem bruising, as mentioned, was severe), but she was very thin and in ill health. Membry told the court that he had heard an outcry on Tower Hill, and found a great 'parcel of blackguards'. He had dispersed them with many a kick, crying, 'Run, you dogs, it is good for your health.' The court acquitted him of any crime.

1719   The millinery-minded Ann Wells was transported on this day, after   **13 OCTOBER**
stealing forty hats from a Whitechapel shop. Ten years later, on the same day, Henry Barnard was transported after seeing a shift hanging up to dry in the same parish of St Mary's, Whitechapel, and unpegging it – he was chased through the streets and captured, still carrying it.

1721   Grissel Murray, wife of Alexander Murray of St James's, Westminster,   **14 OCTOBER**
woke up at 4 a.m. this day to find a servant of Lord Bennyng standing by her bedside holding a sword and a pistol. 'Madam,' he said, 'I mean to ravish you!' He confessed that he had long held a torch for her, but had decided that the great difference in their situations meant he would never have her by any other means. Informing her that he would kill her if she refused, he put down the sword and reached for the bedclothes – at which point she sprang out of the bed, grabbed his pistol with one hand and rang the bell in her room with all her might with the other. He ran for his life. The servant, Arthur Gray, based the defence at his trial on whether he had or had not broken in (the lock was very weak, and the room very often left unlocked), and whether he had or had not come home to hear what he thought was a person in her

Ladyship's room, whom he suspected may have been hiding underneath the bed. Lady Mary Wortley Montagu may have had a somewhat cynical view in mind when she wrote, 'his pistol hand she held fast closed, as she remembers well, But how the other was disposed, There's none alive can tell'. Gray was sentenced to death, but was afterwards reprieved.

15 OCTOBER   1775   At about 5.50 a.m. today, a cry of murder was heard in Silver Street, Bloomsbury. The woman who heard it, Mary Vincent, conferred with her husband and concluded it was simply some of the 'women of the town', who frequently shouted similar things. Then she rolled up the window and saw two men fighting for all they were worth in the street. One whispered, 'Mistress, he has murdered me,' and fell. It was Mr Pratt's coachman, who lived opposite, and he had been stabbed. Mr Younge, the Great Russell Street surgeon, was fetched, but the coachman died two hours later, after writhing in pain so strongly on the way to the hospital that he smashed the glass of the chair that carried him. He said his murderer had broken in to rob the stable. A wig, a coat and a bent bayonet lay in the dust where he had fallen – they belonged to the murderer. A hairdresser, Lawrence Robinson, recognised the wig, which he had altered for a rabbit-seller, Robert Williams. Williams was hanged in January 1776.

In 1806, sixteen people were crushed to death in a stampede at the Sadler's Wells Theatre after a false fire alarm.

16 OCTOBER   1717   On this day, the 'advertisements' at the Old Bailey promised, by the Duke of Boroughs Head, Fleet Street, 'a German, born without Hands, Feet, or Thighs ... who does such Actions, as none else can do with Hands and Feet.' This included shaving, shooting, writing, shuffling cards and 'many other Things too tedious to insert here'.

Also on this day, in 1793, Marie Antoinette approached the guillotine in Paris. Her last words were, 'Pardon me, Sir, I did not mean to do it' – she had accidentally trodden on the executioner's toe.

17 OCTOBER   1720   Captain Edward Lutterell regretted trying to drive off two bailiffs at gunpoint this day when the first, Robert Tranter, pushed him up against a wall and the second, a fat brute by the name of Hugh Reason, stabbed him in the gut. They then threw him to the floor and stabbed him eight or nine times with his own sword, before stabbing him with a new sword when he managed to grab the blade of the first and snap it; they then shot him for good measure. Before he died, Lutterell described how he had begged for his life. 'Damn him,' one replied, 'draw his sword and stab him!' The court found that the two men had been 'very civil' in their treatment of Lutterell, remaining very polite until Lutterell had decided to fetch two loaded pistols and bash one of the men with his cane. The jury found them guilty of manslaughter only, as they were agents of the law, quite entitled to perform their duty and to defend themselves whilst doing so. Both pleaded 'benefit of the clergy', were burnt on the hand and freed.

1818   According to a report published this day, the Bank of England's policy of stamping forged notes and returning them was beginning to cause a minor panic in London. Shopkeepers had taken to pinning up notes that had tricked them in the window of their shops, next to signs saying 'Tradesmen! Beware of changing notes', and many shops would consequently not take notes at all.

Twenty-seven years earlier, on this same day, Thomas Bayne was drinking in the Marquis of Granby, Piccadilly, with his friend George Smith. At just before midnight, Samuel Bromley entered. Smith was a little bit drunk by this point; he got up and ran for the door, where he was dramatically sick just outside. 'How can you be so dirty?' asked Bromley. Provoking him was a bad idea, as Smith was inclined to violence, and the two men began to fight in the street. Smith was eventually forced back into the inn by his friend, but a fatal grievance had begun. Four hours later, Bromley returned to the Granby to eat; the moment he entered, Smith leapt up and stumbled drunkenly over to a shovel, which he began to wave in the air.

'I will cut your bloody head!' he shouted.

'Smith,' replied Bromley, 'I will not be struck and knocked about so!' He chose his own weapon, a long broom, with which he struck Smith on the head. Smith's skull splintered, and he died shortly afterwards. Bromley was fined 1s for causing his death.

1816   A dilapidated house in the Haymarket fell down on this day. An old woman and three others who lived in it were buried in the ruins, but luckily they were not injured. When she was pulled out of the rubble, the old woman was greatly concerned for the safety of her guinea pigs. However, to her great joy, the workmen managed to find them none the worse for wear.

Also on this day, but in 1818, a surgeon named John Harcraves, who was imprisoned at the Fleet (a debtors' prison), was called in on an urgent matter. A little over a week earlier, another prisoner had been walking past the window of impoverished tailor James Learwood's room when he heard a faint cry of 'Murder!' He looked in to see John Daly (42) tear Learwood (50) out of the window seat in his room. The stricken man's eye was black with something like blood. He immediately pulled up the window and said, 'In the name of God, don't kill the man!' Daly's response was less than reassuring: he rolled the bleeding man onto his face and said, 'Damn your head, you old rogue, I will flog your ass!' He proceeded to make good on his words. It turned out that Daly thought the man he was attacking had rifled his room, and taken a letter belonging to him – though they had been great friends before this. The battered thief was picked up and placed in a chair, where he quickly lost consciousness. On the 19th, Harcraves arrived to find the man in bed, half naked and dying. He was covered in sick, and his eye was swollen and black; his face was distorted horribly, and his tongue was hanging out. By the next morning, his pulse had reached 150. Learwood died soon afterwards. A blow to the eye, damaging the brain, was given as the cause of death. Daly was sent to prison for a year.

20 OCTOBER   **1827**   Three lion cubs were born in the Tower of London on this day. For 1s, you could visit the menagerie there, which included lions, tigers, panthers, wolves, leopards, bears, baboons, eagles and snakes. The Bengal lion was known as George, and when small he roamed free in the menagerie; he could be petted and played with by visitors. He ate 8 or 9lb of beef a day, which he ripped to shreds with his claws the moment it appeared. If the lions in the menagerie were hungry, hot or bored, they all started to roar – and sometimes they all roared again after they had eaten. George's sister (and mate) was much more violent: she once escaped, and George Willoughway, the under-keeper, had to drive her back into her pen with a stick – though she resisted fiercely all the way, and sprang on him three times. As soon as she had cubs she went completely wild, and could not be approached with safety. Another 'tyger' may have been the very creature that inspired Blake to write 'The Tyger'. It had a great fondness for drinking soup. A ferocious tigress also lived at the Tower. In 1811, a visiting soldier, hoping to impress his young wife, approached this tiger and stroked its paw. The tiger sprang forward, seized his hand, and dragged him into its den, though his friends grabbed his body and desperately tried to pull him out. Luckily, a brave man present seized hold of a stick and forced it down the tiger's throat, which forced it to let go. The mangled soldier was carried off to a doctor, the flesh of his arm hanging down in shreds. Two leopards lived in the same cage in the menagerie: the female was quite tame, and would lick its keepers' hands, but lady visitors were warned to keep their umbrellas, dresses and hats away from the cage as she tended to reach out and rip them to shreds – several hundred items met this fate. The anaconda, meanwhile, once struck for its food and missed, biting keeper Mr Cops on the hand and leaving its teeth behind when it was forced off. The animals were finally moved to London Zoo at the end of the Georgian era.

21 OCTOBER   **1786**   In 1786, Charles Griffiths struck the head of his mother-in-law, Charity Lee, with a poker after a row. The row had begun when Charles' brother-in-law Samuel – though he had only one arm – punched Charles in the face. The two men had then fallen to fighting; soon one Mr Morgan, a friend Charles had brought with him, joined in – and a general ruckus for ownership of the poker ensued. The fight raged down the stairs, Charles demanding Samuel put down the poker (which he currently held) and fight fair, Samuel fencing with it for all he was worth. Eventually, Charles and his friend were forced to flee. As a dramatic finale to the struggle, Charity then appeared at the top of the stairs, covered with blood, and called, 'Save my child!' However, it was Charity who needed saving: she died a few days later. The court found that she had been struck by accident during the struggle, and acquitted Charles – with a warning against future outbreaks of temper.

22 OCTOBER   **1751**   On this day, Norwich's city bridewell caught fire. The prisoners were released – including one who seemed 'more of the Ouran Outan [sic] species than human'. It was 'Peter, the Wild Boy'. He was only 5ft 3in, and could say only two words: 'Peter', and 'King George'. In 1725, aged about

12, he was found in the woods roughly 28 miles from Hanover. He lived there upon leaves, berries and the bark of trees, running on all fours and climbing up trees like a squirrel. Only the tattered shirt collar around his neck showed that he had once lived with humans. (As the town nearby was a camp for criminals working on the fortifications, it was thought that he might be one of their children.) He was taken to George I, who fed him. After escaping several times back into the woods, he was brought over to London by order of Queen Caroline, and put under the care of Dr Arbuthnot. He walked about the palaces of London in a curious outfit chosen by himself: a green suit, with a red lining and scarlet stockings. He would only sleep in the corner of a room. In 1726 he was baptised 'Peter' in Burlington Garden. He was terrifyingly strong, and attracted to anything bright, smooth or shiny on a visitor's clothes. If somebody made him angry, which was difficult to do, he was terrifying: he would run after the person who had angered him, 'making a strange noise, with his teeth fixed into the back of his hand'. After it proved impossible to teach him, he was handed over to the care of different farmers, with an iron collar on his neck with his name on. He died in 1785, aged 72. Peter loved dancing to music, and frequently ran off into the woods to forage on acorns and leaves. He would then get lost – which is how he ended up in Norwich's prison.

1823 Three men were involved in the awful, infamous crime that happened this day: the murder of London solicitor Mr William Weare. Weare met the men involved in his death, Mr John Thurtell, Mr Joseph Hunt and Mr William Probert, in the smoky gambling haunts of the capital.

23 OCTOBER

John Thurtell (33) was a Norwich merchant and former Royal Marine who fell into bad company through his love of gambling. He was quickly ruined, becoming the victim of every clever card shark in London's sporting underworld. Weare was one of these men. Thurtell's chief love was boxing, and he started to enter and to organise (and also, to fix) prize fights. For a while he had an inn at Long Acre (which, due to the riotous scenes there, quickly lost its licence); he then switched to arson and insurance fraud to make his living. Joseph Hunt (also 33) was a flamboyant and handsome dark-haired swell with an enormous moustache (which he was to shave off after the murder in an attempt to escape detection) and an excellent voice; he made his living by gambling and singing. William Probert (32) was a bankrupted former Haymarket wine merchant.

Weare (it was thought) tricked Thurtell out of £300 with false cards, and a dark and dreadful plan for revenge was laid. Thurtell invited Weare to Probert's cottage in Radlett, about 15 miles outside London, to enjoy a day or two of shooting – a trip from which William was never to return. Weare went to his chambers in Lyon's Inn, where he packed some clothes in a green carpet bag. Meanwhile, John Thurtell and Joseph Hunt went to a pawnbroker's in Marylebone and purchased a pair of pocket-pistols 'to shoot cats with'. Hunt hired a gig, and afterwards a horse, and then procured a sack, a spade (not used, as the ground was too hard) and some cord in Broad Street, Bloomsbury.

They set off from Conduit Street at 5 p.m., and had a very busy weekend: Thurtell set upon Weare in a lane by the cottage, murdered him in a despicable manner, and then dragged his mangled body through the hedge into a neighbouring field. After surprising Mrs Probert (Mr Probert's wife) by turning up unannounced (she had never even met Hunt), they surprised her still further by dragging a weighty rattling bundle down to the garden pond in the night. It was Weare's body. His feet were left sticking out of the water and gleaming whitely in the moonlight, but they pulled them down with a length of rope. In between these tasks, they enjoyed a delicious dinner of pork chops bought in Oxford Street. Thurtell, however, didn't seem hungry – he later confessed that, when he was slicing Weare's throat, so much blood fell over his face that he was 'nearly choked'.

Early the next morning, a labourer met Thurtell and Hunt 'grabbling' in the hedge – allegedly looking for items lost when their gig overturned in a 'lark' (and actually trying to recover the murder weapons, which Thurtell had foolishly left behind in the dark of the previous evening). The labourer returned later that day to see if he could find any money, and found instead only blood, a bloody pocket knife, a handkerchief and a gun. The gun was besmeared with a strange substance – one which turned out to be human brains. Reports of a gunshot heard at about 8 p.m. also began to circulate. Thurtell, Hunt and Probert then returned to London, pausing only to drag Weare's body from its hiding place, cut off his clothes, stuff him into a sack and move him to a pond a few miles away, getting mud and blood all over the gig in the process. The labourer reported his findings, and the road to the discovery of their foul crime began.

Discretion was not the killers' watchword – both Hunt and Thurtell took to wearing William's clothes, whilst Thurtell's hands were horribly scratched (from catching partridges, he claimed). They were arrested soon afterwards: Thurtell in the Coach & Horses in Conduit Street, where his clothes and hat were noticed to be covered in blood; William's clothes, marked W.W., were

William Weare's
corpse transported
down to the pond.

also found. Hunt was caught in King Street, Golden Square. Hoping for clemency, as he had not been present at the actual murder, Hunt confessed where the body was, and it was dragged out: it was stuffed in a sack head-first, with feet poking out; stones were tucked under each armpit to weigh it down. William Weare was buried at Elstree.

On the first day of the trial, some electrifying news came in: Mr Probert was to be allowed to turn King's Evidence. Thurtell and Hunt faced the gallows alone. Probert's hair was visibly turning to grey by the time he reached the court, and his face was thin and haggard. He described what Thurtell had said of William's last moments (recorded in the Newgate Calendar):

> When I first shot him he jumped out of the gig and ran like the Devil, singing out that he would deliver all he had, if I'd only spare his life ... I jumped out of the gig and ran after him; I got him down, and began to cut his throat, as I thought, close to the jugular vein, but I could not stop his singing out; I then jammed the pistol into his head; I gave it a turn round, and then I knew I had done for him.

The skull of the dead man was found to have a hole as large as a finger punched in it, scratched around by the end of the pistol; a large shard of skull was wedged in the brain. His upper row of teeth had been blown out.

When they were condemned, Hunt sobbed; Thurtell was calm, and 'while the very directions for his body's dissection were being uttered ... consumed the pinch of snuff which had to that moment been pausing in his fingers!' Thurtell went to his death on 9 January 1824, with a face as white as a corpse. He bowed to a sporting acquaintance from the gallows, and died a few minutes later, his neck cracking with a sound like a gunshot, and a single groan escaping his lips as he fell. His corpse went on display in St Bartholomew's Hospital for four days, slowly falling into decrepitude; first a finger dropped off, then an eye went missing. At last the display was taken down, though his skeleton remains at the College of Surgeons.

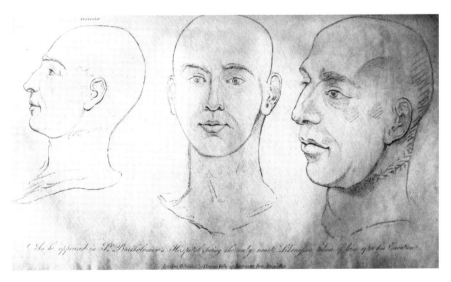

An extremely rare sketch of Thurtell drawn at St Bartholomew's after he was cut from the gallows: the mark of a rope can clearly be seen around his neck.

Hunt, however, had his sentence commuted at the very last second – he was sent to the hulks at Woolwich, and afterwards to New South Wales. After serving his sentence, he married, had two children – and eventually became a policeman. He died in 1861. William Probert, shunned by polite society for his role in the murder and forced to embrace a life of crime to support his family, was later hanged for stealing a horse from Kensington. 'Even the smallest village I went to spurned me as an outcast,' he said. 'I could scarcely move from one place to another without seeing my route marked in the daily papers; every door was shut against me, and every hope of future support blasted.'

The foreman of the jury, William Lamb, 2nd Viscount Melbourne, would later become prime minister, and Australia, where Joseph Hunt would serve his sentence for the wicked crime, named Melbourne after him.

24 OCTOBER   **1791**   Today, according to *The Scots Magazine*, a young man from Bristol visited the lunatics at Bedlam. He looked into one cell and asked the poor man inside what had brought him to this place. When the man remained silent, and only stared sadly at him, he grew angry and spat in the man's face through the grate. The lunatic wiped his face with a piece of straw and replied: 'I am here, Sir, because God deprived me of that blessing which you never enjoyed.'

25 OCTOBER   **1760**   George II died on this day, very suddenly, at the age of 76. After rising at 6 a.m. for his usual glass of hot chocolate, and an early morning walk around the gardens of Kensington, he retired to his water closet. Suddenly, from inside, an enormous crash was heard, as if something heavy had fallen to the floor. His German valet opened the door and found the King sprawled, speechless, upon the floor; a slight wound was on his temple, where he had cut his face falling against the corner of a bureau. Mr Andrews, the surgeon, was fetched, but it was too late: the King was dead. His daughter, Princess Amelia, was called; she was nearly deaf, and leant her face towards the King's to hear his last words – before she realised, to her great sorrow, that he was already gone. Nearly a pint of blood was found in the royal chest when it was opened, which had burst from a hole the size of a little finger in his right ventricle. The King had complained of pain in the chest and a feeling of 'sinking' in the heart for quite some time, but 'the effort of straining which his Majesty had just made in his closet' was thought to have brought about his undoing.

26 OCTOBER   **1718**   In another closet-related tragedy, Anne Buncher, of St Giles', Cripplegate, threw her baby girl into a toilet on this day. The servant boy brought landlady Mrs Taylor the disturbing news: he could see something glinting in the depths of the outhouse. A 'night man' was brought, and he hooked out a baby's body; a midwife swiftly confirmed that Anne had shortly before been delivered of a child. Anne confessed that she had put the dead child in her apron and carried it down to the privy when an opportunity presented itself; she had lost the baby, she thought, in a bad fall six weeks before. The child's father was a lodger from her last place of work, who had seduced her when she went in to make his bed. She was found not guilty of murder.

1729 The Old Bailey records contain the following strange crime:

> John Swart was indicted for the Murder of Elizabeth Hether, by flinging Salt in her Eyes, which so grieved and distempered the said Elizabeth Hether, that she languished from the 10th of October last to the 27th of the said Month, and then died, but as it did not appear to be done with Malice aforethought, the Jury acquitted him.

1817 One of the constables in St George's in the East complained to the Shadwell magistrates that a horse kept stealing hay from the coach-stands in his parish. The horse would turn up, all by itself, every night, eat as much hay as it wanted and then gallop off again. If anyone tried to stop it, it would kick them, run at them or try to bite them. The constable therefore presented the case to the magistrates, who were rather amused by the whole tale. 'Well, Mr Constable,' replied one, 'if you should be annoyed again by this animal in the execution of your duty, you may apprehend him if you can, and bring him before us to answer your complaints.'

Also on this day, Hammersmith fisherman John Bennet agreed to head out to sea with George Sugg. During the trip, carried out the following week, Bennet beat a boy that accompanied them, George Main (11), to death with the tiller of their ship. The sad litany of abuse began when the boy, who had been carrying their catch to shore, slipped and dropped the fish back into the water. Bennet whipped him with a rope for it. He began thereafter to ill-treat and starve him, to strip him and to beat him with a homemade cat o'nine tails. Then the boy, in a rare moment of friendliness, made the mistake of eating more than he was allowed; 'Sirrah!' said Bennet, 'if you offer to eat a bit of Bread without asking my leave, I'll strip your Skin over your Shoulders.' On the return trip to London, Bennet noticed that the ill-treated boy was now suffering from lice – hardly surprising, given that he had been given only one shirt to wear for the last three months. Bennet forced some of the creatures into the boy's mouth. On this, Bennet's fellow fisherman left the boat in disgust, and the 11-year-old was left to face his awful fate alone. When next seen, he was in a 'sad condition'. Blood was running from cuts on his face 'like a spout'. Soon afterwards, the boat sailed up to Hammersmith with the 'blackish' and battered corpse of the boy on board. When Bennet fetched the coffin-maker for him, one Henry Banks responded – and found the naked body of the boy wedged in a tiny space, only 14in square. He had crawled in to escape his vicious master, and died there. The boy had been witnessed in a variety of situations before his death, including working in the frost, soaked to the skin and starving, in nothing but a waistcoat and breeches (if he tried to add any clothing he was whipped). His brain was found to be bruised, but, as the prisoner previously had a very good character, and as he insisted that the boy's death was caused by an accidental fall, he was found guilty of manslaughter only.

1733 On this day, a baby born to Mary Doe (16) died. The next day, a midwife called Frances Crook was sent for; she found that Mary had certainly given birth, but no child was to be found. A great detective mystery began, with a dolorous ending. Stubborn and intuitive, Frances was not to be thrown from the trail: she hounded Mary until she confessed that 'something had come from her, but it was no child'.

'It signify'd nothing to deny it,' Frances told the court, 'for I was sure she had had a child, and therefore a child I would find.' Eventually, Mary agreed that she had indeed given birth, to a boy – but the boy was born dead, she insisted, and had been taken away by her father, a journeyman carpenter. The father entered the room, and the midwife realised, to her horror, that he had been abusing his daughter. The missing child was his. The moment she realised this, Frances angrily accused him – and he ran. Mary confessed that the guess was correct – 'that her Father had lain with her, and that she never had to do with any other Man but him'. The father sent the midwife a note through his wife, declaring that the dead child could be found wrapped in an old curtain and hidden by a pig's house, buried with the horse manure, at 'Tom Turd's-Hole', the place where the night-soil men dumped their carts of London excrement. It was found there soon afterwards. A surgeon placed one of the baby's lungs in a pot of water, and it floated – proof that the baby had breathed before it died. It had bled to death, said the surgeon, when no one tied the umbilical cord. The girl was acquitted, and the father ended his days, when captured, in Reading Gaol.

30 OCTOBER   1816   On this day, Edward Turner (25) was indicted at the Old Bailey for causing the death of his rival, John Curtis, at a prize fight in Moulsey Hurst, a famous Surrey boxing-match arena. The two men fought on the ground for an hour and twenty minutes, and by the end of it Curtis was finished. The dead man's father told the court that Turner had been very fair to his son, and had held his hands aloft when his rival was lying on the ropes so that people could see he was not taking unfair advantage of his near-unconscious situation. Curtis was carried to the Red Lion at Hampton, where Mr Griffin, the surgeon, found his face so battered that he could scarcely recognise a single feature of it; Curtis could neither speak nor swallow. He died four hours later. Curtis had used the most insistent insults to get his rival into the ring, but had found himself much inferior. He had refused to admit this, however, and when carried out of the ring he had simply climbed back into it. Turner was jailed for three months, and fined 1s.

31 OCTOBER   1718   Richard Morgan, of St Clement Danes, stabbed a boy called Humphry Wild in the left buttock with a penknife on this day. The wound was 6in deep and divided several arteries; Humphry died just over two weeks later. Morgan told the court that he had seen the deceased rob a man's pocket, and, when he had charged him with it, the boy had let loose with a barrage of insults, concluding by calling him a 'fat-ars-d-Dick' and threatening to stab him – at which point Morgan had borrowed a penknife and scuffled with the boy, falling onto him and stabbing him as he fell. The verdict was swift: guilty of murder with a sentence of death.

NOVEMBER

Mary Tofts clutching a rabbit – the positioning is clearly a little joke on the part of the artist. As her imposition involved hiding sections of rabbit in very intimate parts of her body, it's no wonder she looks a bit uncomfortable.

1 NOVEMBER   **1749**   'Horatio' Walpole was robbed by the famous Irish highwayman James MacLean (26), a former grocer and chandler of Welbeck Street turned gentleman highwayman and fortune-hunter, in this season. MacLean was 'of person middle Size, well Limb'd, a sandy Complexion, a broad open Countenance, [and] pitted with the Small-pox'. Walpole said:

> One night, in the beginning of November 1749, as I was returning from Holland House by moonlight, about ten o'clock, I was attacked by two highwaymen in Hyde Park, and the pistol of one of them going off accidentally, razed the skin under my eye, left some marks of shot on my face, and stunned me. The ball went through the top of the chariot, and if I had sat an inch nearer to the left side, must have gone through my head.

Mr John Taylor, of the *Sun* newspaper, describes MacLean as a tall, showy, good-looking man. He was finally caught when he tried to sell some lace back to the very man who had sold it in the first place. However, since he was very handsome, and decided to cry in court, he won the hearts of several rich London ladies and lived in a very fine style in the Gatehouse before his execution.

2 NOVEMBER   **1791**   The *Gentleman's Magazine* reported an inferno on this day at the house of Mrs Clitherow, a firework-maker at the upper end of Halfmoon Alley, near Bishopsgate Street. The Clitherow team – two men, plus Mrs Clitherow and her daughter – were hard at work making their 5 November orders when one of the fireworks caught fire during a tea break. Miss Clitherow ran upstairs to wake her three sisters, whilst Mrs Clitherow and one of the men ran down to try and put out the fire. It was too late to reach the sisters, and, when Miss Clitherow tried to escape herself, she found flames blocking the front door. She ran into the yard instead – where she discovered her clothes were on fire. The workman with her threw her bodily into a waterbutt, but then a huge explosion brought a roof-beam down on his arm, shattering it. Mr Gibbs, who lived next door, was blown into the street by the same explosion, and his lodger was blown out of his bed and into the street, splintering his thighs when he landed. The daughter and the other workman were found entombed in the smoking ruins later on, much hurt. They were sent to St Bartholomew's and St Thomas's respectively, but the daughter died on the 14th. Mrs Clitheroe, the three daughters sleeping upstairs, and the young man who had gone into the shop below to help put out the flames, were all killed. The house was completely destroyed; the houses next door were very much damaged, and windows were blown out (and tiles blown off) as far away as Broad Street. The explosion could be heard all the way from Fleet Street, and sounded like an earthquake. The next day, the roasted skeletons of three children were found in the ruins, along with a single arm belonging to Mrs Clitherow. It was recognised by the rings on her fingers. Her husband had been blown up in a firework accident at the same house thirty years before. One of two remaining sons drowned in an unrelated accident on the Thames the next week.

1734   On this day, tobacconists George and John Sutton leapt upon Abigail Bingo in St Peter's Alley and stole a gold ring set with a stone, a black silk glove, a bunch of keys and 20*d*. They came up behind her in the dark and kicked her heels so she fell, catching her middle as she slipped and flipping her over. They then kicked her, shattering her arm, and stole everything she had. Both were acquitted, but remained in jail to answer other charges of robbery across the region.

3 NOVEMBER

1719   On this day, Sarah Nicholson, of St Peter's, was charged with wrapping her newborn baby boy in a linen cloth and putting him in a trunk, whereupon he suffocated. The landlady, Mrs Linegar, had noticed an unusual and awful stench pervading from her lodger's room, and, when she realised where it was coming from, she had called for a constable. Inside the trunk they found the tiny infant wrapped up in a handkerchief. Sarah proved in court that the child had been stillborn, and was dead when she put it into storage; she was therefore acquitted.

4 NOVEMBER

1721   At about 2 a.m., watchmen in Princes Street, St James's, were disturbed by a great shriek. They came running and found Constance Radison sprawled on the floor, rather the worse for drink and screaming out that she had been 'stuck'. They helped her up and she went on her way. A little later, the watchmen saw a man walk into Princes Street with his sword drawn. 'I have stuck an old whore in the arse,' he said, 'and sent her about her business.' They seized him, and he immediately offered them half a crown to let him go. His name was Robert Bembridge, and he was carried off to the magistrate, Sir Thomas Clarges, swearing that he would pay for a doctor, and that his sword had been in its scabbard when he did it. The point of his blade, 'misty' with blood and actually bent at the end, told a rather different story. Meanwhile, the old lady he had stabbed was stretched out on the cold brick floor of the cellar in which she lived, groaning continually and neither eating nor drinking. The rogue who did it, she said, had trampled on her belly and stomach as she lay on the ground. However, in court her continual drinking and the coldness of the ground was decided upon as the main cause of her death; Bembridge was burnt on the hand and released.

5 NOVEMBER

1802   Today, Mr John Cole Steele was robbed and murdered on Hounslow Heath in a very barbaric manner. Four years later, one Benjamin Hanfield lay dying on board a prison hulk at Portsmouth, awaiting transportation, and decided he wished to clear his account before the end. He was carried to Bow Street, pointing out the scene of the crime on the way and naming John Holloway – tall, brutal-looking and aged around 40 – and the smaller Haggerty as his accomplices. The victim was a lavender grower who went missing on his journey home one day. His family eventually discovered his body stuffed into a ditch near to a barracks. He was marked with many wounds, and a thick leather strap had been wrapped around his neck. A bludgeon had been abandoned by him, and he had evidently been dragged into the ditch and left to die by one or more attackers. His skull had been

6 NOVEMBER

The vicious murder of Steele – Hanfield can be seen sneaking away in the background.

broken both at the front and the back, and his right arm was purple with bruising.

The feverish Hanfield described how Haggerty had called out to him from the Turk's Head, Dyot Street, and invited him to participate in a 'Low Toby' – a footpad robbery. As darkness fell, they waited for Mr Steele in a clump of trees on the lonely highway. At first all was amiable: Steele handed over his money, and hoped that the men 'would not use him ill'; as they began to search him, however, he began to struggle, and the robbery took an ugly twist. A carriage began to clatter towards them, at which Holloway swore, and said, 'Take care; I will silence him!' He then smashed Mr Steele's skull with the bludgeon, and dropped him, stunned, to the floor. The coachman later told the court that he had heard two deep groans, one fainter than the other, as he rattled past that night, and that he had remarked that, 'there was something desperate carrying on there...' Hanfield, horror-stricken, left his friends to finish the job on their own. When next he saw them they were modelling the victim's hat. As the public outrage about the crime grew, they disposed of the evidence by throwing the hat, filled with stones, from Westminster Bridge. The two men themselves sealed their doom by falling for the oldest trick of all: Officer James Bishop of the Worship Street police office put the two prisoners in cells next to each other, and then hid himself in a privy attached to both of the rooms, where he could make notes on everything they said to one another.

Unfortunately for them, they decided to talk about certain details of the case. They came to the gallows on 23 February 1807, Holloway kneeling on his way to the rope and declaring, 'By God, I am innocent!'

In a further tragedy, twenty-seven people died and many more were hurt as the enormous crowd surged forward to watch the drop fall. As the crowds cleared afterwards, Londoners who had been trampled over were picked up and carried on boards to St Bartholomew's, where their mangled remains were identified by their weeping loved ones.

1735 On this day, at a silk dyer's house in Fetter Lane (where Elizabeth Brownrigg was to horrify the world with another crime of captivity decades later), the daughter of Anna Maria Thorn, Anna Maria Thorn jnr (15) perished. According to the indictment, she had been locked in a cold room without proper food or heat since March. Anna Maria had three daughters: Dorothy, Charlotte and the deceased. The tale began – as in the Brownrigg case – when Anna Maria was caught stealing food in an attempt to ward off starvation. Her landlady decided to do some detective work: she started to peer through the keyhole at dinnertime, and saw the mother and two daughters eating heartily whilst Anna Maria jnr stood by, 'trembling'. After their meal, Anna Maria was handed a tiny scrap of food – sometimes just a small piece of cabbage. One scrap of liver she ate eagerly, causing her mother to say, 'Hussy! How you cram it in!' When the landlady spoke to the mother about her cruel treatment, she was told she was 'a lying scoundrel'. This made her jump, for the woman was normally 'very civil' to her. The kind-hearted landlady started to hide food for the girl under the 'charcoal dust tub' in the yard. If she complained to anyone, the girl said she was beaten. When the landlady expressed her surprise that she had not heard any of this, the girl shocked her still further: 'My Mamma stuffs her Handkerchief in my Mouth when she beats me.' At last, the girl died: she was 'an Anatomy, as if she had nothing but Skin drawn over her Bones'. In court, the mother produced references to say that she was 'often solicitous when they [her children] had the small Pox', amongst other signs of attention. The jury decided to clear her of the charge.

Also on this day, but in 1783, the very last felon swung at Tyburn: John Austin, a highway robber who had robbed John Spicer. As a newcomer to London, Spicer asked two men to 'help him find lodgings'. Instead, they took him to a field, where they 'chopped at [him] several times' with a cutlass, tied him up and threw him to the floor. Spicer said, '[they] cut me across both hands, and a very bad cut over my wrist, and two or three on my head, and one on my leg.' John Austin told the judge, 'I am innocent, and I do not think much of dying.'

1782 John Barnard died today of the injuries he sustained when James Wellbeloved of Lombard Court (who did not earn his name) punched him in the face. Barnard had pushed James on the 7th after a drunken argument in the street; James had responded by striking him – knocking him to the stones, where he lay, gaping like a fish, for six minutes before he could speak. Blood ran slowly out of his ear. Wellbeloved was fined 1*s* for causing the man's death.

1726 On this day in 1716, the Queen gave birth to a stillborn son. Ten years later, Guildford surgeon and midwife Mr Howard, and the King's own surgeon, Nathaniel St Andre, were duped by one of the most infamous and

7 NOVEMBER

8 NOVEMBER

9 NOVEMBER

imaginative con-women of the eighteenth century: Mary Tofts, the 'rabbit woman of Goldalming'. The story began when Mary, according to the most reputable reports, gave birth to five rabbits. She then gave birth to three more rabbits. Today, the two doctors visited – and 'delivered the poor woman of three more rabbits'. Some literally 'leapt' from the woman. On the 15th, the Prince of Wales' secretary, the Hon. Mr Molyneux, visited to see this marvel. He found Mary at Mr Howard's house, in labour...

> ...dressed in her stays ... I waited for the coming on of fresh pains, which happened in three or four minutes, at which time I delivered her of the entire trunk, stripped of its skin, of a rabbit of about four months growth.

Her right side felt lumpy, as though more rabbits were 'bred in those tubes'. She then produced the skin, 'rolled up and squeezed like a ball', and then 'the head of the rabbit with the fur on it'. All of the rabbits were 'broken into pieces' – delivered as forepaws, liver and intestines, the trunk and shoulders, the thighs, the head, and lastly the skin – and the doctors put them all in jars of spirits. They all had sharp little claws and 'complete numbers of teeth'. On 26 November, 'all of these facts were verified before his Majesty', with anatomical demonstration using four of the foetuses.

Mary explained that she had been working in her garden when pregnant on 23 April, and had seen a rabbit run by. This set up a 'longing for rabbits'

Nathaniel St Andre – looking woebegone, as well he might.

which in turn made her start dreaming of rabbits, and gave her 'a constant and strong desire to eat rabbits'. Mr Howard swore that as he was delivering one rabbit, he could feel the one behind it 'struggling with such violence, that the motion could be sensibly seen and felt'. A pension from the King was promised. Then, when Mary started producing what looked very like a hog's bladder, suspicions started to grow. On 29 November, Mary was brought to Mr Lacey's bagnio in Leicester Fields, where she had 'frequent contractions of her fingers, rolling of her eyes, and great risings in her stomach'. Then Thomas Porter, the porter at the bagnio, told Sir Thomas Clarges that he had clandestinely purchased rabbits for Mary. She tried to claim that these were just for eating, but was eventually forced to confess to inserting sections of rabbits for the purposes of defrauding the general public. She was sent to Tothill Fields but was eventually released without charge. She returned home.

1724   A curious document, written on this day in 1813, records the cost   10 NOVEMBER
of a hanging: 7s 6d for the execution, 4s 6d for stripping the body and 3s 6d for the 'use of Shell' (the coffin).

The famous Spitalfields resident Jack Sheppard (23), one of the most notorious thieves and prison-breakers in the history of Britain, made his last appearance in court today. A housebreaker and extraordinarily gifted escape artist – he had two plans in place even under the gallows – he was finally

Jack Sheppard.

held and executed on 16 November 1724. An apprentice carpenter, he first fell into bad company at the Black Lion alehouse in Drury Lane, where he met Elizabeth Lyon, known to history as 'Edgworth Bess', and started housebreaking – including the house of his own master, Mr Kneebone. Soon after, he started prison breaking: when Bess was arrested, he simply knocked down the beadle and let her out again.

Then James 'Hell and Fury' Sykes handed him over to the law in return for a reward – forcing Jack to smash through the roof of the St Giles' roundhouse and escape. Next he was arrested and sent to New Prison (where he stayed in a room with his 'wife', Edgworth Bess) – where he managed his second escape, by filing off his fetters with tools smuggled in by friends, cutting through the window bars, and climbing down the wall on the classic rope of sheets. Next, after being caught and

Jack Sheppard in his special chains, stapled to the floor – he was out of some of them before the warder even reached the ground floor.

sentenced to death, he escaped again, forcing the ordinary of Newgate to publish his life story without the scenes at the gallows – for Jack was not there. He had cut through the bars of the hatch at the condemned hold's door and wriggled through. Next time he appeared at Newgate, he was put in 'the castle' (the strongest part of the gaol) and loaded with chains, which tied his legs together – and were stapled to the floor. No one who could possibly be carrying tools was allowed to see him – but what the gaolers did not see was a small nail on the floor. Jack used it to unlock the 'great horse padlock' holding him to the floor, and slept very comfortably wherever he wished in the cell. However, one day he was caught out of his chains – and a pair of handcuffs was added to the haul. These he was out of before the warder even got to the bottom of the stairs. Then he twisted a small iron link from the chain between his legs, went up the narrow chimney, and used the iron fragments to break through the bars there. He then took an iron bar up the chimney with him and used it to cut through the doors or walls of all the rooms above him. He made his way onto the roof of the prison, along to the roofs of the houses nearby, in through a window, and down the stairs to freedom – 'Lord, what noise is that?' said a woman there. A man replied, 'Perhaps a dog or cat.'

Wearing extremely fine clothes, rings and a top-class wig, he was then arrested for the last time. He had spent the last two days of liberty drinking with two mistresses, and was blind drunk. As he climbed into the death cart, he had a penknife, facing upwards, in his pocket, ready to cut the ropes that held him so he could run over the heads of the crowd and away. Unfortunately, an officer named Watson patted him down and cut his hand on it – and it was taken away. His final plan – for friends to cut him down swiftly and restore his body to life after hanging – also went awry. He is buried in St Martin in the Fields.

1800   Post boy Thomas Chalfont (17) could not resist temptation on this day, and took a £10 note from a letter containing three such notes. When the letter arrived at its destination a day late, and with the words on the accompanying letter crudely changed to suggest that two notes, worth £20 in total, were enclosed, the customer called in the authorities. The bank traced the missing note to Thomas, who had used it to pay a bill at the post office. He had written his own name on the back. Chalfont was sent to the gallows. He was the second postman to be executed for such a crime.   **11 NOVEMBER**

1740   John Cunningham (14) died on this day. He had been bird-catching with his friend John Robinson (13) in fields near Paddington at about 7.30 a.m. when he realised that another boy, Robert Williams, jealous of his amazing success, had sent a thug named Sharp to smash his traps. Sharp was a hulking teenager, much bigger than the two friends, and, when they caught him bending the twigs of their bird traps, he picked up a stick and began to hit them with it. Angry, the two boys made a revenge attack on Williams' nets, and sat on them all, one by one. When Williams appeared, Cunningham refused to get up – he stubbornly remained, sitting on the   **12 NOVEMBER**

ruins of a trap, even whilst he was kicked and hit. The stick he was whipped with was the width of a thumb; the kick was aimed at his private parts. He lay on the grass for several minutes afterwards, crying, 'Murder!' The two boys then walked sadly home, Cunningham complaining that his groin hurt. Surgeon Thomas Cooper found the boy in 'desperate convulsions':

> He was the next day in very great pain. All he said was, O my belly! O my belly! Not a word how it was done, nor who did it. Upon searching him, I found a rupture: one testicle was swelled, and very black.

Sharp's father brought his son to see the boy before he died:

> Sharp fell upon his knees, and said forgive me. Cunningham said yes, I do: God bless you. I heard him say, Williams! Williams! just before he died.

It was revealed in court that Williams had not been responsible for the final, fatal kick, and so he was acquitted at the very sad court case in December.

13 NOVEMBER **1755** On this day, the governors at the Bridewell Hospital were forced to conclude that their 'Bridewell boys', raised and educated in a trade at the prison, had been particularly riotous at Southwark and Bartholomew Fairs. Several were whipped. Worse, some were whipped and then thrown out – losing all hope of learning a trade and the £10 bonus that went with it.

14 NOVEMBER **1821** On this day, Ann Bantling was taken to the laying-in ward of the workhouse infirmary. Two days later a midwife was sent for, and Ann gave birth to a stillborn daughter. The midwife paid her some ten-minute visits afterwards, but each time she seemed worse – until she died. A neighbour revealed that she had heard cries and the swishing of a stick before Ann went into the workhouse. The cause was Algernon Disney, and he was beating Ann for the crime of 'not opening the door in the manner she was told to'. Ann had then run down the street, but was dragged back by him, grabbing on to the railings all the way. Her nose was bleeding, and she attempted to get passers-by to save her. The next morning she appeared very much bruised. Her neck, shoulders and ear were black with whipmarks. However, though the surgeon at her post-mortem found her posterior black with whipping, they found that an infection had occasioned her death; Disney was found not guilty of murder.

15 NOVEMBER **1716** Augustine Lincoln, who worked at the Swan Tavern in Cornhill, threw a knife at fellow servant Robert Fibbot today after a fight over the way Lincoln ate oysters. Lincoln ended up charging across the bar and kicking at Fibbot, who started to retreat – until Lincoln threw his oyster knife at the man, hitting him in the thigh. He caught an artery, and his friend – for until then they had been great pals – died of the blood loss that resulted. A verdict of manslaughter was given.

1763 John Wilkes published an article describing fellow MP Samuel Martin as having, amongst other attributes, 'a snout worthy of a Portuguese inquisitor'. He wrote in a subsequent edition 'of the most treacherous, base, selfish, mean, abject, low-lived, and dirty fellow that ever wriggled himself into a secretaryship'. Martin was so angry that he dedicated himself to practicing marksmanship; he then challenged Wilkes to a duel. He was lucky enough to be accepted: Wilkes once replied to a challenge with the response: 'Sir, I do not think it my business to cut the throat of every desperado that may be tired of his life.' The line about the snout may have been a bit rich: Wilkes was notoriously ugly. However, he claimed it took him just half an hour to talk away his face before success with any woman he set his cap at was ensured. He had six children by different women. The two men met in Hyde Park on this day, each with a set of pistols. Martin fired and missed; Wilkes' pistol misfired. They then took their second gun and aimed: Wilkes missed, but Mr Martin shot the editor of the *North Briton* in the gut. Mr Graves took out the ball, which had struck Mr Wilkes' coat-button, entered his belly half an inch below the navel, and sunk obliquely on the right side towards the groin. It was extracted from behind and Wilkes made a recovery. One week later, John Wilkes fled to France, with the help of friends, in order to avoid arrest for seditious libel, on order of parliament, for insulting the King.

1770 George Garrick's duel with Mr Baddeley of the Drury Lane Theatre was disrupted today by the latter's wife, the famous actress Sophia Baddeley, running dramatically between the two and crying, 'Spare him! Oh, spare him.' She later left her husband for an extremely remunerative career as a courtesan.

Cornelius Crawley (25) was arrested on this day in 1814 at Perkins's Rents, Pie Street, Westminster – whilst he was in bed with his partner, one Catherine Hall. As he was rattling along to Bow Street, he told the officer that the handbill that had led to his arrest was 'a very bad description'. He was charged with killing George Dixon at Vine Street, Covent Garden, that August. The murder weapon was a poker. Catherine Raine, the pair's landlady, had heard a great noise when Crawley returned home that fateful day and then heard a soft voice calling, 'pray do not.' She had gone up the stairs and found Dixon bleeding, with a fractured skull. Dixon was a former lover of Catherine's whom she had bumped into in the street. After drinks in Round Court, they had returned to the bedroom – only for the husband to return home. In the couple's room, a pool of blood and a poker snapped in half were found. George died in St George's, attended by surgeon Sydney Chopping (!). Mr Crawley got six months' and 1s fine.

1742 A neighbour heard a scream in a single pensioner's house in Fetter Lane and looked up – to see blood fly all over the nearest window. He saw a man in a woollen cap peep through the window, but could not tell who it was. When onlookers broke into the house, they found that blood was dripping down from the ceiling – it was seeping through the floor of the room above. There they found Susannah Dix (74) sprawled on the floor 'in her gore blood'. Her temple was smashed, and her brain wounded. A surgeon was fetched but she could only say, 'O Lord! O Lord!' He said, 'Madam, as you can speak you should tell who did it, but she only said, 'Lord! Lord!' Thomas Homan was found hiding in her cellar. A dirty, bloody old iron bar lay nearby. His hand was 'all over bloody to the finger ends'.

He had only meant to rob her, he confessed, but she had come down the stairs and seen him.

'Tom, what do you want?' she had asked. Then she ran. He grabbed a poker, and she the fire-tongs, and for an electric moment they looked at each other – and then he struck. She screamed, and he beat her to death so she could not discover him. He was executed at the end of Fetter Lane, nearest to the place where he had murdered the old gentlewoman.

19 NOVEMBER   1831   A kidnapping at the very end of the Georgian era came to its conclusion on this day, when a house in Nova Scotia Gardens was searched.

On 5 November, porter William Hill opened the door of the dissecting rooms at King's College, Somerset House. He found John Bishop and James May standing at the door. May, swaying rather drunkenly, told the porter that he had 'a male subject' for him – a boy of about 14. He asked for 14 guineas for the corpse. Mr Richard Partridge, the demonstrator of anatomy, was fetched, and, after haggling over the remains, a price was fixed. The men returned that afternoon, carrying an ominous hamper. Another man was with them, one Thomas Williams. Inside the hamper was a sack containing the small body, which May upended casually. The corpse's left arm was stiff, and his fingers clenched. No signs of a coffin's sawdust could be seen upon him. Bishop remarked that Partridge could not find a fresher corpse; the porter, looking closely, realised that the body was indeed fresh – particularly fresh. He asked what the boy had died from, and they replied that they did not know – 'it was no business of mine or theirs'. Whilst the men waited for their payment by the fire, the surgeon and several students were called – and they all agreed that it was very suspicious. On the pretence of fetching change, Partridge went for the police. Struggling all the way, the men were taken to the watchhouse.

Mr Partridge told the court how his suspicions had been raised when he saw the body, and noticed his swollen face, bloodshot eyes and rigid limbs. The next day, at the station in James Street, Covent Garden, together with Mr George Beaman, he made a fuller post-mortem. He found the body still rigid, suggesting that the boy had been dead but thirty-six hours. His bloodshot eyes were protruding from his face; his tongue was forced out between his lips and blood was trickling from his mouth. Inside, a stranger sight awaited: all of his front teeth had been ripped out, taking sections of gum with them. The stomach was full, and smelled slightly of rum. He had eaten about three hours before he died. Dentist Mr Mills later returned twelve teeth, which he had bought from the prisoners for 12s.

Joseph Sadler Thomas, superintendent of Division F, interviewed the three men. May told him that the corpse was Bishop's, and that he had merely gone along to fetch the money; Williams told him that he had merely gone along 'out of curiosity, to see the building'. Bishop said that he had the body because he was 'a bloody bodysnatcher'. All three were drunk – May was so drunk that he was actually carried into the room on all fours, 'scuffling' and with his shirt over his head.

The police found the fatal cottage in Nova Scotia Gardens on this day. In a back room they found a trunk, and the next day a 'hairy cap'. Tools covered in blood were found (with which the men had forced out the teeth), and clothes with more blood (and clay) upon them were discovered at May's lodgings. Behind the house, softness in the soil (which they probed with rods) revealed a bundle of small clothes, with blood upon the collar and a shirt torn right up the front.

Waiter Henry Lock of the Fortune of War, Giltspur Street, told the court that he had seen the men with a silk handkerchief – a handkerchief filled with human teeth. As he watched, May had washed them, one by one. They were worth £2, he had told the astonished man.

It turned out that Bishop and Williams had been hawking the body all over London: the porter at Guy's told the court how he had refused it, though he let them store the body there, where it remained (with one foot sticking out of the sack, and one knee poking through a hole) overnight. James Appleton of Mr Grainger's anatomical theatre, Webb Street, Southwark had also turned it down.

Then Augustine Broom entered the Old Bailey, and described how he had brought 'Italian boy' Carlo Ferrier over to London to be his apprentice. He had last seen him alive on 28 July 1830, at Mr Elliot's in Charles Street, Drury Lane. Organ player Joseph Paragell had seen him at the Quadrant, Regent Street, and others had seen him in Oxford Street. Both Broom and Paragell recognised the body, and others his clothes and cap.

In a sign of things to come, bodysnatcher Bishop – who, in twelve years, had sold between 500 and 1,000 bodies – begged the jury to try and forget any press coverage they might have read which had prejudiced their minds against him. Bricklayer and fireman Williams (26) said he knew nothing of the body, and butcher May (30) of the Strand, with six years in the procurement trade, claimed that the blood on his clothes came from a pet jackdaw which had been accidentally pinched by a door and had then flown around the room. All three were sentenced to death.

John Bishop confessed in Newgate to luring the boy to his house on the promise of work. They had then given him bread, cheese and rum laced with laudanum. When the boy passed out, they lowered him by a rope around his ankles into the depths of a well in the yard. He struggled and made the water bob and bubble. Three quarters of an hour later, after a stroll, they hauled him out, stripped him and put him in a box wrapped with cord. The clothes were buried where they were found. They had bumped into May that same morning, and he offered to help them get a fair deal for the body. He also showed them how to force out the teeth before sale for an even better return, levering them out with an awl. However, May did not know how this fresh-looking corpse had been obtained: he assumed the body had been stolen from a grave, as was usual in their trade.

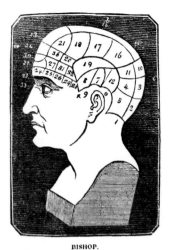

BISHOP.

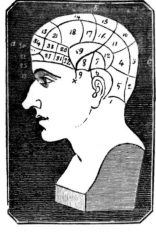

WILLIAMS.

Phrenological
studies of Bishop
and Williams'
heads, with the
crime scene and
a portrait of the
victim, Carlo Ferrari
/ Ferriers.

BISHOP'S COTTAGE.

As the end approached, Bishop also confessed to murdering Fanny Pigburn (35) – thin, tall and much marked with the smallpox – on 9 October 1831 after he and Williams had spotted her sitting by a church in Shoreditch. Fanny had been thrown out of her lodgings with her 5-year-old daughter, and had nowhere to go. They had offered her a seat by their fire, and then arranged to meet her again soon. She too went down the well, and was left there so that the rum and laudanum might run out of her mouth into the water. The whereabouts of her child were not known.

They had also murdered a 10-year-old boy named Cunningham on 21 October, after finding him huddled under the pig-boards by the pigs at Smithfield Market. A few cups of warm beer and laudanum, and he too went into the well. He slipped into unconsciousness in one of Bishop's children's chairs, and was sold to St Bartholomew's for 8 guineas.

The crowd at their execution was enormous and 'exceeded all calculation': barricades were thrown up along the route, and houses with even a partial view were let for an extraordinary price. The gallows went up opposite the debtors' door, Newgate. Three chains were put up, but then one was taken down – May had been respited. Hoots and jeers rumbled through the crowd when this was announced. When May himself heard the news, he dropped to the floor 'as if struck by lightning', and suffered such a violent fit that the officers thought that his 'warrant of mercy had proved his death-blow'. When he was restored, he shook hands with limbs that were shaking violently.

Bishop was led to the press room and pinioned, and Williams followed, his face pale as ice and with tears standing out in his eyes. As they ran down his cheeks, he said, 'I have made my peace with God.' Bishop walked unsteadily onto the boards beneath the gallows first – and, as he did so, 'the most astounding yells, hooting, and cheers that we ever heard resounded through the immense crowd'. They cheered until the drop fell – and then the crowd surged forward so strongly that a barrier towards Smithfield came down. The board collapsed across the chest of three people, injuring them dreadfully, and the crowd's feet ran over many more in the crush. Every bed in the Compter Ward of St Bart's was filled. Williams came next, to even louder cheers. An hour later, when the executioner came to cut down the bodies for dissection, the crowd cheered again, and followed the cart of corpses all the way to Hosier Lane. Bishop went to King's College, and Williams to St Bartholomew's, to serve the very men they had themselves often supplied with material.

1755 On this day, Isabella Buckham, spinster, called out for the bed pan from her sickbed in Faith's Ward of St Bartholomew's Hospital. She could be heard groaning and being sick. Later that night, at between 1 and 2 a.m., a strange noise was heard in the ward – a shriek. 'Do you not hear a child cry?' was the question that flew around the room. All agreed they did, but no one could account for the sound. Isabella then called for the nurse, Ann Smith. 'Nurse,' she said, 'my sheets are all wet.' When Ann turned down her bedding, she found her covered with blood and water. 'I said, God bless me, here has been a child,' she informed the Old Bailey. Isabella insisted that she had had no such thing. The afterbirth in her bed said something different, as did her flannel petticoat, which had the 'print of a child' upon it. Clots of blood fell from the sheets as they were lifted, and bloody footprints could be traced from her bed to 'the vault'. Mr William Clutterburg poked inside this hole with an iron rod until he cleared a space, and this was searched. A 'fine male child' was discovered dead inside, with tiny nails and curling hair: 'It was as fine a child as I ever saw,' he said. Isabella at last confessed – the man who drove the Bethnal Green stagecoach was the father, and, had she been in her senses, she would never have treated her baby so. She was acquitted of murder on the 22nd.

20 NOVEMBER

1767   On this day, an event that would terminate in one of the most shocking crimes in all of London's history began. On the top floor of a flat in Tenter Alley, Little Moorfields, lived shoemaker Mr John Williamson (46) and his wife Anne (25). The woman in the flat below, Elizabeth Farringdon, had grown used to hearing Anne cry out, and occasionally begging Mrs Cole, Anne's stepdaughter, 'Don't let him use me so.' Then, one day in September, Anne came down to see Elizabeth. She cut an extraordinary figure, for her hands were behind her back – and they were held by a pair of iron handcuffs. She asked Elizabeth if she could take them off with a nail or the point of a fork; Elizabeth and her husband tried, but to no avail. 'I must go up and stay in misery as I am till he comes home,' she said, and trooped back up to her lonely attic. After this, Elizabeth told Mr Williamson that he was a 'bad man' as often as she dared, but the screams still echoed from the top floor with depressing frequency. Muffled shouts of 'Will you go in?' were heard, and thumps shook the ceiling as a body hit the floor. Williamson also began to spread filthy tales about Anne, claiming 'she was so swarming with vermin that he could not come near her'.

Then a new twist: a child, John's daughter Mercy (15), was heard crying out 'Pray father, dear father, don't do it!'

'Damn her for a bitch, I will!' was the reply.

Following that, on 15 December, strange dragging sounds were heard scraping across the ceiling. 'I thought sure the poor creature was dead,' Elizabeth told the Old Bailey. The next day, word came at last: poor Mrs Williamson was indeed dead. A gang of neighbours, Elizabeth included, crowded upstairs to view the body. 'She looked more like a skeleton than anything else,' they said. Her ankles, wrists and middle were covered with red marks, and her cheek and forehead were marked by blows. She was, as suggested, covered in lice.

Elizabeth then noticed an ominous door in the corner. She opened it, and found inside a pile of rags, and a staple driven into the wall. This closet had been Anne's home since 21 November. In court, one Anne Hart described a visit to the couple. Mr Williamson had been planning to go out for a drink, when his wife burst out, 'For God's sake, Mrs Hart, beg of him not to handcuff and tie me up, and I will be very good.' When Hart expressed horror at this, the husband had replied, 'I know best what I have got to do, I shall do it.' He then showed them a pair of iron handcuffs. 'The bitch has broke the lock of them,' he said. He also showed them the closet with the staple inside. A cord was tied to it. He bid Anne turn round, and without a word she did, placing her hands behind her back as she did so. The handcuffs went on, and she was roped into the closet. The staple was rather high, so that she had to remain on her tiptoes, and called out, 'Oh Mr Williamson! Oh Mr Williamson! You draw me so tight, you'll cut my hands asunder.' Williamson said that 'she always made that noise, and if she did not hold her tongue, he either would knock her head against the wall, or against the partition'. He then went out, leaving the miserable woman, her daughter and Mrs Hart in the room. Cuffed to the wall, Anne begged for a stool to stand on and a pinch of snuff to take. Mercy would not do it for fear of her father, but Mrs Hart obliged. She then told Williamson what she had done. 'I will break every bone in my daughter's skin for letting you put it under, for the bitch will get out of the closet!' he replied.

When the case came to the Old Bailey, Mercy gave evidence. She told of her mother going into the closet 'pretty often', and for 'a great while'. How long? she was asked. 'A month, I believe,' was the chilling reply. In all that time, Anne had not been let down, nor out to sleep or to use the bathroom. 'As far as I could I helped her, and so did Mrs Cole,' Mercy said. They were too frightened to let her down, lest she refuse to go back in again and they should all be beaten. She ate only once a day, when her husband placed a bit of bread on a shelf that she could reach with her mouth. The stool was not allowed into the closet during this entire month. Sometimes the door would be opened, and the husband would force his family to throw pints of water in her face 'by way of punishment'.

Poor Mrs Williamson in her cupboard. Other depictions of this same scene in rival editions of the Newgate Calendar include a basin of water poised in front of the door, ready for the water torture which became a new and horrible feature of her captivity shortly before she died. In this case, the basin is tucked rather demurely under the table. A piece of bread can be seen on the cupboard shelf.

The Sunday before Anne died, she was finally let down and fed. She was very weak, and staggered; she could eat but little. Sitting on her rags in the closet, she managed what she could with her swollen hands. The cuffs at last came off (they were never to be replaced). She remained in her closet that night, and the following day was allowed to shuffle towards the fire. She kissed her husband on the cheek – but when she tried to kill some of the lice that swarmed on her, she was ordered back into 'her kennel'. By the next morning, she had fallen into convulsions that shook the door of the closet. When it was opened, she was found with her face pressed against the wall; her face was working in a terrible fit. Foam and blood came out of her mouth. She had been subject to fits for years, and smaller fits shook her regularly as she stood in her cupboard. Her teeth were clenched tight, and no substance could be given to her. She shook for an hour and a half, slept for a brief moment and then awoke as a mad woman, calling her abuser 'Daddy'. A client came up that day to have a shoe mended, and must have been astonished to hear a voice from the cupboard saying, 'Daddy, let me out.'

'No,' said Williamson. 'Dress yourself and then you may come out.'

She had no shoes or underwear on, and so could not. That night was to be her last. Later that evening her husband touched her head, and found she had lapsed into speechlessness; her family gathered around by candlelight and touched her arms, which were warm. They suspected that she had not long to live, and they were right: she died at about 5 a.m. She spent the last hours of her life still stretched out in the gloom of her stinking cupboard.

Williamson was hanged at Moorfields on gallows facing Chiswell Street. He confessed to the crime just before the cart drew away. Around 10,000 people watched him drop. His children went into the Cripplegate Workhouse.

22 NOVEMBER **1721** A man called Thomas Burton walked into the Vine Tavern in Long Acre on this evening, rubbing his hands and declaring that he had set all the old women of the neighbourhood talking by firing off his pistols. Unfortunately for him, the road was very uneven and jolted him as he fired; it turned out that the bullets had struck an old woman as she was coming out of the Bull Head opposite. She died shortly afterwards.

23 NOVEMBER **1805** Thomas Burton (30) was imprisoned for a week for his first ever crime: the theft of 43 quires of paper from a printer in Fenchurch Street. A servant sent the errand boy running after him, who managed to corner him in Leadenhall Market. 'O Lord, David, did you see me take it?' Burton said. He was carried back shamefaced to his employer, and fined 1s to boot.

24 NOVEMBER **1774** 'Clive of India' died on this day. Walpole wrote, 'His constitution was exceedingly broken and disordered, and grown subject to violent pains and convulsions.' An excessive dose of laudanum to ease the pain saw him off.

Also on this day, a man revived as he was about to be anatomised. In September 1740, William Duell (16), the son of an Acton shoemaker, instigated an appallingly violent assault upon a young woman sleeping in a barn in Horn Lane, Acton. Six or seven of his friends joined him in this crime, and he was sentenced to death for it. The victim died soon afterwards. Duell repented of his crime, was hanged on 24 November, and came shortly afterwards to Surgeons' Hall, to be anatomised. As his naked body was being washed, however, he suddenly began to breathe; he was placed in a chair and looked after, and returned to Newgate in the evening, where his punishment was amended to transportation for life. (Other fantastic tales of London's revived include a very clever forger, who inserted a silver tube into her neck – presumably in the form of a tracheotomy that allowed her to breathe despite the clutch of the rope – and thus was restored to life by her friends after her date with the executioner.)

1788   Today, a terrible frost began that lasted for seven weeks. Whilst Londoners made merry on the ice, tens of thousands of men were thrown out of work. Several of the more unscrupulous watermen smashed holes in the ice and then charged people to use their planks to cross them. When the ice eventually broke, enormous lumps of ice went spinning down the Thames, causing damage to everything they passed. All of the boats were tied up, but the water ran so fast that some were ripped free. One at Rotherhithe tore off the supports of the house it was tied to as it went, killing five people inside.

   Also today, but in 1819, a gravedigger at St Botolph was buried up to the chin when the grave he was working on collapsed. 'For God's sake take me out, or I shall die!' he shouted. And die he did, a few hours later. *25 NOVEMBER*

1721   Isaac Ingram of St Andrew's, Holborn, fell out with his wife Mary this day when she would not come to breakfast. Eventually, she declared that she would not come even if it should kill her. Isaac was very piqued, and threw the iron poker he was holding at random towards the curtain. Unfortunately, it hit Mary on the head and cracked her skull, and the wound proved to be fatal. 'For God's sake, call a surgeon,' he called, 'for I believe I have killed my wife!' As he had no malice against her, nor any design or thought of hurting her, he was found guilty of manslaughter. *26 NOVEMBER*

1752   On this day, Sarah Pool had a drunken row with her husband John and accidentally killed him. They lived in King's Head Yard, Shoreditch, and were fighting over whether she would or would not go upstairs. She cried, 'I will not be pull'd about!' She then kicked him in the private parts, picked up a lump of brick lying nearby and threw it at his head. He clapped his hand to his face and said, 'I believe you have done it for me now.' Sarah was very frightened, and together they bound his head with a handkerchief, but to no avail: John had to go to London Hospital shortly afterwards, where the bone of his skull was showing; he was trepanned, but died the same day. His brain was proved to have mortified under the bruise, and his wife was found guilty of manslaughter. *27 NOVEMBER*

1740   This dark and rainy night, shoemaker Daniel Jackson of St George's, Bloomsbury, shot his wife in the back with a pistol in the middle of the street. As cabdriver Michael Moore was letting them out at St Giles', Jackson pulled *28 NOVEMBER* out two 10in pistols and 'flashed them'. His wife screamed, and Moore then heard two shots: he turned to see the woman crumpled on the floor, the pistols next to her and Jackson's right hand covered with blood. He had treated her brutally for two years, breaking her lip and nose and blacking her eyes more than once. He had also been witnessed forcing spirits down her throat, in an attempt to kill her through drink, and had been heard firing a pistol at her in their lodgings. She had taken to hiding his sword to prevent him from murdering her. However, she could not stop pieces of shot from two discharges drilling into her forehead and into her back, splitting her vertebrae and breaking her ribs. The edges of the two hideous wounds were actually burnt by the powder. Jackson claimed that the guns had gone off by accident as he pulled them from the bag, but the court disagreed and sentenced him to death. However, he cheated the gallows by secretly stabbing himself in the gut on the same night that he was committed to Newgate, using a slim shoemaker's knife to do it. He suffered in silence for a few days, and then confessed when one of the Newgate attendants found some bloody rags in his cell. A large lump of flesh was also discovered there, which he had cut off from the ragged wound when it began to rot. He died shortly afterwards. He was buried in Christ Church's Yard, with a letter in his pocket asking that his mother bury him with the remains of his wife.

29 NOVEMBER   **1779**   Charles Fox fought Mr Adam MP in Hyde Park at 8 a.m. after a sharp exchange of words in the House of Commons. When Fitzgerald, Fox's second, told Fox that he needed to stand sideways, his answer was comical: 'Why? I am as thick one way as the other.' Fox declared himself satisfied and refused to fire, so Adam shot him in the chest, wounding him but slightly. They then parted as friends, with the famous line, 'Egad! Adam, it would have been all over with me, if you had not been charged with Government powder!' (Government powder was notoriously poor.)

However, the most famous event of this day was the barbaric, immoral and disgusting behaviour of Captain Luke Collingwood, of the *Zong*, who threw 132 slaves overboard in 1781 so he could claim their insurance value – £30 per head. Showing the magnificence of the human spirit, the last ten refused to be pushed, but leapt overboard together – and 'leaping into the sea, felt a momentary triumph in the embrace of death'. Throwing slaves overboard was common practice: an estimate in 1825 gave the number of slaves thrown overboard in the Middle Passage per year – half of which were alive – as 3,000. A shortness of water was given as the captain's rationale for ditching his cargo into the ocean, but it was proved in court that not only had it rained a great deal throughout, but that not one sailor had been put on short-water rations. Collingwood died shortly afterwards, and no officers or crew were ever charged with murder. However, the case grew more and more notorious – especially when the solicitor general said that there was not even 'a surmise of impropriety' in the act: 'Blacks are goods and property; it is madness to accuse these well-serving honourable men of murder ... The case is the same as if wood had been thrown overboard.' Some slaves were subsequently 'rescued' in London by people inspired by reading about the case. These included one poor man who was kept on the Thames in conditions so cold that both his feet mortified, and he had to have them cut off at St Bartholomew's. Reading the details of this case inspired abolitionist Thomas Clarkson to his great work, one that harrowed him so much that he said, 'Sometimes I never closed my eyes [at night] for grief.'

1774   The man who robbed Dr Bell, Princess Amelia's chaplain, came to the gallows this day. Dr Bell had heard horses galloping towards him and turned, not expecting trouble of any kind. The two men had then stopped his horse, and demanded his money.

30 NOVEMBER

'My money?' he replied, surprised.

'Yes, or I will blow your brains out!' the first man answered.

Bell handed over his meagre possessions and his watch, and was allowed to ride on. One of the crooks turned out to be the famous 'Sixteen-String Jack' (the name deriving from the strings he wore on his boots, one for each time he had appeared in court and been acquitted). He was an extremely handsome man, and once the coachman to the Earl of Sandwich. When he stepped onto the gallows platform, in a coat of bright green, he had an immense bunch of flowers handed to him by women in the crowd.

Sixteen-String Jack, with laces around his knees.

DECEMBER

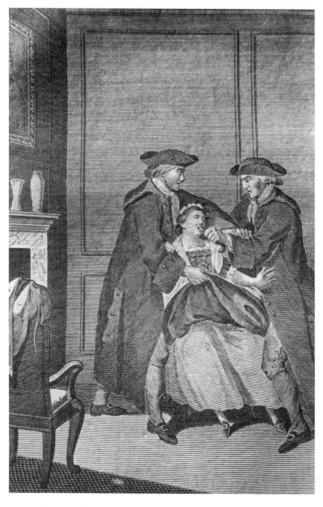

Levi Weil preventing mad fellow home-invader Lazarus
from shooting Mrs Hutchins at Chelsea.

1725   The Society for the Reformation of Manners reported that they had prosecuted 2,506 persons for keeping lewd and disorderly houses, swearing, drunkenness, gaming and proceeding in their usual occupations on Sundays in the preceding year.

1816   A group of would-be reformers, inspired by the French Revolution, met in Spa Fields on this day, leading to a riot. Henry 'Orator' Hunt was the ringleader – the famous Radical speaker who was scheduled to speak at the infamous Peterloo meeting three years later, now known as the Peterloo Massacre – and he demanded universal male suffrage, annual general elections and a secret ballot. A man called Watson waved a tricolour and ordered the crowd, made up mostly of sailors carrying weapons stolen from a Snow Hill gunshop, to follow him to the Tower. They were met at the Tower by troops who dispersed the meeting, but not without a death in the crowd. The three leaders were acquitted of all charges when it was shown that a government infiltrator had spurred on the mob and acted as an *agent provocateur*.

1745   On this day, £1,000 was subscribed by the London Chamber towards supporting soldiers trying to quell insurrection in Scotland – the infamous '45 rebellion. With a voluntary subscription, this raised enough to make 12,000 breeches, 12,000 shirts, 10,000 woollen caps, 10,000 woollen stockings, 1,000 blankets, 12,000 pairs of wool gloves, and 9,000 'spatterdashes'.

1799   Six wagons of Spanish treasure were carted through the streets of the capital on this day, from Piccadilly down St James's, Pall Mall, the Strand, Fleet Street and Cheapside. When it reached the Mansion House, the Lord Mayor and his wife toasted it with golden cups, whilst the crowd cheered and sang Rule Britannia. Twelve or fourteen more similar wagons of treasure later arrived in London, amounting to a vast quantity of 40 tons.

1758   Widow Sarah Metyard (44), and her spinster daughter, Sarah Morgan Metyard (24), cut up the body of their apprentice, Ann Nailor (13), who they had starved to death; the pieces were found on this day.
   The tale began when Ann tried to escape the vile conditions she was kept in: she was forced into the attic, beaten, and tied to a door. By the end of her third day there, she hung 'double' from the door and did not move. 'I will make her move!' said the daughter. She slapped Ann with a shoe, first on the backside and then upon the head – but still the girl did not stir. The other three apprentices in the house, who had worked in the attic whilst Ann moaned in the corner, were quickly sent downstairs, and never saw Ann again.
   Then, on 5 December 1758, two watchmen of Holborn came to the overseer, Thomas Lovegrove, and told him that they had found some parts of a dead body lying in a hole in Chick Lane. They brought a wooden coffin on a cart from the workhouse, and, by the swinging light of the lanterns, Lovegrove saw a sight of horror: the trunk of a human body, surrounded by scattered body parts; after a grim search, all but the hands were found. It

The Metyards cutting up Ann's body. Her hand is about to go upon the fire.

stunk 'prodigiously'. At the workhouse the parts were washed, assembled and examined. They were then buried.

It was a terrible mystery, and one that would have remained unsolved but for one thing – the mother's hot temper. The Metyards had a violent relationship, and the mother often beat her daughter. Two years after the murder, Metyard jnr left with former lodger Mr Richard Rooker. Mrs Metyard was terrified that her daughter would betray the crime, and started to stalk her. She 'insulted' the pair 'without intermission, day and night', and even followed them when they moved. Finally, however, she went too far, and the daughter began to make strange allusions. 'You are the Chick Lane ghost!' Sarah Morgan shouted (a play on the famous Cock Lane imposition). 'Remember the gully-hole!'

When the mother was gone, Rooker demanded an explanation. What he heard terrified him, and sent him straight to the authorities: the daughter described how Ann had been killed, and how her body had been dragged to a box in the attic. It had remained there until it putrefied, and 'maggots came from her'. This occasioned a smell that could not be easily disguised – so the mother took out the melting corpse and cut off the arms and the legs. One of the hands (with a distinctive missing finger) went on to the fire, which 'told no tales'. She then wrapped the torso and head in one bundle, and the limbs in another, and threw them, by night, into Chick Lane gully hole (after an attempt to sling them over a wall proved abortive). On the way home, soaked with unmentionable fluids from her journey, she stopped for a restorative at the inn of Mr Inch, a publican from Temple Bar – who instantly declared that there was 'a stink' in the house; she replied tartly that 'he had it all to himself, for she smelt none'. Then she quickly swallowed her drink and left.

The Metyards had to be separated in the prison, lest they attack each other, and would always blame the other if asked about the crimes. Unbeknownst to the gaolers, the mother had been starving herself (a fitting fate) in an attempt to cheat the gallows; a few days before the due date she fell into a fit and swooned away. She never spoke again. On 19 July 1762, before 9 a.m., the women were put into the cart. The ordinary had to fight to get to them through the enormous crowds, and found the mother stretched out like a statue, not even seeming to breathe, though her chest twitched convulsively now and then. The daughter begged for prayers from the crowd (over the jeers and boos), and looked about for Mr Rooker. She added that 'she died a martyr to her innocence'. Both were hanged at Tyburn shortly afterwards.

1797   Today, 'passionate' Maria Theresa Phipoe (40), otherwise **6 DECEMBER**
known as Mary Benson, was charged with the murder of Mary Cox in Garden Street, St George's in the East. Landlady Munday had gone to fetch the pair a drink, and returned to hear a great groaning, 'and a rattling in the throat'. Ten minutes later, the door of Mrs Benson's room creaked open to reveal just a bit of Benson's face and gown. 'You may come in, Mrs Munday,' she said, 'but nobody else.' Mrs Munday, quite understandably, was too frightened to do so: she ran for a surgeon instead. When she returned, she found Mary Cox leaning on the kitchen table, holding her 'singer', which was bleeding profusely. Her throat had been cut. The stricken woman made a weak motion across her throat, and then pointed upstairs. She was then carried to hospital – as the whole neighbourhood tried to crowd into the house to see what was going on. One neighbour had actually pushed open Mrs Benson's door in the landlady's absence, and witnessed a horribly gory scene: Mrs Cox sitting on the floor pressing an apron to her weeping throat. The dying woman had also been stabbed several times in the chest. The neighbour ran down the stairs, crying, 'Murder!' Unnervingly, the wounded Mrs Cox followed her down the stairs, gripped her and 'made a noise like t–t–t–t–t'.

John Dunbar, the beadle, came up the stairs to the crime scene, where Mrs Benson told him, 'I believe the Devil and pashon [*sic*] have bewitched me.' He then realised why Mrs Benson was clutching a handkerchief over her left hand – half a finger lay on the table. Mrs Cox had cut it off. The bloody murder weapon was found concealed in Mrs Benson's bosom at the London Hospital.

Naturally, the women gave different versions of the event. Before she died, Mrs Cox claimed that Mrs Benson had cut her throat as she reached for a cup, crying out, 'You bitch! I will kill you out, that you shall not be able to tell your own story.' Mrs Benson claimed that they had rowed over the price of some trinkets, rising to hot words about whether Mrs Benson was or was not 'a whore' – before Mrs Cox chopped her finger off with a case knife. This happened so quickly that she 'did not know what happened till I picked my finger off the ground', causing her to slip into a fugue state. 'A little while after,' she claimed, 'I found myself alone in the room, covered with blood, and on the table I perceived my finger.' The surgeon suggested an alternative – that she had chopped off her own finger after the murder to help justify her crime. Maria Benson/Phipoe was hanged on 11 December 1797. She gave the executioner a guinea for his work, and blamed her violent temper on laudanum. She had already spent a year in prison for tying a man to a chair, making him sign over £2,000 and then telling him to choose between having his throat cut, swallowing arsenic or a bullet. He chose to escape instead.

7 DECEMBER **1715** Elizabeth Flood appeared before the Old Bailey today to answer the charge that she had robbed a 'lunatick' in her care, a woman by the name of Susan Shepherd, of hundreds of pounds of her inheritance, before taking away all food, candles and any form of heat so that the lady starved to death. In her defence, Elizabeth pointed out that she had, in fact, been a very dear friend of Mrs Shepherd. Shepherd had also told anyone who would listen that she planned to reward Mrs Flood for her many kindnesses to her, and that her own family – who, cut out of the will, had brought the prosecution – had been very rude and uncivil to her. The jury cleared Elizabeth of all charges.

8 DECEMBER **1733** The *Weekly Register* of 8 December 1733 declared that a group of roguish Hackney drivers had taken to attacking all rival chaises: they received a hearty payment for every one they managed to force into a ditch or otherwise wreck. (They had also taken to 'particular saucy impudent behaviour' by charging far above the set fee, 'affronting gentlemen [and] frightening and insulting women'.) The death toll from this and other abuses, it was declared, was rising. Watermen too had taken to unscrupulous driving, drowning Londoners in the process. One even visited a woman he had widowed to beg a coin, 'by way of satisfaction for a pair of oars and a sail he had lost the night before, when her husband was drowned'. It was said that if the passengers looked frightened on their journey across the river, then the watermen grew 'saucy and audacious', and took the most ill-advised route they could manage across the Thames.

9 DECEMBER **1766** The body of Mary Hobbs (10) was found today in Old George Street, Spitalfields, in the house of loom-keeper Jane Collins. A neighbour, John Cobb, had previously heard 'the melancholy cry of a child' echoing across from the Collins' house. It was Mary: she was standing under a tree branch, whilst a man folded up a piece of rope – to pretend to hang her by – and Mrs Collins watched. Cobb ran across and said, 'Mrs Collins, what in the name of God have you been at?' He was informed that the little girl was a 'naughty wicked hussey [*sic*]', and had stolen a handkerchief and a knife. The 'hussey', it seemed, was frequently naughty – for the rattle of stick blows could often be heard after that day. The two washhouses were connected, and, through a knot hole in the wood, the Cobbs saw the 10-year-old beaten with a mop. They drummed on the partition and shouted for all they were worth, but the blows kept coming – despite a male voice – Mr Collins – saying, 'Leave off beating the girl.' Mrs Collins was notorious for returning home late, drunk, and roaring for the girl to bring her a candle: 'Moll, Moll, you bitch, light me, let my neighbours see I have not murdered you yet!' she once shouted. The child was half-starved: 'I have seen the poor child eat cabbage leaves and candles,' said a lodger. On the 9th, she died, and a searcher was sent for, Elizabeth Cotton. She could not get in, but returned the next day and lifted the coffin lid: there she saw a mottled body, with scratches on both legs where Collins had rebuked the apprentice for sitting by the fire. She lifted the body from the coffin and put her, naked, on top of a bed – where she found extensive bruising on the face, and the right arm raw and black from elbow to wrist. Her back had two red stripes, 'like a pair of horns'. Mrs Collins claimed that the girl had tripped over the broom and hurt her arm, the bruise which was said to have caused her death. As Mrs Collins had put the child's name on her tiny coffin, the court decided that she could not be all bad and acquitted her.

Seventeen years later, in 1783, the first executions outside Newgate took place. They were: John Burke, highwayman; George Morley, highwayman; Simon Wilson, high treason for coining: John Wallis, Richard Martin and Frances Warren, who made off with 108 different small items in one go; John Lawler, burglar; William Munro for uttering; and two people – William Busby and Francis Burke – who had both returned from transportation before they were meant to. Busby had been sniffed out in a Kent ditch by a small dog.

1771   Today, four skeletons went on display at Surgeons' Hall, each with a bushy beard glued on. They were Dr Levi Weil, Asher Weil, Jacob Lazarus and Solomon Porter. They had murdered Joseph Slew at a farm on the King's Road, Chelsea, and were hanged on the 9th at Tyburn. On the night in question, the men had stormed in and ill-used maid Mary Hodgkin. When her mistress, Elizabeth Hutchins, had heard the ruckus downstairs and gone to help, they pushed her into a chair, pulled her petticoats over her head and told her to leave them there 'as she valued her life'. All the while, Elizabeth could hear her cook screaming, and the men threatening to cut her throat. The intruders then went upstairs. She heard rustling and screaming – as if they were throwing a servant down the stairs – and then two pistol shots. When she tried to run for the door, she found it blocked by men who threatened to blow her brains out. Joseph Slew then staggered down the stairs in nothing but a shirt: 'How are you, Ma'am, for I am a dead man!' he said. His shirt was actually on fire where he had been shot, and Elizabeth was forced to put it out with her hands. He then dropped, with blood running down his legs. The thieves came over to steal her shoe-buckles, pistol-whipped her and pushed the gun in her face. They then ran, with all the valuables in the house. They were quickly identified and sent to Triple Tree.

1811   On this day, one of the most disgusting crimes in London's history took place. Mr Marr, Mrs Marr, their baby and their servant were found murdered in the family shop in the most horrible circumstances imaginable.

The family's female servant had gone to fetch some oysters at about midnight, leaving Mrs Marr feeding her baby, and Mr Marr getting ready to close the shop in the Ratcliffe Highway. Half an hour later, when the servant returned, all was in darkness and the doors were locked. She rang and rang, but no one answered. A watchman, hearing all the commotion, came along and tried the door too. Nothing was heard from within. Eventually, Mr Murray, the pawnbroker who lived next door, was woken. He climbed over the wall to the back door, where he entered the house and found a sight that was to haunt him for the rest of his days: stretched out in the hall was the mangled body of the Marrs' servant boy, who was just 14 years old. He had been struck so violently on the head that his brains were discovered on the ceiling, and 'the counter,

10 DECEMBER

11 DECEMBER

Finding the body of
Mr Marr.

which extends the whole length of the warehouse, was found bespattered with his blood and brains from one end of it to the other'.

Petrified, Mr Murray shouted for help. Then, hefting the light he had taken from the landing where the servant's bleeding body lay, he continued on into the silent shop. Lying by the street-door he found Mrs Marr, dreadfully wounded and lifeless. Her head had been struck repeatedly, her skull was shattered above her ear. Huddled behind the counter he found the body of Mr Marr, whose head had also been fearfully mangled. His nose was broken, his skull smashed and he had been struck with great strength on the left eye. One more body was yet to be discovered, one that was worse than all the horrors he had yet discovered:

> ...he then advanced into the kitchen, and petrified with horror, he saw the little babe in the cradle, with one of its cheeks entirely knocked in from the violence of the blow, and its throat cut from ear to ear.

The Marrs were a young couple, aged about 24, and their baby was about 14 weeks old. They were buried together in one grave in St George's churchyard the following Sunday.

Just a few days later, another disgusting crime was to occur nearby. On Tuesday 19 December, New Gravel Lane was alarmed by shrieks of 'Murder!', and a half-naked man was seen to climb out of a house on a rope made of twisted sheets. He screamed out, 'They are murdering the people in the house!' Three men broke into the house, along with a local constable. A horrible sight was waiting for them too. According to the Newgate Calendar:

> On looking round the cellar, the first object that attracted their attention was the body of Mr Williamson, which lay at the foot of the stairs, with a violent contusion to the head, the throat dreadfully cut, and an iron crow by his side; they then proceeded up the stairs into the parlour, where they found Mrs Williamson, also dead, with her skull and her throat cut, blood still issuing from the wound; and near her lay the body of the servant woman, Bridget Harrington, whose head was also horribly bruised, and her throat cut. Mr J. Williamson was about fifty-six years of age, his wife, Mrs

C. Williamson, about sixty; and Bridget Harrington, fifty years of age. The master and mistress were both very corpulent, and the former very stout.

Mr Williamson's leg was smashed, and his hand was cut; the servant girl, legs in the grate, was more battered than her mistress, and her throat had been cut almost to the bone. None of the bodies were yet cold. Upstairs, sound asleep, was the Williamsons' granddaughter. The window was open, the sill covered with blood, and the murderer or murderers unknown had again made their escape.

Suspicion soon fell on an Irish seaman named John Williams, an 'idle, dissolute and quarrelsome' fellow who had once served on the same ship as Marr, and who had been seen many times in the Williamsons' public house. He lived at the Pear Tree Tavern nearby. The evidence against him began to mount steadily: the woman who did his laundry described how his shirts had been ripped and covered with blood around the time of the murders; John Cutherson, a fellow lodger, described how he had found his stockings, borrowed by Williams, covered with fresh mud on the day after the murder; John Fred Richter, another fellow lodger, described how Williams had tried to dramatically alter his appearance after the murders by shaving off his prominent sandy whiskers.

The circumstantial evidence was strong. However, an earthly judgement was never to be given, for, on 31 December, Williams was found in his cell at Coldbath Fields Prison, hanging from a hook on the wall by his own handkerchief. His body was carried through the streets strapped to a slanting board; his face was still ruddy with congested blood. He was without a coat, hat or shoes. Above his head were placed the iron maul and the iron crow with which he had committed his brutal crimes. Behind his head was the stake which was to be driven into his heart with the very maul he had used in his atrocities. Thousands watched as his body was taken slowly through the streets, pausing outside the scenes of the crimes, till the procession reached St George's Turnpike. There waited a hole, deliberately dug too small so that his body could not assume a dignified position. His body was crammed into it, and the stake smashed into his heart. Unslaked lime was thrown into the hole, which was filled with earth. The paving stones were then replaced. The world was not to look upon the face of the diabolical murderer Williams again – until a gas company dug up the skeleton, stake through heart, in 1886, just two years before another throat-slashing multiple murderer was to horrify all of London. The skull remained in a nearby pub for many years afterwards.

1768 William Bear, John Aldridge, Walter Stoaks and Daniel Asgood committed murder at the Last & Sugar Loaf, Water Lane, Blackfriars. The landlord served the rowdy lightermen (dealers in coal) with beer, which they claimed 'stank'; then he served them with gin, on which they declared him 'a booger' and punched him. They then told one customer that they would like to throw him on the fire and broil him, which sent the landlord running for a watchman – William Ridley. When the landlord returned with more help, he found the watchman in the street. Ridley had not had a good

12 DECEMBER

time of it in his absence: 'I have been sadly used,' he said, and, lifting his wig, he pulled out a clot of blood from his ear and threw it on the floor. The men had hidden in the houses by the reeking Fleet Ditch, and leapt out to attack as Ridley passed, shattering his lantern and his skull – with his own watch staff. He went home to his wife, cried in bed and died in hospital on the 12th – after bleeding at the eyes, mouth and ears. Asgood swung at the next possible hanging day.

13 DECEMBER   **1790**   On this day, artificial-flower-maker Renwick or Rhynwick Williams of St James's parish – a strange stout figure always to be seen in a powdered wig – was brought from Newgate to Clerkenwell Green to take his trial for several assaults. He was finally brought to book after being recognised in St James's Park and seized on the orders of one of his victims. History remembers this man as 'the London Monster', and more than fifty attacks are laid to his name. He became so famous for a time that men began to wear 'No Monster' badges to show that they were not the madman, and women to wear copper-protected skirts.

He was charged with slashing the right thigh of Ann Porter, spinster of St James's Street. The Monster was in fact well known to Ann, as he had taken to abusing her family when he passed them in the street, with language 'the most horrid, and the least sufferable to human ears'. He had 'a shivering sort of voice', and his usual talk was 'of drowning them in their blood, and of blasting their eyes'. His language was overall 'indecent, inhuman and

abusive'. The whole family found him so strange and disturbing that they had dubbed him 'the wretch'. On the day of the attack, as they proceeded from the ballroom at St James's, Ann and her sister Sarah must have felt their hearts sink when they realised that the wretch was once again on the prowl. The light was dim, but it was enough to see the prisoner by – though Ann said she would have known him with less light. He approached Ann and her sister – and then, with a sickening punch, ripped a long

Williams, the alleged London Monster.

THE MONSTER

knife through the back of Ann's skirts and into her thigh. Miss Sarah felt a 'stroke' as he passed, and then he struck again at her sister – and they ran. Another friend was struck on the left side of her face, and saw 'a light like a flash of fire from her eye'. Their brother John told the court that he had opened the house door and found the terrified girls on the doorstep, and the Monster standing just behind them, 'looking in'.

Mr Tomkins, the surgeon, thrilled the court when he said...

> ...he had been in many scenes of horror, but never saw anything that affected him so much before; that the room was full of blood, and the poor girl laying [sic] like a dead corpse; he said that if he had made an incision as a surgeon, he could not have made a cleaner wound; the instrument must be very sharp; she had a fever, and [it] was five or six weeks before she could walk.

Williams was then charged with the wounding of Elizabeth Davis of Clarke's Court, Holborn. On 5 May, between 9 p.m. and 10 p.m., she had been returning home by the intermittent light coming from the shops when a man had suddenly spoken to her. 'Where are you going?' he said. He began to follow her, and at the top of Chancery Lane he stopped her with a bunch of flowers and said, 'Are these not very pretty flowers?' He pushed the flowers (which appeared to be fake) into her face and said, 'Will you smell them?' She refused – and it was lucky for her that she did, for some reports suggest that a knife was hidden amongst them. Her refusal was to no avail, however: he caught her by the throat with one hand and struck her thigh with the other. She heard her clothes rip, and struggled free, whereupon he punched her in the chest. She choked out, 'Murder!' and he ran. She stumbled home, and fainted on the bed of Sarah Garrison, her landlady. (Sarah later told the Old Bailey that she had not recognised Elizabeth's voice as she 'halooed aloud' outside her lodging, and had in fact taken her 'for a common prostitute.') Her only words were, 'Oh the man! The man!'.

Williams was then indicted for a similar assault on Elizabeth Baughan, which took place on 6 December 1789. She had been walking along Bridge Street towards Parliament Street when a man came along, 'grumbling' aloud. He had suddenly pushed himself between Elizabeth's sister and the rails they were walking by, and whispered, 'Blast you, it is you!' in her ear; he then punched them both about the small of the back with a sharp, small knife. Both girls' clothes were cut to pieces, and the sister was pitched to the floor. As she watched, horrified, Williams knelt to the floor and struck at Elizabeth. Elizabeth recognised the Monster, after she recalled that he had once followed her from King's Palace to May's Buildings, forcing her to slap him in the face.

The court sentenced him to two years for each of the crimes, each sentence to start only when the last ended. He was also fined several hundred pounds. Whether Williams was truly the Monster or not has never been agreed.

14 DECEMBER **1724**   Journeyman Richard Coats, of the parish of Stepney, was indicted for the murder of servant Alexander Tailor on this day, after he grew angry with the boy's 'saucy and reviling' language and his 'saucy carriage', and threw a throwster's star at him in a shop for the same (a throwster twisted silk into yarn), cracking his skull. The boy looked likely to recover until the nurse gave him 'ale and brandy', which tipped him to his doom. Coats, normally extremely placid, was burnt on the hand for manslaughter and released.

15 DECEMBER **1714**   John Norman, of the parish of Edgware, opened his barn today and found his two geese gone – but a strange dog in their place. He found out who the dog belonged to and went to their house – where he found his two geese, hidden in the room of one John Edwards. Edwards said he had bought the geese for 3s, and, since Mr Norman could not swear that the geese were his, the probable thief was acquitted.

16 DECEMBER **1784**   On the eleventh anniversary of the Boston Tea Party, 'a daring attempt at robbery was made at Mrs Rice's house in Tooting', according to the *London Magazine*. A gang rang the bell, but the footman would not open the door for them. Then, when reinforcements appeared (in the shape of a passing bricklayer, a blunderbuss and the coachman), he did – and the gang were on them in a second, cutting and slashing with their swords. The coachman was cut down. The bricklayer was shot in the head. The footman turned tail and ran back through the house, screaming for help, and the gang were forced to run for their lives – taking away nothing but the coachman's blunderbuss for their efforts.

17 DECEMBER **1731**   On this day, Mary Vezey (55), the wife of weaver Corbet Vezey of Stepney, was examined by a man of the court. The tale that had led to this moment was an extraordinary one. In mid-December 1731, Christopher Best, the beadle, had been walking towards Mr Finlow's house at the Four Swans, Mile End when – to his astonishment – he saw two legs poking out of the top of the house. A girl then fell out of the top floor and onto an old shed below; she rebounded from the building and crashed, stunned, to the floor. Her body was quite black, and her legs appeared to be covered with white mould. She was dressed in nothing but a thin old gown and a bit of a red petticoat. A woman – Mr Vezey's mistress, no less – then came out of the house, picked up the extraordinary figure and carried her inside. Understandably, the policeman followed and began to rail at the man waiting inside: 'Are you not ashamed to keep your wife so? She's nothing but skin and bone!' Eventually they allowed the beadle to go upstairs, and he found a dusty old attic containing a mouldy old piece of bread hanging on a string. The woman then came to, saw the beadle and exclaimed, 'For God's sake stay by me! I have been used barbarously! I am starved to death!'

Best returned the next day and found that the attic had a key in the lock, and that several pieces of old cheese had been scattered about. Mary told him that she would eat them if she could, 'but in the weak condition I am in, I might as well try to eat a piece of board.' Normally, her small dinner was left just inside the door: if she was too weak to move, she starved, and if she made it to the food, crawling over the wooden boards, she often found her strength would not allow her to return to her bed. Sometimes her fingers grew so cold that she found she could not eat the food she had crawled to get. No fire, candle or sheets had ever been seen in the room. No filth or waste had left it: her toilet was the fireplace, and the smell of more than a year's worth of human waste drove her to distraction. She was usually forced to lie with her nose underneath her pillow. She then showed the beadle a piece of paper: in it were long, mouldy white strips of her own skin, peeled off by sheer malnutrition. She was a skeleton, nothing but skin over bone; one witness said that she 'look'd just like an Anatomy that I have seen at a Surgeon's'. Her whole skin was either black or white with mould, and vermin had eaten 'holes' in her head. She said that if she ever tried to cry for help, she was horsewhipped. The husband's sole comment to her was that if it was not for the law, he would murder her.

She then began to spit blood, and died soon afterwards. Her cousin, heartbroken, came to visit her before she died, but had to turn down her offer to kiss him for a last time because of the noxious smell. Her escape had been an attempt to end her own life, as she could bear no more. After an attempt to cut her own throat had failed, she had rolled herself out of her window. The motive behind her treatment was the fact that she would not sign over a small estate she owned: she refused to do so, despite a horrendous confinement that lasted more than a year. However, a long parade of neighbours and friends appeared who swore that the woman's life was not that bad, and so the court brought in a surprising verdict – Mary's death was not due to her ill-treatment, but instead the result of a 'visitation of God' in the form of an asthma attack!

1786   On this day, three men – Michael Walker, Richard Payne and John Cox – were hanged opposite a pawnbroker's shop in High Holborn for the murder of Duncan Robertson in a robbery gone wrong. They had lashed a knife across his left shoulder, forehead, nose and wrist. His nose was nearly cut off. They then all cheered. Surgeon James Horsefall found Robertson 'lying in a bath of blood'. The man was very weak, and fell into a feverish delirium. He tore off the bandages in the night, and was terrified and disturbed; then he started having fits, and eventually had to be straight-jacketed. The next day, he was found snoring and torpid; he died half an hour afterwards. All three men were found guilty and sentenced to death. The judge, Baron Hotham, said: 18 DECEMBER

> You have gone forth like wild beasts, to prey upon the innocent and unoffending, determined to wade through blood, if necessary for the accomplishment of your purpose. You have ... proceeded with the utmost cruelty with a dangerous weapon to mangle and wound the unfortunate deceased ... [and] you are found in the most flagitious manner, huzzaing and glorying in your crime.

19 DECEMBER   1740   Abraham Benbrook, of Westminster, accidentally knocked Samuel Masters into a stone step in the Tyburn Road after a quarrel over money. The blow echoed around the court, and blood flew out as Benbrook's head cracked upon the stones.

20 DECEMBER   1829   On this day, Mr Murray the bookseller was forced to pay restoration for libelling two men from Jamaica, Escoffery and Lecesne, by describing them as 'most infamous characters, convicted felons and miscreants' in his publication *Annals of Jamaica*. The *Gentleman's Magazine* wrote: 'For this foul charge there did not appear to be the slightest ground and a verdict of guilty was returned.'

Also today, a paper was read at the Royal Society which attempted to demonstrate that a pair of bellows was enough to sustain a head after decapitation.

21 DECEMBER   1717   Highwayman Nathaniel Hawes (19) finally came to the gallows today. He had previously refused to enter a plea until his handsome clothes were returned to him to wear at his execution, 'For no one shall say that I was hanged in a dirty shirt and ragged coat.' After seven minutes spent suffering under an agonising weight in Newgate's press yard, he relented and pleaded not guilty. He was hanged nonetheless.

22 DECEMBER   1753   The danger of entering London's rookeries was exhibited on this day when Thomas Mott came to Angel Court in search of a through passage. A woman accosted him and suggested a drink, and he proceeded to enter her house. All of a sudden, a man entered the room, caught him by the throat and said he would kill him if he spoke. He then took his watch and his money, and some women took his handkerchief – before they blew out the 'glimm' (the candle) and let him go. Mott ran into the court and shouted, 'THIEVES!' A passing soldier advised him to grab anyone who tried to leave the house. He seized the first, a 'ragged girl', and her neighbours helpfully pointed out that she was hiding money in her mouth. She then spat 4s into his hand, given to her by Mott's male attacker – who was hanged.

23 DECEMBER   1775   On this day, apprentice William Ringrose was sent to Bridewell for trying to escape his vicious master, hairdresser Stephen Self. A week before Christmas, a neighbour had flung a piece of mutton bone to a dog in the Porter's Arms. To his astonishment, he saw William begin to chew on it as though he had not eaten for a month. He then left – with other scraps and bones tucked under his coat. He looked half starved. Others told how the boy would come to their house to shave them, and look 'very wishfully' at any food that was lying around. When the boy was released from Bridewell he was very ill, and his legs were 'exceedingly bad'. He died on the floor of his master's house on 22 January, on a scanty bag of straw, after his master gave 'the nasty dog a good kick'. He groaned so loudly that he woke the neighbours, who found him with soaked feet, covered in blisters – left untreated by the master – and in stockings which he had not been allowed to remove for weeks; they had eaten into his feet and 'tore his flesh away'. His toes were all dead and covered with ulcers. His feet smelled of rot, and were much swollen. The prisoner's defence was that the boy had been 'bad and wicked' for running away. He was found guilty of manslaughter only.

1813 Mr Thomas Aris, the partner of Sarah Evans of Clerkenwell, was ordered, on this day, to pay support for their illegitimate child, George. He refused, and a fatal set of events was set in motion. On 14 March 1814, Coldbath Fields cabinet-maker, Charles Baldwin, was on a Sunday stroll near Islington Road when he saw something odd caught upon the grate through which the water rushed into the New River's reservoir. It was a tiny body, dressed in a dirty bed-gown, small stockings and shoes. The figure had a small black hat upon its head, covered with mud. Underneath there was a black silk cap. Baldwin dragged the body from the river and laid it upon the railings – where he realised, to his horror, that a handkerchief was twisted around the loins and neck; there was a half brick in it. The handkerchief was taut, like a rope, cutting into the tiny neck. The knot was tucked under the left ear. It had been tied there before the boy came into the water. Gravedigger Mr Clayton, of St James's Church, was sent for. The body was washed and displayed in the vault of the church, and a vast number of people came to see it. At 2 p.m., Sarah's landlady, Ann Blakey, recognised the body as belonging to 4-year-old George Evans. At about 3 p.m., Sarah Evans entered the room. She stared in silence at the corpse for about a minute, and then she said, 'That is not my George ... That is too big for him.' Each item of clothing was shown to her. She claimed to recognise none – though when she was shown the shoes she could not speak. The court was, however, forced to admit that the water had swollen the body horribly, making identification difficult. It was, in fact, 'in a putrid state' – or, as the man who displayed it tactfully put it, 'Death stretches, and the water swells.'

Sarah was known by all as a most affectionate mother, and a 'mild, affectionate, humane woman'. George had been a 'very fine boy; a fine, cheerful, playful boy'. Evans was taken to Coldbath Fields Prison, then on to Newgate. Sarah told the court that she had delivered the child to his father on the promise that he would take care of him. Thomas had thirteen children, and had fallen on hard times trying to pay for them all; when his washerwoman identified the handkerchief around the boy's neck as belonging to Thomas, Sarah was declared not guilty. The judge suggested that Thomas be most closely investigated.

1807 Coachman Richard Prince opened his door at dusk on Christmas Day and received a knife through the eye for his trouble. It had been thrown by Elizabeth Godfry (34).

'Why should you be so malicious as to hurt a fellow creature in that way?' she was asked.

'Serve him right,' was the reply.

The pair had quarrelled earlier in the day, after Richard had heard her arguing with a man over payment in her room. When you learn that 'several

24 DECEMBER

25 DECEMBER

unfortunate women' were in the house, and that it was 'a noted house for women of the town', it is not hard to guess why. Her defence was that she had swept up the knife without realising what it was, to defend herself against intruders. She was hanged the following February.

26 DECEMBER　**1783**　On this day, Edward Whitehead was found not guilty of the murder of John Vanderplank after a pub brawl. Vanderplank had used 'very abusive' language to Edward. They had fallen to fighting, until watchmen burst in – and Vanderplank toppled over, dead. As no surgeon was called by the court, the judge declared that, 'When men are in violent passions, it may occasion the breaking of a blood vessel, and may bring on deadly symptoms.' Whitehead was freed without charge.

27 DECEMBER　**1718**　Two women, Mary Ipsley and Elizabeth Rickets, allegedly murdered an unknown woman at 'Tumbledown Dick's' lodging house in Brentford on this day. The victim, a fellow lodger, was heard to scream at nearly midnight, whilst someone said something about 'knocking out her brains'. Nothing more was heard of her until two men, who slept in the woman's room, mentioned that there was a corpse upstairs. It was the unknown lady. One of the lodgers dragged her body down the stairs and into a coffin – and she was carted off for burial. Mary Ipsley – who was overseeing the box's transport – seemed to be rather nervous. When the cortège reached the graveyard, she told Mr Tille, the curate of Ealing church, that she had applied to have the corpse buried. Sadly for her, however, he had been at the churchwarden's house all day, and knew she had not. He then declared, 'I much suspect you: I will see the Corps.' She tried to stop him looking at the body by claiming that the woman was 'nasty' and 'full of Plague Spots', but to no avail: 'pox or plague', he would see the body. The moment the top section of the coffin was opened, Mary flew forward and seized the corpse around the neck – and shook it violently! When asked why, she confessed it was to make it 'purge' and 'stink them all out of the church'. She did not succeed, and the corpse was viewed: stark naked, and covered in 'Marks of Violence and barbarous Usage'. Her hair was bloody and clotted, and blood ran from one ear and one nostril. In a further horror, a dead baby had been tucked under the corpse's feet. The baby's face was covered with a caul (i.e. the thin membrane which covers the baby in the womb), which one of the women pulled off – revealing that 'there was no Nose ... only two Nostrils'. In fact, the whole face was 'as flat as the back of the hand'. Blood then 'flew out of the child's mouth'. Lower down the woman's body was 'such a Vacancy that no Child ever made in a Woman by its Birth'. The baby appeared to have been cut out. Looking at this truly awful spectacle, one of the searchers declared that 'somebody deserved to be hanged'. In their defence, the prisoners said that the mysterious lodger had arrived at Christmas time, and had gone upstairs – where she started fitting, delivered a dead baby and then perished. The damage to her lower body had been caused by giving birth during a violent convulsion, they claimed. As the evidence of foul play was 'strong, but presumptive', both women were set free.

James Greenacre meets his doom outside Newgate Prison. (With kind permission of Neil R. Storey)

1837   On the afternoon of 28 December 1837, Constable Samuel Peglar was stopped by a terrified passer-by and taken to a pathway near Edgware Road. There he found a dusty sack containing the trunk of a human body; the head and lower limbs were nowhere to be seen. The arms were tied with a thin cord. He found a wheelbarrow and wheeled his disgusting find to the Paddington poorhouse.

The head believed to go with this torso had already been found in the Regent's Canal; when the lock-keeper tried to shut the gates, he found a small bundle – 'a 'dead dog', he thought – blocking them, and hooked it towards him. To his horror, he saw what he knew instantly to be a human ear bob to the surface – his hook was caught in the long and dirty tangles of hair on a severed human head. It was missing its right eye, and the jawbone poked whitely through the left cheek. The head looked as though it had been in the water for four or five days, the lock-keeper thought – in his time he had hooked out 'several' different bodies, and was something of an expert on the topic. The legs and thighs were found in a reed bed on 2 February.

Eventually, the victim was identified as large-handed mangle-working laundress Hannah Brown (47). She had been struck in the eye with a rolling pin by her fiancé, James Greenacre (42), on Christmas Eve (the day before she was due to marry him), after she proved to own less property than she had claimed. He had then sawed off her head, tucked it in a handkerchief and taken two different bus rides with it on his knee before he reached the canal. The torso he took in a cab to Pineapple Gate, Edgware Road, and the legs he carried himself.

His housekeeper – and mistress – Sarah Gale was transported for life for her part in helping to cover up the crime. Greenacre was executed on 2 May.

28 DECEMBER

1716   In St Giles in the Fields parish, a man with no name (he is recorded in the Old Bailey records as simply C—— G——) stole fourteen silver spoons, two pairs of shoes, some roast beef and some mince pies on this day. The owner heard that someone had been seen at Colebrook with just such a list of items, and caught the mysterious thief at Piccadilly. He was branded on the hand.

29 DECEMBER

30 DECEMBER   **1814**   Ann Simpson died on this day after her partner of six weeks, William Freeman (41), struck her on the top of her head with a pewter pint pot in the Golden Chain public house. He had raised his glass to another woman, causing the 'passionate' Ann to snatch his glass and throw the contents in his face. He was so angry that he snatched it back and brought the mug down smartly on her head – twice. Blood flew out and she was dragged off to the London Hospital. The wound suppurated, erysipelas spread across her body, and she died. Freeman was sentenced to six months' imprisonment in Newgate and a 1s fine.

31 DECEMBER   **1828**   On this day, servant and widow Betty Jeffs waved goodbye to her master, John Lett Esq. She was looking after his house for him, as she had done for some eighteen years. The next day, when he visited, he found her dead in a room below stairs. Her throat was cut. 'Her countenance,' said the surgeon who examined her, 'had a strong expression of horror upon it – her eyes were open, and her hands hard clenched.' An empty razor case and a pair of scissors lay nearby. Knuckle-print bruises covered her collarbone, and a dirty shoeprint could be seen on her face. The shoe had pushed her neckerchief into the hole in her throat. Tiny spots of blood were found on each thigh. One William Jones (22) was arrested shortly afterwards, and was found to have a cut on his thumb and the marks of a bloody hand on the back of his own hand. However, the case could not be proved, and the murder remains a mystery to this day.

Judge Jeffreys seized at Wapping, in the disguise of a sailor. His coffin was uncovered in Georgian London.

Today, in 1810, the coffin of the notorious Judge Jeffreys was uncovered by some workmen repairing St Mary's, Aldermanbury, in the City of London. A large, flat stone was removed near the communion table, and the lead coffin was found in a vault underneath. A nameplate told them who it was. Jeffreys had been attacked by a mob at Wapping, and died in the Tower where they had carried him. The coffin was examined by the public, and then reinterred in the vault.

BIBLIOGRAPHY

Magazines

British Magazine
Classical Journal, various
European Magazine and London Review, various
Examiner, various
Gentleman's Magazine, various
London Critical Review
London Journal, various
London Magazine, various
Monthly Magazine, various
North Briton, various
Spectator, various
Famous Crimes, Past & Present, various

Georgian (and Early Victorian) Books

Allen, Thomas, *History and Antiquities of London Westminster*, Southwark, and Parts Adjacent, 1828
Anon, *The Georgian Era: Memoirs of the Most Eminent Persons, who have Flourished in Great Britain*, various vols
Anon, *The Fatal Effects of Gambling Exemplified in the Murder of William Weare*, 1824
Anon, *The Newgate Calendar*, various editions
Borrow, George Henry, *Celebrated Trials and Remarkable Cases of Criminal Jurisprudence*, 1825
Foot, Jesse, *The Lives of Andrew Robinson Bowes, Esq. and the Countess of Strathmore, Written from 33 Years Professional Attendance*, 1815
Hervey, John, *Memoirs of the Reign of George II*, various vols
Malcolm, J.P., *Anecdotes of the Manners and Customs of London During the Eighteenth Century*, various vols
Walpole, Horace, *Journal of the Reign of King George III*, various vols
Wilkinson, George, *An Authentic History of the Cato Street Conspiracy*, various vols, 1820
Wilson, Henry, *Comprising Memoirs and Anecdotes of the Most Remarkable Persons of Every Age and Nation*, 1834

Modern Books

Brooke, Alan, and Brandon, David, *London: City of the Dead*, The History Press, 2008
——— *Tyburn: London's Fatal Tree*, The History Press, 2005
Craven, Mary, *Famous Beauties of Two Reigns; Being an Account of Some Fair Women of Stuart and Georgian Times*, 1906
Cruikshank, Dan, *The Secret History of Georgian London*, Windmill, 2010
Flanders, Judith, *The Invention of Murder: How the Victorians Revelled in Death and Detection and Created Modern Crime*, HarperPress, 2011
Fyvie, John, *Noble Dames and Notable Men of the Georgian Era*, 1911
Halliday, Stephen, *Newgate: London's Prototype of Hell*, The History Press, 2007
Howse, Geoffrey, *The A-Z of London Murders*, Wharncliffe, 2007
James, P.D and T.A. Critchley, *The Maul and the Pear Tree*, Faber and Faber, 2010
Linnane, Fergus, *The Encylopedia of London Crime and Vice*, The History Press, 2005
Low, Donald A., *The Regency Underworld*, Sutton, 2000
Moore, Wendy, *The Knife Man: Blood, Body-Snatching and the Birth of Modern Surgery*, Bantam, 2006
Roud, Steve, *London Lore: The Legends and Traditions of the World's Most Vibrant City*, Arrow, 2010
Shoemaker, Robert, *The London Mob: Violence and Disorder in Eighteenth-Century London*, Hambledon Continuum, 2004
Storey, Neil R., *London: Crime, Death & Debauchery*, The History Press, 2008

Websites

http://www.capitalpunishmentuk.org/
http://www.georgianlondon.com/
http://www.londonlives.org/
http://www.oldbaileyonline.org/
http://rictornorton.co.uk/

ABOUT THE AUTHORS

Graham Jackson is an engineer who has been assembling digital libraries of old books, including one called 'Georgian Villains', hence his co-authorship of this volume. He has recently launched TheGentlemanAngler.com website, which presents the views of a Georgian gentleman returned to the twenty-first century.

Cate Ludlow is a Commissioning Editor at The History Press. She has been collecting antiquarian books on London and on true crime for several years, and her previous volumes include *Dickens' Dreadful Almanac*, which also contained a horrible event for every day of the year. Her friends are starting to give her funny looks, and her family have requested 'something nice' for the next book. They will not get it.